Walker, Herschel.

Breaking free

Breaking Free

Herschel Walker

with Gary Brozek and Charlene Maxfield

A Touchstone/Howard Book
Published by Simon & Schuster
New York   London   Toronto   Sydney

HOWARD
BOOKS

Touchstone and Howard Books
A Division of Simon & Schuster, Inc.
1230 Avenue of the Americas
New York, NY 10020

The author is represented by the literary agency of B&B Media Group,
Inc., 109 South Main, Corsicana, Texas 75110; www.tbbmedia.com.

First Touchstone and Howard Books hardcover edition April 2008

TOUCHSTONE and HOWARD BOOKS and colophons are registered
trademarks of Simon & Schuster, Inc.

For information about special discounts for bulk purchases,
please contact Simon & Schuster Special Sales at
1-800-456-6798 or business@simonandschuster.com.

Designed by Carla Jayne Little

Manufactured in the United States of America

10   9   8   7   6   5   4   3   2   1

Library of Congress Cataloging-in-Publication Data

Walker, Herschel.
    Breaking free / Herschel Walker.
        p.   cm.
    "A Touchstone Book."
    1. Walker, Herschel—Mental health.   2. Multiple personality—
Patients—United States—Biography.   I. Title.
RC569.5.M8W35 2008

362.196'852360092—dc22
[B]
            2007038547
ISBN-13: 978-1-4165-3748-9
ISBN-10:   1-4165-3748-1

A Note to the Reader

This book is also the story of my life with Dissociative Identity Disorder (DID). My goal is to educate people about DID. However, I am not a doctor or psychiatrist. My experiences, opinions, and ideas about DID are not those of a professional. They are not a substitute for personal medical care and attention.

For those who have been diagnosed with a dissociative disorder, or who are struggling with the negative aspects of dissociation, it is my hope that this book will inspire you to accept your diagnosis or to make the decision to seek professional help if you are not already in therapy.

To my son, Christian Walker,
I love you.
Thank you for helping me to mature as a man and a father.

I want to acknowledge Charlene Maxfield. Thank you for all your help. And also, my thanks to Gary Brozek for his time and talent in developing this book.

It is not the critic who counts, not the man who points out how the strong man stumbles, or where the doer of deeds could have done them better. The credit belongs to the man who is actually in the arena, whose face is marred by dust and sweat and blood; who strives valiantly; who errs, who comes short again and again, because there is no effort without error and shortcoming; but who does actually strive to do the deeds; who knows great enthusiasms, the great devotions; who spends himself in a worthy cause; who at the best knows in the end the triumph of high achievement, and who at the worst, if he fails, at least fails while daring greatly, so that his place shall never be with those cold and timid souls who neither know victory nor defeat.

Theodore Roosevelt (1858–1919)
26th President of the United States
The Man in the Arena
Paris, France
April 23, 1910

Author's Note

William Shakespeare, in Act II of *The Tempest,* wrote, "What's past is prologue." For most of my life, I believed the exact opposite was true: "What's past is past." I've spent my life looking forward, not backward. That's one reason why writing this book has been a challenge. I've also spent much of my life overcoming challenges; in fact, I relish a challenge and some would say I've gone out of my way many times to take one on instead of taking the easy way out. I'm not so sure about the going-out-of-my-way part, and I'll leave that for you to decide after you've read this.

You may find it surprising that I'm familiar with the works of Mr. Shakespeare. As you'll see, there's a lot more to me than my ability to carry a football, sprint to the finish line, or any of my other accomplishments on the field of play. It's interesting to me that we use the word *play* to describe what I did for most of my adult life. To me, whenever I stepped out onto the football field, the track, a bobsled run, or even in playing a video game with my son, what I was participating in was a matter of life-or-death seriousness. I'm that competitive. Most people who know me off the field have a hard time reconciling that fact with the reality they know firsthand—that I'm a southern gentleman born and bred, meekly humble, devoted to God and my family, and about as unlikely to enjoy wreaking physical havoc on myself and others as a Buddhist monk.

The truth is that I am all of those things. The truth also is that for most of life, from childhood onward, I had a form of mental illness that enabled me to be simultaneously a fierce competitor, consumed by a desire to be the best and to dominate, and a quiet unassuming man who let his actions do the talking. When I was diagnosed with dissociative identity disorder (DID) shortly after I ended my playing career, I wasn't certain if what I was being told about myself was true. After all, I had heard about multiple personality disorder and I felt like none of those Jekyll-and-Hyde images and associations applied to me. When my doctors explained to me that I had developed other personalities (alters) to help me cope with and survive the pain, alienation, and abuse I experienced as a child and adolescent, I was skeptical. I did some digging to investigate their claim more fully, in an attempt to understand what role the disorder may have played in how I had lived my life.

This book, then, is a part of my coming to terms with this diagnosis. As I said, I'm not someone who is prone to reflecting on and examining the past. By necessity, however, I had to be this way in order to write this book. I want to be sure that readers understand how difficult this is for me, not as an excuse for failures in fact or omissions of details that others might recall, but simply to let you know that as I was experiencing these events growing up and as an adult, I wasn't aware of the multiple personas who existed in my mind. For me, like most of you reading this, my experience was a seamless stretch of events narrated by a single person. I didn't realize then that there was inside of me a kind of chorus or a cast of actors each taking their turn to step into the spotlight to take charge. I now understand that there may have been as many as twelve distinct alters enabling me to cope with my reality. Some of them were aware of the presence of the others, some were not.

In looking back, I can see how these many alters may have acted on my behalf at certain points in my life, but I also have to say that I was unaware of their presence in those moments. I was simply being Herschel Walker and doing what I thought was best. As I relate these events to you in the pages that follow, I hope that you will keep this distinction in mind. I am recounting my life as best as I can recall it through the filter of this diagnosis of DID. I often find myself puzzling over how I behaved back then, the choices I made, in the light of this relatively new information I've come to understand about myself. I guess that one way I can make you understand how this feels to me, the strangeness of it all, is to ask you how you might view your life and your past if, say, you were to learn at the age of thirty-three that you were adopted. You'd have a lot of questions regarding how your life would have been different if you'd known that essential fact about yourself.

One of the things my alters did for me was to make me forget most of the awful things that had happened to me. They worked very hard to bury those memories in secret places that the essential, more vulnerable me couldn't find. As a result, I don't have strong and clear recollections of most of those painful moments. In digging them up now, after more than twenty years, they show the ill effects of having been buried for so long—those memories are mostly composed of a patchwork of faded and decomposed images. Simultaneously, what DID also did for me was to preserve the more pleasant experiences—and there were many—by placing them in a kind of sealed jar. I can remember some things that happened very clearly, but what I did or how I felt about them at the time is murky at best. One of the symptoms of DID is a disconnection from time and events, and my lack of recollection, my disconnection from many of the most traumatic experiences, was one of the key diagnostic points my doctor used to confirm his claims about the nature of my mental illness.

I'm still struggling with the knowledge that I have a mental illness, and making sense of my life knowing what I know now remains a real challenge for me. I've taken on as my life's mission not just understanding DID for my personal benefit, but understanding it so that other people may enrich their lives, lessen their level of pain, and find comfort in knowing that even with all those different alters as company, they, and I, are not alone.

Foreword from Dr. Jerry Mungadze

I met Herschel Walker for the first time while participating in the *Dallas Times Herald* indoor track meet at Reunion Arena in 1980. Carl Lewis and Herschel Walker were featured to compete in the forty-meter dash, while I was slated to run the two-mile race. Before the race, I remember the intensity between the two athletes. Carl and Herschel didn't speak. They just warmed up—pacing and staring at each other. Seconds after the starter gun sounded, Herschel had won the race, and instantly the tension melted away. As he relaxed, Herschel introduced himself to me and my African runner friends. I immediately connected with him, and through the years, we developed a friendship as we chatted at various meets in which we would both compete. Little did I know that this same passionate sports hero would one day walk into my office, facing perhaps the greatest challenge in his life.

Trying to understand what was happening to him, Herschel bluntly asked me, "Doc, am I crazy?" And so our journey together began. For the past twenty years, I have guided hundreds of people struggling with dissociative disorders on the difficult path of recovery. But doing so with someone like Herschel Walker has truly been an extraordinary experience—not because of his celebrity status, but because of what he brings to the journey for himself and all others who share similar experiences.

Herschel did not *have* to share his personal battles with anyone outside his family, but he is courageous and caring enough to do so. Inviting you, the reader, into the compelling story of his life, Herschel poignantly shares how he has used adversity to inspire him to be successful in his running career, his professional football career, his Olympic career, and in his business life.

For those readers who may have been diagnosed with a dissociative disorder or are struggling with the negative aspects of dissociation, *Breaking Free* will inspire you to accept your diagnosis, to work with your alter personalities, and to seek help if you are not already in therapy. For those readers already being treated, this book will open doors to self-help ideas you have not thought of before.

Finally, *Breaking Free* will also help your family members obtain a better understanding of dissociative identity disorder (DID) and how it works. It will drastically change their perceptions of the disorder, as well as help them lovingly embrace their loved ones who daily live with DID.

Jerry Mungadze Ph.D.

Dissociative Disorders expert, Mungadze Trauma Programs

Adjunct Professor in treatment of trauma-related disorders,

Baptist University Graduate School, Dallas, Texas

Prologue

The day had started like most others in my life. I rose well before my wife, Cindy, and son, Christian, were awake. I slipped quietly down the stairs of our suburban Dallas home and stepped into what I consider in some ways to be my safe haven—my workout and exercise area. I got down on the floor and began my usual routine—2,500 sit-ups and 1,500 push-ups. I'd been following that same pattern for more than twenty-eight years, 365 days a year come rain or shine, feast or famine, on the road or at home. Only today, in the process of writing this, did I calculate what that all meant: 17,500 sit-ups a week; 910,000 per year; 25.480 million since it all began back in Wrightsville, Georgia, as a chunky sixth grader. By my calculations, it will take me a little more than twelve and a half more years to reach 37 million—the number of miles the Earth

1

is from Jupiter. My allusion to another planet is deliberate; for a lot of my life, I've felt like an alien, and tried to put a great distance between other people and me.

After I finished my workout, I took a quick shower and then I sat and read the newspapers with the television turned to CNN, to catch up on the world's events, just as I did nearly every morning. That routine comforted me; my playing days were over in one sense but in many others they never ended. I folded up the papers and put them in the recycling bin. I brushed my teeth and checked on Christian before going to my home office, where I spent the rest of the morning. Cindy came in at one point to let me know that she was going out with some friends for lunch, and she'd be taking Christian with her. I kissed them both good-bye and returned to my work.

A few hours later, I was still seated at my desk, reviewing some paperwork I'd taken home regarding a potential deal I was hoping to make. I was determined to make Renaissance Man Food Services and Herschel's Famous 34 major players in a very tough industry. Since I'd stopped playing football three years before in 1998, I'd been focusing much of my competitive energy on making my many business interests flourish. Things were going well. I really didn't need to work, money was not an issue for me, but I'd been relentlessly restless for the last twenty-five years of my life, and I wasn't about to slow down.

I'd sat there checking and rechecking some numbers, when I glanced at the calendar on my desk. The date was February 24, 2001. In exactly seven days, I was going to turn thirty-nine years old. Hard to believe that time had passed so quickly. I'd enjoyed a stellar college career, won the Heisman Trophy, finished up my professional days as the number two player in all-purpose yardage (number one if you considered, which the NFL didn't, my yards earned in the USFL), represented my country in the 1992 Winter Olympics in Albertville, France, been paid millions of dollars for playing a game, and earned millions more from endorsement deals. I'd been able to help family and friends, met with presidents and business leaders, was married to the only woman I'd ever loved, had a son I adored. Considering all that, what was about to happen made little sense to me then, and only now can I understand my actions at all.

The phone rang. It was my friend Robert Jones's wife, Natalie. When I heard her voice, I suspected what the call was about. I looked at the calendar again. It had been almost six days. Natalie and I exchanged hellos.

"Herschel," she said, "he's here but Bob isn't around. What do you want me to do?"

I felt as though someone had thrown a switch in my head. "Natalie, whatever you do, you tell that man not to do anything. He's to stay right there. He better not even think about unloading that car."

"Herschel, I'll talk to him, but—"

I cut her off. "Natalie, I'm telling you, that man had better not touch that car or move a muscle."

"I'll see what I can do."

In one part of my brain, Natalie's frightened tone registered and made me even angrier. Not at her, but at the guy sitting in her driveway. He'd jerked me around long enough. I was going to put an end to that. What's right is right, and what this man had been doing was wrong. Way wrong. I could never abide by people taking advantage of someone else—especially me. Another part of me felt bad about putting Natalie, an innocent bystander, in a tough position and for alarming her. That didn't stop the downhill slide I felt, the rapid acceleration of my emotions.

"I'm getting in the car, and I'll be there in twenty minutes. He better be there when I get there."

I slammed the phone down, grabbed a set of keys, and literally ran out of the house to the garage. I stood in the weak February sunlight, pressing the button on the key fob, listening for the distinctive blip that would tell me which car's keys I'd grabbed. I hustled over to the far bay and waited impatiently for the opener to raise the door. I was tempted to grab the handle myself; instead, I waited for what seemed minutes for the rattling mechanism to do its work. Sliding behind the wheel of my Mercedes E Class sedan, I felt like there was a war raging inside of me.

Natalie had called to let me know that a car that I'd ordered from a man in Philadelphia had arrived. I'd originally asked that it be delivered to Robert's house because I was scheduled to be out of town. Well, my trip had come and gone, and still no car had been delivered. Six days had passed, and this man had not honored our agreement. I'd spent three days sitting at home waiting to hear from him, expecting that he'd be honorable enough to at least keep me posted on the status of the delivery. And now this? He doesn't even return my calls, but instead calls my friend's house, completely ignoring my message that it should now be delivered straight to me? Was that any way to do business? Did this guy think he could get away with not keeping his word? I couldn't let him get away with that.

I could feel my jaw pulsing and my teeth grinding as I sped down Church Road toward Robert's house. I wondered for a moment if my Beretta pistol was still in the glove compartment. I'd been a licensed and registered handgun owner for years, had permits to carry a concealed weapon, and had even gone to the FBI academy during two off-seasons to do some training. I'd majored in criminal justice in college and had dreamed of serving in the FBI. The logical side of me knew that what I was thinking of doing to this man—murdering him for messing up my schedule—wasn't a viable alternative. But another side of me was so angry that all I could think was how satisfying it would feel to step out of the car, pull out the gun, slip off the safety, and squeeze the trigger. It would be no different from sighting on the targets I'd fired at for years—except for the visceral enjoyment I'd get from seeing the small entry wound and the spray of brain tissue and blood—like a Fourth of July firework—exploding behind him.

Every few seconds, I'd hear a voice telling me, "No, Herschel, that's wrong. You can't shoot a man down in cold blood over this." Over that voice I'd hear another urging me on: "You've got to take care of business. This guy has done you wrong. You can't let him get away with that. Kill him." Over and over these two voices were shouting at me, each one pleading with me. As I made the turn south on the four-lane highway that would take me to the subdivision where Robert and Natalie lived, I began to pray to God. For even longer than I'd been doing my daily routine of exercises, I'd been praying. As a born-again Christian, I believe God actively and directly influences me to action. I asked that He help stop me from what I was about to do.

"Lord, Jesus, I do not want to kill this man. Please, dear God, somehow show me what it is that I should do."

My hands were crushing the steering wheel, and when I caught a glimpse of myself in the rearview mirror, I saw the veins and sinews in my face and neck standing out like rivers and streams on a relief map. My face was contorted and it was difficult for me to believe that the person I saw in that mirror, eyes darting furiously from the mirror to the road ahead, was really me.

"Do it."

"Stop it."

"Do it."

"You can't."

"Do it."

Like the pulsing rhythm of a chorus, the two voices kept up a relentless beat. Simultaneously, I felt frightened, exhilarated, disgusted, at peace, and resigned. Motoring up to Robert's house, I felt as if adrenaline was being pumped by the gallon into my system. Everything came into such sharp focus. Every red petal of the flowering burning bush that lined the driveway stood out in stark contrast to the boxwood evergreens that squatted in front of them. Red. Green. Go. Stop. Do it. Don't.

I repeated my plea to God for guidance. As always, He was there for me then.

I stopped the car and slammed the shifter into park. As I was reaching for the glove compartment to check for my gun, I could see through the web of steel that made up the carriage of the auto transport trailer to the back window of the semi's cab.

SMILE. JESUS LOVES YOU read the sticker plastered there.

I had my answer. I sat in the car for a few minutes, head in my hands, giving thanks to God. The voices quieted and then fell silent. All I could hear was the ticking of my turn signal. Lord knows how long it had been on, but I knew that I needed to take a new direction in my life.

The Herschel Walker who had driven to that house with murder in his heart and mind was not the Herschel Walker I had been for most of life. Something was clearly wrong with me, and I had to figure out what it was. And quickly.

All my life I've faced life's battles head-on and at great speed. I was about to embark on a challenge I'd never thought I'd have to face, but one that I was determined to win. For a while then, and at various periods of my life, I felt like I was losing control, spiraling downward, acting out in ways I'd never thought possible. I'd been wondering if I needed professional help in answering this question: "Doctor, am I crazy?"

Before I would see a doctor, though, I had more push-ups

and sit-ups to do. Why was that 37 million miles to Jupiter and the number of exercises I completed so important to me? Because for a lot of my life I've felt isolated from the rest of the world. I'd been running for most of life, from what only I really knew but seldom talked about. It was time to stop running and face some harsh realities.

Chapter One

Diagnosed but Not Defined

In the days, weeks, and months following my asking (and mind you, not for the first time) that question about my sanity, I got my answer. Doctors told me that my behavior and history indicated that I had dissociative identity disorder. That is the term that mental health professionals now use in place of multiple personality disorder. I can understand why the American Psychiatric Association, in 1994, in its definitive guidebook to identifying mental illness, the *Diagnostic and Statistical Manual of Mental Disorders-IV,* changed that name.

As advanced as we like to believe we are, when it comes to mental illness, many people react with shock and horror when they are diagnosed with it. Worse, when we learn that a loved one, a friend, even someone we know casually or not at all has been diagnosed with mental illness, a part of us recoils. We don't want to believe it, and yet we're fascinated to learn the news of the diagnosis, searching our memory banks for telltale clues to fortify our suspicions that something wasn't quite right with the person all along. In rural Georgia of the 1960s, we sometimes talked about people, relatives or neighbors, who we sensed "weren't quite right" or "touched in the head." Most often we simply referred to these poor folks as "tetched." All those attempts at softening the language of mental illness represent our efforts to avoid the sometimes harsh reality of what it does to those with the condition and to those who know them. The term *multiple personality disorder* was another distortion of the reality of the condition. I don't know how any of us in my family would have reacted if we had heard that term applied to any one of us.

My family wasn't one for gossiping and spreading rumors, but I can remember all of us gathered around for one occasion or another and one of us making a passing reference to Mrs. Johnson. She lived in town, and was, it seemed to me at eight years old, an elderly, stooped woman. I remember her as a woman who walked around town always dressed to the nines. Clad in her Sunday go-to-church suit, a necklace with pearls as big as marbles strung around her neck, and a red smear of lipstick that didn't so much cover her lips but thickly trace the outlines of them, she was hard not to notice. What I remember most is that she always seemed to be involved in a conversation with herself, that gash of a mouth in constant motion.

Now, I can't say for certain that she suffered from DID, but I do remember my mother telling me just a year or so ago that Mrs. Johnson had passed. That shocked me, and I thought the woman surely must have been nearly a hundred and twenty years old when God called her home. Turns out she was only seventy-three. Whether my mis-estimate of her age was typical of a young child's view of an elder or an accurate perception of Mrs. Johnson's physical transformation as a result of mental illness, I can't say for sure. But I do know this: whenever Mrs. Johnson was mentioned, the adults reacted one of two ways. They either rolled their eyes in pity, or dropped them in shame—both accompanied by a sad, slow shake of the head. Pity and shame live in the same run-down neighborhood, and I don't ever want to live there, let alone visit.

The shame and pity of it all is that we view mental illness the way we do—most often as a failure of the person's will, a weakness of character. In recent years, some mental disorders have come out the closet, so to speak. We now recognize that mood disorders like depression and bipolarity afflict many people and their origins are chemical in nature and not a character flaw. We can all sit and watch the commercials the pharmaceutical companies and their advertising agencies put out touting the effectiveness of their latest antidepressant compounds—Cymbalta, Lexapro, Paxil, and others. We may even know the difference among monoamine oxidase inhibitors (MAOIs), tricyclics, and selective serotonin reuptake inhibitors (SSRIs), thanks to the frequent newscasts, magazine articles, and books about depression. That makes sense when you consider that according to the National Institute for Mental Health, approximately 20.9 million people over the age of eighteen suffer from various mood disorders. That number translates into nearly 10 percent of the American population. That accounts for less than half of the 26.2 percent of Americans over the age of eighteen who may be diagnosed with a mental disorder in any one year. That means 57.7 million people in this country alone have some form of mental illness.

Increasingly, we have heard in the last few years about what the NIMH classifies as "anxiety disorders." Among these are the various phobias, panic disorder, obsessive-compulsive disorder, post-traumatic stress disorder, and general anxiety disorder (GAD). The NIMH estimates that nearly 40 million Americans experience the symptoms of any one of these anxiety disorders each year. That is slightly over 18 percent of the population.

We've come to accept mood disorders and anxiety disorders as a part of our culture—they may be a product of our intensity and the fast-paced and uncertain nature of our lives. They've come to be so normalized that television audiences have embraced the actor Tony Shaloub's portrayal of an obsessive-compulsive detective on the show *Monk*. We view the outward manifestations of his mental illness as endearing quirks. While I'm glad that in one sense our responses and reactions to some mental disorders have changed, I'm not certain that the same can be said for DID or another kind of personality disorder, schizophrenia.

In fact, if you go to the home page of the NIMH Web site, you will find that while schizophrenia is listed, DID isn't. If you dig a little deeper into the Web site and search for the term *DID*, you will only find one entry—and that is on mental health and mass violence.

My hope for this book is to educate people about DID. Truth be told, until I was diagnosed with the disorder in 2002, I had never heard of it. When I was told that the disorder was once called multiple personality disorder, immediate images of the movie *Sybil* sprang to mind. I had never read the book by Flora Rheta Schreiber that the TV miniseries was based on, but I did watch Sally Fields as she played the shy young graduate student with sixteen different personalities. Sybil's so-called waking self was a fearful, nerve-racked young woman who had to rely on other personalities or "alters" to deal with most everyday situations. When she needed to be aggressive and assert herself, Peggy Ann or Peggy Lou would step out of the shadows and help Sybil. If she needed to be friendly and engage other people in conversation, then Vicky took control. Depending upon the situation and what it demanded of her, Sybil could call on any one or a combination of those sixteen distinct personalities to take on the task. For most of us, our impressions of DID or multiple personality disorder are shaped by that movie, or the classic *Three Faces of Eve,* or maybe by a more recent movie, *Primal Fear,* starring Edward Norton as a conniving, violent murderer who may or may not suffer from the disorder.

Like all fictionalized accounts, those films contain elements of truth as well as fiction. In order to effectively show what is going on as each personality reveals itself, characters are often shown speaking in different voices, with very different mannerisms and accents, and other very distinctive physical and vocal traits. In reality, only people with the most severe cases of DID will behave in that way. In my case, I may have acted out in ways that were out of character for me (as I did in the car purchase incident) but it wasn't as if I walked, talked, or looked very much different from my "usual" self. Most people would have made the assumption that I was having a bad day, not that a Bad Herschel had taken over. In truth, there was a bad, angry Herschel inside of me, just as there is inside all of us. What made me different, and what characterized my distinct form of DID, was that for the majority of my life, the alternate personalities that I developed did far more good than harm. That I believe DID can be a powerfully effective tool for some people is likely to be the greatest shock you will encounter in reading this account of my life and the role DID played in it.

Since there is so much "information" out there about DID that I believe is distorted or inaccurate, I've decided to risk the shame and potential pity my revelation will elicit in order to come forward to reveal the truth about my mental illness. I can remember very clearly the moment I decided to take this step. I was looking over my collection of vintage watches. I held a Patek Philippe in my hand, one of the finest Swiss timepieces ever made, and began to wonder about the men who had worn it previously. Was time kind to this person? Did the passing seconds and minutes bring them happiness or sadness? Did they bring great wealth or debt? Did they bring freedom or bondage?

Our lives revolve around time, either wanting it to go faster or to stop it. Time is a very valuable commodity, and what we choose to do with it will make a difference in our lives as well as the lives of other people. I was raised to believe that each of us is responsible for choosing the kind of imprint we leave on this world.

You can have fame and be known around the world. You can have more money than you will ever be able to spend. You can live in a million-dollar mansion and drive a Mercedes-Benz. But if you can't or won't help others, all of that's in vain. Your life will be like someone who carries his money in a bag riddled with holes.

I feel there is a specific plan and purpose for every person on the face of the earth. I have accomplished many goals in my life, and because I have received so many honors and awards, some may think I have fulfilled my destiny. I feel that the greatest achievement of my life will be to tell the world my truth, from my perspective, about dissociative identity disorder.

I hope my legacy will be more than what I have achieved on the football field and on the track. I would rather be remembered for opening my heart and sharing my experience with DID so that others can understand this condition.

A lot of research has been conducted and many books have been written concerning DID, none of which have cast it in a positive light. My goal is to help bring freedom to the lives of those who have it and understanding to those who have never experienced it. I want to show that dissociative identity disorder can sometimes be a positive tool for good rather than something always negative and destructive. In many ways, my belief about DID is a lot like the condition itself. DID is a coping mechanism that we use in the face of something that could potentially destroy us—in that sense, it is a very positive thing we use in the face of something over-whelmingly negative.

Just as depression is just one type of mood disorder, DID is just one type of dissociative disorder. To understand what it is, we have to understand what dissociation is. As the word suggests, dissociation is a mental process in which we don't associate or connect one idea(s) with another or others.

For example, we all daydream, and have all probably had the experience of driving in a car and looking down at the odometer, the clock, or a passing road sign and realizing that a significant chunk of miles or minutes has passed of which we have little or no recollection. The same may happen when we "get lost" in a good book or a movie. We're not aware of the passage of time, or maybe even the entrances or exits of others in the room. We lose touch (disconnect or dissociate) with the context of our surroundings. If we experience that, does it mean that we are mentally ill? Of course not. I use those experiences just to show how the mental process of dissociation works. When that process is more complex and chronic, then we've moved along the scale from mild to more severe and entered into the realm of dissociative disorders. The most severe cases of dissociative disorders can prevent people from fully functioning, while others with dissociative disorders, like me, can hold down full-time jobs and appear to be leading a typical, "normal" life.

The key word in DID is *identity*. When a person has DID, they either consciously or unconsciously create another identity (often referred to, as I will throughout this book, as an "alter") in order to dissociate from some painful, traumatic events. To illustrate the difference between the general term *dissociate* and DID, let's use the example of a young woman who is the victim of incest. In order to cope with that incredibly traumatic experience, the mind dissociates or disconnects the person's thoughts, emotions, memories, actions, or even identity from the circumstances. For example, a young woman who is sexually abused (as was Sybil) may dissociate the room, the time of day, from the ongoing memory of the attacks. This offers a kind of temporary emotional escape from the horror, the fear, and the pain, of what has happened to her. If you've ever wondered how a victim of incest can remain living in the same house with his or her abuser, it's often because of the process of dissociation. It can be as simple as "blocking out" those memories or as complex as creating an alter who suffered the abuse. When DID is present, that alter is the one present during the abusive episodes, but is not the one seated at the breakfast table the morning after the attack chatting away as if nothing had happened. To that victim of DID, it really is as if nothing had happened to her—it happened to that alter who was momentarily, or even much of the time, not present. That lack of connection or association is what marks all dissociative disorders regardless of the severity. Again, what makes DID distinct from other dissociative disorders—post-traumatic stress disorder (PTSD) is the most widely known of them—is the creation of that other identity, personality, or alter.

PTSD and DID are very closely linked, and most people with DID are also diagnosed with PTSD. The reason for that should be obvious—DID is the result of a trauma, and the alter or alters developed in response to it are initiated during and after that trauma. Not everyone with PTSD develops alters, but everyone with DID has suffered, to one degree or another, some kind of trauma, usually in childhood. For children, DID and any other form of dissociation are an extremely effective defense against pain—physical and emotional—or the fear of that pain being inflicted on them. It allows them not just to endure the pain, but to function as though the trauma hasn't happened to them at all. What a wonderful thing the mind can do for us; we can survive what would seem to be overwhelmingly hopeless situations and live to fight another day. That is the way that I prefer to look at it. I have to admit that there is a downside to it—that persons with DID continue to suffer the abuse, dissociate from it, and, as a result, not report the abuse. Another downside is that over time, because the escape is so effective, those with DID get so good at using their coping strategy that they overuse it. I hate to use a football analogy for fear of trivializing this, but I think you will understand the point better if I do. If a team has success with a particular running play—a halfback toss, for example—they may start to call it more and more. The defense will make an adjustment, and as a result, the play will break down and the running back will be thrown for a loss.

What also happens frequently with DID is that the person will continue to use a coping mechanism long after the traumatic circumstances are in the past. If you continue to use that same dissociation or have developed those alters to help you, and your circumstances have changed, then your coping mechanism is no longer effective. My father, Willis, used to say, "If you think of yourself as a hammer, you start to see everyone and everything as a nail. Some people and some situations don't call for being pounded on." In other words, you need the right tool for the right job.

What is also important to keep in mind is that all of this takes place at the level of the subconscious. I was never aware that I was using a coping mechanism to deal with the abusive treatment leveled at me. I just responded. When the choice I made to deal with the pain worked, I used it again when a similar kind of threatening situation occurred. Through repetition, the habit of having an alter take over became a routine, and the brain is a marvelously efficient machine that likes to take any process we are engaged in—from driving a car to walking to insulating ourselves against hurtful negative comments—from the conscious to the subconscious level. That is what DID did for me, and why as I was growing up, I didn't consciously realize what I was doing—I was just doing it because it worked.

In my case, it took me a long time to realize that as much as DID helped me, it also, in some circumstances, pounded me on the head and cost me dearly. Over the years, I have also come to realize that through dissociative identity disorder, I have gained confidence, true friendships, freedom from fear and loneliness, relief from pain and hurt, and an ability to retreat into a world of my own whenever I choose. Knowing when and how to use that hammer is, I believe, the key to living a healthy life. Knowledge is power, and it is my deepest desire to share what I have learned about myself and DID with you.

You may not have any personal experience with DID, but from what I learned through research and the events of my own life, you've probably had some experience with a form of mental illness. I want to do what I can to help remove the stigma of mental illness, to demonstrate how once it is understood, DID and the mental process of dissociation can be channeled into something positive. To do that, we've got to back to the beginning and the cause of my DID. To do that, we've got to head to Wrightsville, Georgia, a place that, oddly enough, given all that I've just told you about DID, holds many wonderful memories for me.

Before we go on, though, I want to make something else clear. I've been diagnosed with DID, but I have chosen not to let that diagnosis define me or limit me. I don't think of myself as a "victim" of the disorder, nor do I "suffer" from it. Quite simply, I have it. It doesn't have me. Knowledge has given me even more power. Power has given me control. God has given me all things, and through Him and with Him, and for Him, I can do all things. And so can you.

Chapter Two

Signs and Wonders

Ｐeople with DID, in particular those with the most severe forms of it, have suffered a great trauma in their life, particularly in early childhood. As I said before, I don't have perfect recall of my childhood, but I do know one thing for certain—I was born into a loving, supportive, and God-fearing family. I know with the same certainty that I just drew a breath that I was not physically or verbally abused by any member of my immediate or extended family. I suffered no sexual abuse at the hands of anyone. I state this so emphatically because many DIDers have experienced that particularly horrible brand of trauma. I feel fortunate to not have had to deal with that reality.

I don't know if it is a blessing or a curse to not remember with any clarity a single defining incident or series of incidents that caused the onset of my using DID as a coping mechanism. I do sometimes wonder if that faulty memory is a function of DID itself, but doctors have told me that there really is no such thing as a perfect textbook case of DID—or any other mental disorder, for that matter. I've taken a microscope to my memory banks and not come up with a definitive incident that I can call a cause. I'm very much a perfectionist, and it sometimes troubles me that I'm not that perfect textbook case.

What I can tell you with perfect clarity is that I was born on March 3, 1962, in Augusta, Georgia. My father, Willis, met my mother, Christine Taylor, when she was only sixteen or seventeen. They married shortly thereafter. My father was comfortable around women, having grown up in a house filled with them. His father, my paternal grandfather, died when my father was still a child. He had six sisters and a mother to tend to, and I suspect I got my sense of duty and responsibility from him. He had to quit school before he got his high school diploma so that he could help support them. What I got from my paternal grandfather was my first name. I also shared my birth date with him and with my father. I don't put much stock in coincidences, but I've wondered if there is some significance to the three of us sharing a birthday like that. With six siblings, my mother came from a large family herself. In my family, holiday get-togethers and Sunday-evening meals (church services took up most of the day) were always boisterous, crowded affairs. We were churchgoing people, but we also knew how to laugh and have fun.

By the time I came around, my parents had already had four other children in somewhat rapid succession. Willis Jr., Renneth, Sharon, Veronica, and I averaged being separated by about fourteen months. Later on, my brother Lorenza, and little sister, Carol, joined the fold. Not only were we close in age, we were a very tight family. We lived outside the small town of Wrightsville, some fifty miles east of Macon—the home of

Little Richard. While Wrightsville wasn't a one-stoplight town, you could probably have counted the traffic signals on one hand. There was a Piggly Wiggly grocery store in town and not a whole lot else. Neighboring Dublin, seven or so miles south of Wrightsville, was considerably larger, having three high schools, a couple of grocery stores, and a more thriving downtown area. We seldom made the trip up route Route 57 to Macon. First, we didn't have much money, and second, just about anything we needed we could get in Wrightsville or Dublin.

We didn't live in Wrightsville proper; instead, we lived in a house about five or so miles outside of town. To get to our place, you had to cross three sets of railroad tracks. I never had the sense that we lived on the proverbial wrong side of the tracks. I also never felt poor, though that was the reality of our situation. When I was very young, my father worked the fields for a white landowner by the name of Mr. Jackson, and my mother was the housekeeper for the Jackson family. She treated those kids (a boy and a girl) as though they were her own. The good Christian woman that she is, she also taught all of us that color was invisible. Whether a person did wrong or right was what mattered and not pigmentation. I can't say that everyone shared that feeling, this being southern rural Georgia in the 1960s, but in our house and to this day, that is what I believe and put it into practice. It wasn't always easy to believe that and put into practice. Wrightsville is in Johnson County, and of the four thousand or so people in Wrightsville itself and the seven thousand in the county, 80 to 85 percent were white, and racism's long legacy in rural Georgia was still deeply rooted.

Our little wood-frame house sat about three or four miles away from our closest neighbor. We were isolated geographically, and our closest aunt or uncle lived nearly ten miles away. Our property wasn't all cultivated land. Surrounding the house were stately pine and oak trees, some draped with Spanish moss. When I was old enough to be out on my own, I loved wandering around those woods and fields. I listened for the welcome sounds of brown thatcher birds singing nearby, and the squirrels chattering among themselves as they scrambled for acorns. The thorns of the Cherokee rose vine would seem to reach out and grab my pant leg. This was a beautiful, delicate white flower with a gold center that reminded me of my mother. Sometimes I pricked my finger attempting to gather them for her.

I can't say that I was a mama's boy, but I do adore my mother. In looking for links to DID, I sometimes wonder if it was my separation from her that triggered some early predisposition for the disorder. My mother fell ill immediately after I was born. She had to take her bedrest, and my mother and father thought it best that I go to live with my maternal grandparents, Alfred and Ann Lee Taylor. I often tell people that if, after I die, and I'm waiting in line at the Gates of Heaven and I see that Ann Lee Taylor has been turned away, then I'm going to get out that line and follow her, because if that woman can't get into heaven, there is no hope for me.

As far as I'm concerned, Grandma Ann Lee asked Jesus to set the moon and the stars in the heavens for me to enjoy and to keep me safe. I needed that sense of safety because I was horribly terrified of the dark as a child. *Petrified* is a good word to describe my fear—it dried me up and froze me solid in place. I don't know why I had such a strong reaction to the dark, but it was real and it was severe.

As kids, one of our favorite things to do was to climb trees. We also helped Dad cut down some of the trees that had been marked for firewood, and chopped and split the wood in preparation for cold winter nights.

I remember sitting around the fire with my family, soaking up warmth and listening to the crackling of the wood, taking comfort in the sound and scent. When the fire burned down, sometimes Mom or Dad would send me outside to bring in more wood. I dreaded going outside, but I did as I was told. I'd pause at the door for a moment, take a deep breath, and plunge into the unknown. During the day, the trees were my friends, but they seemed to be my enemies in the dark. The movement of their branches quickened my pulse and constricted my throat. I imagined that the tree limbs were arms reaching out to grab me, take me to some even darker place to do things to me that I could not begin to imagine. Stepping off the porch to cross the lawn to the woodpile had my chest thumping and my ears ringing. If I stepped on a twig or over a rock, it was as if I'd snapped some dead person's limb or trod on a skull. I'd quickly gather up the wood, and make the stomach-churning, bladder-burning journey back to the light. My mother and father would look up from the television, or whatever else they were doing, and see me standing there beaming.

"Thank you so much, little man," my father would say.

"Thank you, son," my mother would add.

They thought I was smiling with pride, looking for a compliment, but the reality was that I was glad to be back in the light and alive.

I never told anyone that I was so frightened of the dark. Keeping my emotions to myself, of not letting anyone in my family know about what was troubling me, was a trait I shared with the rest of the family. Though we were very close, we weren't ever really openly demonstrative about our emotions—especially as we got older. I knew I was loved, and I knew I loved my mother and father and siblings, but none of us ever really showed those feelings openly. As far as my fear of the dark was concerned, I stuck with what seemed to be a family rule: suffer in silence.

Later on those evenings, Mom would tuck me into bed, say a prayer, kiss me good night, and turn out the light. Lying in the silence as darkness infiltrated the room, I would sometimes feel engulfed and swallowed up by it. Having my brothers in the same room with me didn't help ease my anxiety or lessen my fear. I was not about to cry out, crawl next to one of them, or otherwise seek comfort.

I was tortured by what I assume were nightmares, but what I experienced lacked the unreal qualities that typify most bad dreams. At the time, and even now, I'm still not sure if I was asleep or awake when these visitors came to me. I know that kids often see a frightening movie or read a scary story and go to bed, and shadows and light transform themselves into shapes. That's not what happened to me. Instead, the images I saw in front of me were as real as any of Hollywood's most expensive visual effects. Most often, I saw animals in my bedroom—wolves mainly. They weren't immediately threatening me, but I could see them sitting and staring at me with baleful, pale yellow eyes. I could feel their hot, fetid breath and hear their soft yet menacing panting. I wouldn't cry out because I was afraid that would make them spring into action, and I didn't want to wake anyone in my family. I lay there rigid, fighting back sobs, until, my energy completely spent, I drifted into a restless sleep.

Describing your dreams or nightmares is difficult, and I can never capture the visceral nature of them and my fear. I tried lots of things to escape them, but sleeping with the blankets pulled over my head, counting to myself, or any other attempt to take my mind off what I knew was out there lurking failed—at first. Over time, I didn't so much lose my fear of the dark and those visions as I escaped them. When I was young, I didn't know about the power of dissociation and how DID works, but that is what I must have employed to get over my fear. I wish that I could tell you that I had a switch that I could flip, or that eerie music played to signal the entrance of one of my alters, but that didn't happen. Just as I sensed a presence in my room, those animals, in time I became aware of another presence, but this one calmed and reassured me. It never spoke aloud, but I did hear it. I can't say that it was speaking to me, because that core self, the frightened one, was gone. In its place was this new being who wasn't afraid of the dark or the animal images I saw. He was brave and courageous and whatever fears or other emotions my frightened self must have experienced were gone and I had no memory of them. Only in talking to my doctors and in thinking deeply about my past am I really able to recall these incidents. I'm as mystified by the process of the formation of this alter as you probably are.

Unlike the stereotypical depictions of people with multiple personality disorder—when we see the alters being aware of the presence of one another and interacting with one another or commenting on the others—with my form of DID, I had no conscious awareness of there being multiple forms of me. I was always just me, except I exhibited different behaviors. Many researchers into DID talk about the ability of a child to "go there." Where the person with DID is going is to some safe place he's carved out for himself and left another version of himself behind to deal with the pain or fear. The way I understand it is that if you remained conscious of the fact that this alter was being left behind and suffering, you'd be in pain as well—and also feeling guilty for having sacrificed one of them to spare you. If you had any conscious awareness of what was going on, then the coping mechanism wouldn't be very effective. In other words, you can't, on a conscious level, say to yourself, "Okay, I've been beaten in the past and it hurts me a lot, so I'm going to send 'Bob' in there to take the abuse while I go off someplace else."

All of the dissociation and formation of alters takes place at the subconscious level, and whenever a new alter steps in, you aren't aware of that transformation taking place. It just happens. What makes this a really tricky concept to understand is that my alters were self-created. I was responsible for them coming into my consciousness and becoming a part of me. At some point, and I have no memory of doing it, I did "go there" for the first time and experienced relief from my fear. Once I figured out how to do this, and in my case that meant forming an alter who was more or less fearless, I did it with greater and greater frequency. I was not entering into any kind of psychotic state, fugue state, or any of the things that constitute schizophrenia and a true break from reality. Everything was still happening to me in the real world. I wasn't imagining that I was no longer afraid of the dark or of those animals: I—this newly created self—truly was no longer afraid of those things.

To better understand how this concept works, here's how a *conscious* thought process would go:

> I am experiencing something painful.
>
> I don't like the emotions or physical pain I'm in.
>
> I feel powerless to escape from it physically.
>
> I can't endure it any longer.
>
> I need help to get out of this situation.
>
> I am going to go somewhere in my mind that is very far from this real experience.
>
> I am going to imagine that this is happening to someone else.
>
> I am going to enlist the aid of someone who is stronger than me to ward off these feelings.
>
> The strategies I've used have been successful—I am no longer conscious of the pain.
>
> I'm going to use these strategies again when the need arises.

Of course, none of those thoughts registered in my conscious mind, but that's essentially the process I went through at a subconscious level to get through the bad stuff.

If all that I had experienced as a child was this fear of the dark and nightmares or night visions, then it would be pretty easy to chalk up my overcoming those fears to maturation. Many of us have fears of the dark and are troubled by nightmares, and most of us simply outgrow those troubling aspects of childhood. In my case, only when you take into account additional adaptations I made to overcome other more serious obstacles does the DID diagnosis make sense.

I come from a very athletically gifted family. Not only were my older brothers and sisters standouts on the playing fields and courts, but many of my cousins were as well. For the longest time, it didn't seem as though I was ever going to even approach the kind of athletic success any of them enjoyed. To put it simply, I was fat. Couple that with a severe stuttering problem, and you have a recipe for a schoolyard disaster. Everyone in my family did their best to treat me just like any other kid, and my mother did her best to help me to read and to speak well, but my stuttering persisted. I spent hours in front of the mirror reading aloud from books and practicing tongue twisters. As many sit-ups and push-ups as I would do later on, that was how many times I've said, "Sally sells seashells by the seashore."

Stuttering and its causes remain a bit of mystery to medical researchers. Speech pathologists have been able to identify different types of stuttering, but what causes it still isn't known. In general, a stutter is one of the several kinds of communication disorders that produce something specialists call a "disfluency." Most of us produce disfluencies on a regular basis—we may punctuate our vocalizations with *ums* and *ahs* or other speech sounds to produce a pause while we think of and get our vocal production mechanism ready to produce the sounds necessary for the next word. In my case, and in the case of most severe stutterers, I repeated certain words and sounds as well as practicing prolonged enunciation of certain sounds. The type and degree of repetitions vary from stutterer to stutterer, and in some of the most severe cases, the person appears to be running out of breath while speaking and the muscles and joints used in speech appear to be tense, distorting the individual's face as she speaks.

As you can imagine, when kids from outside the family discovered that I stuttered, I was in for a lot of t-t-t-eeaa-sssing. If I'd only been overweight and stumpy, I might have gotten just a little grief; after all, there were other kids in my school who shared that characteristic. Unfortunately, I had the fat-kid sin and the stuttering sin in combination, and I was the only one at Johnson County Primary and Elementary who stuttered. If any of you reading this are parents of school-age children, then you know how cruel other kids can be and how the cruelest kids have a finely honed sense that enables them to identify and target any characteristic that sets a child apart as different from the pack.

From my very first days at school until I entered high school, I was subject to a daily assault of verbal and sometimes physical abuse by my classmates. In some ways, it seems like harmless teasing. What kid doesn't have his name used and abused and twisted into some insulting form or other. "Herschel is a 'girl-schel' " isn't really all that bad, even when it's drawn out in stuttered singsong form to last half a minute: "H-h-h-h-h-er-sch-sch-sch-sch-el is-is-is-is-a-a-a-g-g-g-g-irl-irl-sch-sch-sch-sch-el!" Repeat that over and over again for the duration of the time we were gathered on the playground before school and the first bell rang, and you can understand how, in time, the song of the playground swings was replaced in my mind by that mocking music. Of course, the other kids employed other insults, most of which I've long since forgotten, but I'm sure you get the point.

I wish that I could tell you that, in TV movie-of-the-week fashion, I discovered a sensitive, compassionate classmate or teacher who rushed to my defense and protected me. In that make-believe scenario, the student would be a popular girl, one of the leaders of the top-tier social clique who is willing to risk her own social status to befriend me. If it was instead a teacher, she'd be a young idealistic woman, fresh from a radicalized campus up north who came to rural Georgia bound and determined to wipe out injustice wherever she found it. Not only would she take me under her wing, she'd eventually get me to the point where I would stand triumphant in front of the whole school as the district speech tournament champion—the two of us holding my trophy aloft, faces beaming. A quick cut to my mother dabbing at the corner of her eye with a handkerchief, my father on his feet slamming his hands together, telling everyone, "That's my son."

This, however, is reality, and the only true part of that scenario is that I did have incredibly supportive parents. The harsher truth is that my fellow students most often treated me like I had the plague—and in the cutthroat world of adolescence, the truth is that I did. No one wanted to associate with me because I was an outcast, a stuttering-stumpy-fat-poor-other-side-of-the-railroad-tracks-living-stupid-country boy. To be seen with him was to be stained with his original sins and to be cast out of the garden of acceptance. I didn't blame those kids then, and I don't blame them now. Saying that doesn't diminish the hurt I felt or the longing I experienced. I craved contact with the other students, and that's probably part of the reason I took the brunt of their verbal abuse without complaint. Even though the Herschel-the-girlschel chant was irritating and pointless, at least I was hearing my name spoken aloud, I was getting some kind of attention from someone at school.

To my teachers, I was as transparent as glass. They saw right through me, not in the best sense of seeing how my outward calm masked my inner hurt and anger, but in the sense that in their eyes, I wasn't even there. In their defense, I should point out that this was rural Georgia in the early 1970s. These teachers were well intentioned but likely ill prepared to deal with someone like me. Johnson County schools had no speech pathologist on staff. We were a poor rural school district, and I'd be surprised if my teachers even made $10,000 a year to educate kids who frequently came to school empty of belly and devoid of much hope for a better life. I know I wasn't aware of all the socioeconomic factors then, but, according to the 2000 census, the median income for a household in the city is $17,750, and the median income for a family is $21,429. About 33.7 percent of families and 35.5 percent of the population were below the poverty line, including 52.6 percent of those under age eighteen and 26.4 percent of those age sixty-five or over. If those numbers are at all comparable to the time when I was in the lower grades, then my stuttering set me apart, but there were plenty of other kids with other disadvantages in my classes. If so many other kids were downtrodden, then they didn't need to look far to find someone in worse shape. A sad truth, but kids mirror the society they are brought up in. Everybody is looking for somebody to put down as a means to feel better about themselves.

Again, I'm not excusing what was done to me or how I was treated. I'm simply saying this is the reality that I deal with. Believe me, I hated the idea that everyone thought that I was stupid because I stuttered. If you think that notion about stuttering and low intelligence is ridiculous and no one would believe there's a correlation between the two, the Stuttering Foundation of America lists "Five Myths" on the home page of its Web site. The number one myth, even today, is the one about stuttering and low intelligence. That belief had to be even more pervasive back when I was in elementary school. I can remember being in the sixth grade in a social studies class. We were in the middle of a lesson about the Greeks, the Romans, and the Spartans. I had developed a love of history, and, in particular, I loved to read about these three ancient civilizations. I especially enjoyed reading about their martial practices, their wars, and the physical preparations the members of the warrior class undertook. The teacher asked if anyone knew where the word *gymnasium* came from and what it meant in Greek culture. Of course I knew the answer, and I could have cited chapter and verse about the athletic and educational nature of the institution, what the related institution *palestrae* was, that both were under the protection and patronage of Heracles, Hermes, and, in Athens, Theseus. I knew that athletic training and competition were integral parts of the social and spiritual life of the Greeks from early on, that the contests took place to honor heroes and gods, and sometimes as part of the funeral rites of a fallen chief. I also knew that many of the athletic rites and practices the Greeks took part in had their origins in Sparta.

All of those words and concepts came fluidly into my mind, but I didn't raise my hand. I'd learned early on that speaking aloud in class brought me more ridicule. I guess my teachers were trying to protect me, and a lot of times even if I did raise my hand, they didn't call on me. Why risk my embarrassment and their having to try to restore order to a classroom outburst spawned by my stuttering response?

So I sat there with my mouth shut and my mind racing with ideas.

That's not to say that some folks weren't trying to slow me down by throwing obstacles in my path. In the fourth grade, a teacher, whose name I've not forgotten but I will not share with you, walked back into the school building with me after recess. I don't know if she'd seen me sitting off by myself or what, but she put her arm on my shoulder and said, "Poor Herschel. Life is going to be tough on you."

I looked up at her, and she had a sad, hound-dog look—the jowly sunken-eyed look of a bloodhound who'd lost the scent. "You ain't going to amount to much in this life, child. Maybe you'll get your reward later on."

I was so used to being put down that I didn't respond immediately. I simply filed it away along with all the other insults, petty and painful, that I would eventually use as kindling to ignite the fire in me. Maybe other people didn't believe in me, but I developed alternate personalities who did, ones who insulated me from the harshness outside my family circle, who let me know that I could amount to anything I wanted to. Fortunately, in time I'd have demonstrable evidence that this was the case, that other people had underestimated me and my scholastic abilities.

At least by the time I reached the sixth grade, my marks had improved greatly and I was pretty sure that my teachers didn't think of me as stupid. It was just easier for everyone concerned if Herschel remained a spectator and not a participant. But man, how I wanted to participate.

We didn't have much money when I was real young, but every now and then my mother or father could spare a nickel or a dime or a quarter. Now, I'm no angel and I'm as tempted by the offerings of the flesh as the next man or boy. Having that bit of metal in my pocket triggered fantasies of being able to stop at one of the local service stations in town that had a candy counter. (Keep in mind that I was a fleshy youngster.) With a dime I could get a couple of caramel Bull's Eyes, peanut-buttery Mary Janes, the sweet hot torture of an Atomic Fireball, the sophisticated flavor of black licorice whips, or the velvety goodness of a chocolate-covered—well, just about anything chocolate covered was good.

As sorely tempted as I was to spend that money on candy, I wanted to taste something sweeter—connection with one of my classmates. At recess, I'd go out on the playground, and while all the other kids climbed over the playground equipment, played Chinese tag—a variation on the game in which you have to place your hand on whatever part of your body the person who is "It" has touched—jumped rope, or stood in a gaggle gossiping, I'd target someone. I usually picked someone who wasn't involved in one of the activities or larger groups. Stealth wasn't really necessary, but it helped. I'd slink (as much as someone of my size could) up to one of the younger kids and tap him or her on the shoulder. I always hated how their look of surprise and delight turned to disappointment when they saw it was me. Undaunted, I'd hold out the sweaty coin in the palm of my hand and offer it to them. At first they'd look at the coin and then at me, suspicion clouding their face. What could this guy be up to? Then I'd ask them, "Talk to m-m-me?"

Once they understood the nature of the transaction, they'd take the coin and we'd talk for a few minutes. I don't recall that we discussed the great issues of the day, we just chatted about the mundane things that kids do. I can't describe how good it felt to step out of my usual isolation tank and into the fresh air of human interaction.

As kids, we spend the better part of our day at school, and to be shut up and shut out of so many things each and every day made school excruciating. Those few moments of respite from that isolation, even if I had to pay for them, were what kept me going to school. I was used to being treated normally at home, so the contrast between school and the rest of my life was so great as to be painful. I would sit in class, and have the sensation that I was like a guppy or blue tetra that someone had brought in and neglected to take home from show-and-tell. I was submerged in my own environment, glassed off from the rest of them, subject to the torturous tappings on my fishbowl walls by the most belligerent students, ignored by most others, and fed infrequently whenever someone noticed me or I made enough of a splash to get their attention.

In a lot of ways, being relegated to oblivion would have been better. The verbal attacks lost their sting after a while. The physical attacks were something else. I played a violent body-contact sport at the highest level, I've attained black-belt status in several martial arts, but the blows that I remember having taken in those activities don't seem to have the same impact on me as those earlier beatings do. I really don't like to dwell on the past, but in the interest of getting at the truth about DID, I've had to examine some of these elements of my past. The truth is that I was frequently the subject of beatings throughout my early school days.

My refusal to let other kids see that their words hurt me infuriated them. Early on, I made the decision not to respond when teased. In my family, we jokingly teased one another. My mother didn't like it much, so we restricted it to when we were out of her earshot. We never said the kind of really cruel things my schoolmates said to me. (If I had a dime for every time someone chanted "Herschel, Herschel, fatty, fatty two-by-four, can't fit through the bathroom door," I could have hosted a United Nations of conversations during those playground recesses.) I did develop a bit of a thick skin, and I knew the difference between the kind of loving, though purposeful teasing my siblings and cousins practiced and the kind meant to hurt that my peers employed.

When I wouldn't flinch and show that I'd been wounded by their remarks, a lot of the boys resorted to violent sneak attacks. Even that started as small-scale skirmishes—guerrilla-warfare tactics. I became infinitely familiar with "Chester" (a quick fist thump to the chest), "Charlie" (a similar blow targeting the front or back of the upper leg), "Green Frogs" (a raised knuckle punch to the biceps designed to produce an immediate blue-green bruise), "Indian Sun burns" (the skin of the forearm twisted in opposite directions), and a host of slaps to the back of the head. I was a frequent target of "bookings"—having your books slapped or kicked out of your hands. I knew better than to clutch my books to my chest—in the manner that girls did—since that style of book carrying improved security but also lowered your level of masculinity exponentially.

Again, when I stoically endured those kinds of assaults, my enemies had to raise the stakes. The physical confrontations became more like actual fistfights and wrestling matches. Despite some bloody noses and fat lips, and a few torn shirts, I was able to keep the knowledge of all of this from my family. I had older siblings at school, and they may or may not have heard about what was happening to me, but I know that they didn't hear a thing from me about it.

My response to the verbal and physical assaults of my classmates is fairly strong evidence that I used DID to rescue myself from those bad situations. I didn't go to teachers, my parents, my older siblings; I relied on myself to get through it all. I just kept hearing this voice in my head that was telling me, "It's okay, Herschel. Don't worry none about what they're saying to you. It's not true. You're not a bad kid. You're not stupid. You're okay. Don't let none of this hurt you. You're fine." And I was, or at least that part of me was, content and happy. Just as when I was afraid of the dark and a voice soothed me, this alter, who, if you want to put a name to it, could be called the Consoler, came to my rescue.

Today, I know that psychologists and psychiatrists use the term *self talk* to describe this phenomenon of the internal conversations we have with ourselves. It can be either positive ("You're going to be okay, don't worry about it") or negative ("You're such an idiot. How can you be so stupid?") and we all engage in it. With me and my form of DID, that kind of talk took on a more extreme form and this voice, over time, developed a kind of identity of its own. In order to cope with the beatings, the verbal abuse, and the isolation, that consoler became a kind of parent or friend figure in my life. Those consoling words became a kind of mantra, ones I repeated so often that eventually they became like white noise and I didn't really hear them but felt their effect.

As a result, as was true of overcoming my fear of the dark

and my torturous daydreams, in the place of the one who was afflicted, the Hero alter emerged. That Hero alter was the one who put on the facade of not being affected by what was being said or done to me. The core, central Herschel was hurt, but he was on the sidelines, so to speak, while the alter took the field. Again, this took place on the level of the subconscious, so I wasn't really aware of how all of this was transpiring. At that subconscious level, it was working something like this: I had a coachlike alter who would recognize what was going on—I was being beat on, for example—and he would point to one of the other alters on the bench. The Consoler would get up and enter the game. Once he'd done his job, then the Coach would send in the Hero alter to take the place of both the essential, central self and the Consoler. All of this took place in nanoseconds in real time. The Coach or, as I sometimes like to think of him, the General, was aware of the presence of the other alters. Not all of the alters knew of the existence of the others, but some did. For example, the Hero alter knew that the Consoler existed and was aware as well of the presence of the Frightened/Wounded alter. He didn't much care for the weakness the Frightened/Wounded alter exhibited.

Other members of the "team" contributed to helping me "go there" and to cope directly and indirectly. I don't want to compare myself to a comic-book superhero, but its useful to think of how those superheroes formed an "alter ego" as a result of some trauma they experienced. Bruce Wayne witnessed his parents' death, and as a result, he formed that alternate identity of the Batman. In a sense, that was what I was doing—creating a stand-in who could do some of the things I may have felt my essential self was incapable of. An indirect result of how I was treated and how I coped with that treatment was that I developed a highly sensitive sense of right and wrong. Along with that, I formed a very black-and-white, yes-and-no moral and ethical sense that has both helped and hurt me to this day.

When I got so angry at the man who didn't deliver the car to me on the day that I specified and in the manner I requested, that was that Judge identity coming into play. And he's not a very impartial kind of guy. He sees things in very stark terms. You said you were going to do something for me on a date and a time and you failed to do it; therefore, you must be punished—and punished severely. I guess he's a hanging judge.

On a more positive note, I developed a great deal of empathy as a result of the harsh treatment I received as a kid. I can't stand to see other people get taken advantage of or hurt. I have that same mentality as those superheroes or wounded healers we see a lot in cop shows who live their lives seeking revenge and to right the wrongs they see in the world. As a kid, I wasn't able to do much about the many injustices I saw in the world, but I was busy collecting and cataloging them for later use. The Judge eventually needed an enforcer, and he wasn't yet fully developed. He'd eventually emerge as a prominent part of my personality.

Why I didn't tell my parents or siblings about what was happening is a confounding mystery. Maybe I was ashamed to admit that I wasn't strong like my brothers and sisters were. My lack of communication skills, my stuttering, were also a part of it. Not being able to express myself fluently in words contributed to my lacking emotional fluency. I didn't really have the words or the means to express to anyone else what I was feeling. I was all stuffed up with pain and anger and gave it no outlet. I was not about to cry. That wasn't a possibility at all.

We're a pretty independent bunch, my family, and, as I've already said, a group who didn't express their emotions easily or openly. I don't blame anyone for that, and I know a lot of people who had similar upbringings in emotionally guarded surroundings who didn't develop DID. All I know is that in my earliest years, I formed another kind of family, one who nurtured me and enabled me to survive. As the habit of "going there" and not responding emotionally transformed itself from a subconscious choice into a way of being, it was like cement setting and then hardening over time until it formed the solid, nearly impenetrable foundation of my personality and being. I learned some lessons as a result of that survival—that I could endure most anything, that I didn't really need anyone else. Those lessons were both good things and bad things—as I was to learn much later in life. I am also a very quick study, about my myself and my schoolwork.

Another identity emerged as a result of those experiences, one who served me well, or so I thought, for nearly all my life. In looking back on this, I think of him as the Sentry. Because of how I was treated because of my weight and stuttering, I never let anyone get really close to me. I was then and remain a very guarded person, carefully evaluating people in my life, always asking myself what these people want from me, what they are doing stepping into my territory, what harm they might do to me. I'm less certain that this Sentry alter had working along-side him a Guard Dog—someone with a ferocious bark who warned off intruders. I haven't spoken to many people about my DID, and I don't know if part of the reason for my lack of close ties (and I'm not even sure if that "lack" exists—what is a normal number of friends?) was that I scared people away. Did they view me as aloof, cold, arrogant? I can't say, but when I was a child, I don't think any of those words could describe me. I was aching for real attachment to people, particularly out-side my family, and I understand now that this is a critical part of establishing our identity as we move into adolescence and adulthood. That process is called individuation, and I wonder if maybe because my process of individuation was so skewed by what had happened to me and how I coped with the circum-stances of my youngest days, I developed those other identities in place of a more cohesive single identity. I'm still learning, still puzzling.

Breaking Free

I didn't like school all that much at the start, but I loved learning. I also looked forward to getting home after school to the pitcher of Kool-Aid that my mother had prepared before setting off for work. By the time I was in the middle elementary grades, my mother was working as a seamstress in a clothing factory. My dad had gone to work at a chalk factory over in Irvington (birthplace of the actress Victoria Principal) and he'd come home with his coffee-colored skin sprinkled with what looked like dry creamer.

Waiting for them to come home, I enjoyed watching *Gilligan's Island* on TV, writing poetry, and reading *Cowboy Sam* books. We didn't seem to be suffering financially. We had three meals a day, my mother was talented enough with a needle and a thread to make many of our clothes, and the flow of hand-me-downs kept all of us kids in reasonably fine fashion. So what did I have to complain about? I could put up with those kids messing with me at school, no problem. I'd learned that there was a place I could always go to in my head—along with my house—where nothing bothered me at all.

I wasn't even that lonely and isolated. I had friends in my head who supported and encouraged me and made me feel safe and wanted. Really, what more could a young boy ask for?

When boredom set in, I still had time to escape to my favorite place, the railroad tracks. I'd cut through the woods, and when I reached the tracks, I'd jump from tie to tie, carefully balancing myself on the rails to avoid falling. Here I was in a world of my own, far from the ridicule and harassment of my classmates.

I used the rocks in the bed of the tracks as a distraction to relieve the frustration and rejection of my traumatizing day. I carefully selected my stones one by one and threw them at the signs along the tracks. Day after day, I spent endless hours at the railroad tracks waiting for the next train to come through. I loved the locomotive with its power and might. I marveled at the huge engine and its ability to pull the entire train with such ease. I loved running along beside it, the ground vibrating under my feet as I imagined that I was a similarly powerful engine. As much as I enjoyed this exciting pastime, the whistle of the retreating train would quickly bring back feelings of loneliness.

Watching trains go by, I observed the separation of the cars and felt my own detachment, disconnection, and isolation; feelings similar to what I had experienced when I had been separated from my mother. I fantasized about getting on the train and going somewhere, anywhere. I knew the only way to get on that train was in my imagination. I wondered, "Where is that train going?"

I knew I couldn't afford to buy a ticket on those passenger trains and the freights were far too dangerous a place for me to spend any time, but running alongside them gave me a temporary sense of peace and contentment.

I probably had more of an active imagination than most kids my age because of my enforced isolation and silence. One of the places I could go to, along with my alters, was a rich and protective cocoon of my imaginings. Very often my mind would wander or I would narrate some scenario in which I described the Hero's exploits in which I envisioned my imagined best self. I suppose that most children daydream, but my mental wanderings were much more purposeful; they were another form of escape, another more healthy way of "going there." In concert with my developing alters, they allowed me to flee when I wasn't yet as fleet of foot as I would become.

At that time, I could not have known that my travels would extend far beyond the boundaries of the places where that train could go. Since then, I have traveled the entire globe, and my destiny has transported me far beyond the railroad tracks of Wrightsville, Georgia, all because I decided that I needed, and wanted, to run.

Chapter Three

A Manchild on a Mission

If it's somewhat hard for me to pinpoint the exact incidents and experiences that triggered me to develop alters to deal with the harsh treatment of my peers, I have a much easier time identifying those people and events that helped trigger my physical transformation. As an adult, I became aware of Charles Atlas and the ads that kids used to find in the backs of comic books and magazines. You know the ones I'm referring to—the ninety-eight-pound weakling getting sand kicked in his face who blossoms once he sends away for, then receives, and follows the exercise routines that Mr. Atlas recommended. I never sent away for Mr. Atlas's program, but I did undergo a radical transformation starting when I was in the sixth grade from a much-larger-than-ninety-eight-pound ugly duckling into one of the finest athletes to come out of Johnson County.

41

I didn't do it alone, but it sure felt like it. My alters fostered an us-against-the-world mentality that had me thinking I couldn't let anybody else in on our secrets.

A concept that many people seem to neglect when undertaking a weight-loss program or a fitness regimen is how important it is to change from the inside out before you can hope to effectively change your health, weight, or appearance. In my case, a spiritual transformation was also necessary.

I know that one of the key events of my radically changing the course of my life had to do with shoes. Shoes are about the last thing you would think of when you consider re-forming your mind and spirit, but on one particular Sunday, I didn't feel much like going to church. To avoid having to go, I hid my shoes in the closet. I was fortunate to have a pair of hand-me-down go-to-church shoes. There were a lot of times when we couldn't afford any kind of shoes at all.

I don't recall why I didn't want to go to church that particular Sunday. That was very unusual for me, and not going was something my mother and my grandmother wouldn't tolerate. Ranger's Grove Church of God and Christ was the sun around which our lives orbited come the Lord's day. Both my mother and grandmother sang in the choir, and churchgoing was an all-day affair. I'd grown up hearing Bible stories from Mother and later reading them myself. I found strength and comfort in them. The meek inheriting the earth sounded good to me, so I don't know why I hid my shoes that Sunday when I was fourteen. My nickname among my family is Bo, and my mother followed me around the house saying, "Bo, you got to go, you got to go."

I kept saying, "I don't have my shoes."

She'd been helping me search for them for a few minutes, she was down on one knee peering under the bed when she looked up at me and said, "Bo, you got to go. It don't matter if you don't have your shoes. Jesus don't care what you look like."

I'd heard the story of Saint Paul, the reformed Roman soldier named Saul, who once persecuted Christians. He was on horseback and on his way to Damascus, when God struck him down with a blinding flash of light. Jesus later instructed a man named Ananais to heal him. After that, Paul became a devoted follower of the Son of God. Now, I didn't experience a blinding flash of light when I heard my mother say that Jesus didn't care about what I looked like, but I thought that was unusual because it seemed like everybody else cared what I looked like. If I hadn't have been so overweight, the kids would have had far less to tease and torment me about. I also thought, "This Jesus really sounds like a cool dude." So I went to church that day and paid extra-close attention to what Pastor Edwards had to say about Jesus. Three hours later I walked out of services knowing that I was going to be on a new spiritual path.

I had been a believer before; the solid values and the ethical foundation my parents had instilled in me from the very beginning had been implanted in bedrock. Now it was time for me to build on that foundation. I don't know if I can say exactly that I decided to become a born-again Christian, but I did decide that I was going to fully accept Jesus as my savior, confess to Him all of my sins, and become a brand-new person. I asked God to come into my life and to help me. He was going to help me separate the wheat from the chaff in my own life. I was going to put behind me, as Saint Paul tells us in First Corinthians, my "childish ways." Spiritually, that meant that I had to be baptized and washed with the blood of Jesus. I underwent that process and have remained an active and devout member of the church ever since. With God fully in control of my life, I've been able to accomplish the many things that I have. Without that spiritual transformation, I don't know what might have become of me. Having God and Our Lord and Savior Jesus Christ in my life has meant that I can focus on the present and the future.

Once I made that spiritual choice, it seemed as if a giant ball started rolling, and momentum was going to carry me. It only seemed that way, and there were more than a few bumps in the road to keep this transformation from being something that Jeannie from the TV show *I Dream of Jeannie* could have done with her arms folded and a magical blink. The spiritual part was willing, but the flesh was still weak. I still enjoyed coming home from school and plopping in front of the TV set or going out along the railroad tracks and throwing rocks. There was that time in his life when David was regarded as a mere shepherd boy tending his father's flock. However, when God looked at him, He saw the king David would become.

When the train engineer passed my house, he saw just a little boy who lived and played by the railroad tracks. How could he have known that boy would some day dine with presidents, kings, and other dignitaries? How could I have known myself that these things would come to pass? Though these ideas of transforming myself were just beginning, I can see now how my spiritual life was going to help me change the circumstances of my earthly life. Though I had only vague notions of how I wanted things to be, Hebrews 11:1 helped put things in perspective for me. "Now faith is being sure of what we hope for and certain of what we do not see." I was just beginning to hope and only beginning to see some results. The faith I had in God wasn't nearly as strong yet as the faith He had in me.

By the time my sixth-grade year rolled around, I was a pretty good student, and was managing to get most of my homework done while still at school. That left me with plenty of free time—except for the chores that I had to do. My mother was no feminist, but she was an equal-opportunity chore assigner. Didn't matter if you were a son or daughter, she taught you to cook and clean, wash, hang out, and fold the laundry, and a bunch of other domestic chores. My ideal life of leisure wasn't going to happen in this lifetime, not with my mother around, so I was kept pretty busy, but still managed to sit in front of the old Zenith TV we had in the living room for at least a few hours each night, if not immediately after school.

I was usually the oldest one in the family at home after school. All of my older siblings were involved in after-school activities. Since they weren't at home, they weren't doing any of the after-school chores that I was doing. In my head, an equation formed. Sports = no chores. I'd begun to shed some of my excess weight as I grew taller, not a lot of it, and wasn't a particularly stellar athlete like my older brothers and sisters were. That was okay. I wasn't in it to set records, just get out of doing some of the work I had to do around the house. That was my motivation at first, but over time I did want to start setting records.

Before I could do that, I had to set some goals for myself. Even though I was that dumpy little kid who everybody picked on, I had a taste for challenges—self-imposed and otherwise. At the end of each of the three school years spanning sixth through eighth grade, I gave myself a test—a kind of final exam—to see how I measured up.

The summer between my sixth and seventh years of school, I began to eat, sleep, and breathe running, dreaming of the day I could zip past my sister Veronica. She was on the track team, and her being a girl and all, I figured she would be the best target to start with. The very first thing I did was to put that active imagination of mine to better use. I visualized myself running past my sister, running past an opponent in the opposite lane, and then running beyond myself. I asked my younger brother, Lorenza, to be my training partner. For the next few weeks, every day after school, instead of heading into the house for a glass of Kool-Aid or sweet tea, we'd go over to the railroad tracks for a training session. I'd run along the tracks, with Lorenza at my side, and I'd keep that image in my mind of racing past Veronica. I swore Lorenza to secrecy, and he kept his end of the bargain. No one knew what I was up to, and I don't think anyone really noticed the changes in my behavior, and certainly not in my appearance—they were far too subtle at this point to be visible. I knew that I was going to have to have faith in myself and do these things without anyone else's help beside Lorenza's.

I understand much better now why I chose running. Not only did I have role models around the house, but I really was trying to run away from my past and the verbal abuse and beatings I'd taken. If my words couldn't flow smoothly from my mouth, I could at least move my feet fluidly. Instead of simply "going there" mentally, I could now go somewhere physically. If I felt constrained by my weight and stuttering issues, then running gave me a small taste of freedom and escape that was like an elixir.

Sadly, as I look back over those early days, I'm struck by how much of myself I withheld from others. I didn't want to tell any of my older siblings about my plans to run for a couple of reasons. Number one was I knew they'd be supportive, but I'd also get more teasing from them. I wasn't about to open myself up to that. Number two, I instinctively felt that I had to do this myself, that no one else was ever going to care as much about my success and progress as me. Number three, and here is where the DID really kicks in, I felt like I didn't need anyone else—here was the Sentry and the Consoler coming into play. I don't think it even occurred to me at that age to share any of my dreams or aspirations with anyone. I was so used to being isolated, and so used to having the Consoler telling me I was going to be okay, that I didn't need anyone else. Lorenza was the exception, and I probably asked him along as much out of a sense of responsibility as I did out of a need for companionship. He was my younger brother and I needed to look out for him. Duty and responsibility were so important in my family, and along with my genuine affection for him, I did feel those additional pulls. Most of all, though, through the influence of those alters, I felt like I had to develop faith in myself, by myself, for myself.

That faith was severely tested early on in my training. Toward the end of the summer of my transformation, just as I was about to enter the seventh grade, I experienced two things whenever I ran—my nose bled and I felt terrible pain and stiffness in my knees, and at night they'd swell terribly. I put up with the discomfort and kept running, but in time my mother noticed the bloodstains on some of my T-shirts and other workout clothes. I had to tell her what was going on. If the bloody clothes weren't enough of a red flag, I would sometimes hobble around the house like a stooped and elderly man from my knee pain. It wasn't just the pain; the swelling in them had formed into hard knots. My knees and lower legs started to look like gnarled and twisted tree limbs.

Despite my protests, my mother insisted that I go to see a doctor. She got time off from her bosses at Paracraft—the textile plant—and took me to nearby Dublin. I don't remember much of the car ride, except that I was filled with dread. I wasn't afraid of the doctor or needles or anything like that, or of the pain I might have to go through in being examined; instead, I was afraid that I was going to have to take time off from my routines. School was about to resume, and I'd shed a few pounds and added some muscle and vertical inches. I didn't want to experience any setbacks now that I was on this mission.

Dr. Thomas's office was in a squat white clapboard house that had been converted into a medical facility. The waiting room, what had once been the living room, had only one window, which was partially covered with a pair of deep maroon velvet curtains. What little light filtered through tinted everything the color of Mercurochrome. It was as if all of us sitting

47

in the waiting room had already received first aid for whatever wound we were suffering from. Dr. Thomas only had a few magazines sitting on a scratched and wobbly coffee table—*Highlights,* a few *Time* magazines, and one dog-eared copy of *Reader's Digest.* I lost myself in a story of an earthquake and tidal wave that had swamped the Alaskan coastline some years before. My mother darned a few pairs of socks.

When it was time for us to go into the examination room, my mind was still back in Alaska, with a man who ran a lumber mill. Dr. Thomas came in a few minutes later. He had me drop my pants and get into a gown so that he could look at my knees more closely. He asked me a few simple questions and poked and prodded the angry swollen joint. I mostly just answered with a simple "Yes, sir" or "No, sir." From the first moment I saw Dr. Thomas, he had a scowl on his face, like he'd just eaten something he didn't like, so I couldn't tell from his reactions if he thought what I had was serious. His nurse assistant brought me to another room after the doctor was through with me. I had to hold a big padded device in front of me, what looked like an umpire's chest protector, while she took X-rays of my lower legs. When she was done, I was asked to put my pants back on and sit in the waiting room. I was surprised that my mother wasn't out there waiting for me.

I really felt nothing the whole time I was with the doctor, having the X-rays taken, and while I sat in the waiting room after. That detachment from the events and the possibilities I faced was fairly typical for me at this stage in my life. I'd developed enough defenses to keep out most bad thoughts. I don't know why I had been so filled with anxiety on the drive to the doctor's office. In a way, I think of that as the anticipation before the game or the battle. Once I entered the fray, I was fine. My mother didn't have to say much to calm me or to soothe me, since the alters were telling me that everything was going to be fine.

All of those defense mechanisms crumbled when I was finally called into the doctor's office. He was seated behind a cluttered desk, and he had his hands folded behind his head. My mother would barely make eye contact with me. She was seated in a chair, half turned from me. I looked at the doctor. Above his head, a clock in the shape of a University of Georgia football helmet ticked loudly.

"Young man, in most regards you're an extremely healthy individual. I'm afraid, though, that it would be inadvisable for you to run. In fact, I don't think you'll ever be able to run again. Doing so would put you at great risk of losing whatever mobility you have in your legs currently."

Each of his words pierced the shield of detachment I'd held in front of me. I cast a glance at my mother, and she seemed on the verge of tears. That's when my lips started to quiver and my throat tightened.

"Thank you, sir," was all I could manage to say.

Looking back, I can see that my mother and I were very naive in the ways of medicine. Neither of us asked any questions or even thought of getting a second opinion. We simply accepted what the doctor told us. Doctors weren't to be questioned, and to this day, I don't know what Dr. Thomas's official diagnosis was, and maybe I've exaggerated how dire his prognosis was. I've since learned that a lot of active young kids who go through a so-called growth spurt develop something called Osgood-Schlatter disease. All I knew then was that it was as if someone had chopped me, and my dream, off at the knees. I walked out of the doctor's office and into the waiting room and I felt smaller, diminished, like the tables and chairs had either grown in size or I'd reverted to my toddler height. My mother took my hand once we were outside and held it until we reached the car: "I'm so sorry, Bo." As I've said, my family wasn't big on displays of physical affection, but she held my hand and then held me close to her. I didn't want to cry or to let her know how upset I was and I put up a good fight, conquering my tears quickly.

I rolled down the window and felt the breeze flowing across my face. That's what I loved about running, the feeling of abandon and freedom. As the green fields of southern Georgia rolled past me, I closed my eyes. I heard my mother saying a prayer, and when she was through, she said again, "I'm so sorry, Bo. I wish there was something I could do. I surely do. Anything at all."

"Me, too, Mama. Me, too."

Chapter Four

Using My Feet

An old African proverb states, "When you pray, use your feet." My mother's prayer on the car ride home from Dr. Thomas's office only included one part of that two-part formula for getting what you want. To me, the proverb means that it is important to ask for God's help and guidance, but you shouldn't just sit around and wait for Him to do everything for you. I guess that the American equivalent of that expression is "God helps those who help themselves." When things get tough and get out of control, I tell Jesus that I need His help. I make that request with a pure heart, not with malice, not with anger, but a pure heart. That is what my mother always told me. You may not make the right choice, but if you decide based on a pure heart, Jesus will help guide you and direct you. He knows that you aren't doing it for any reason other than just because it is the right thing to do.

At the age of twelve, it's hard to remember those simple truths when faced with what seems to be a situation in which you are getting the exact opposite of what you want. I can't say that being told I couldn't run anymore was a death sentence, but if I had been taking that first of three final examinations I was going to eventually administer myself, then I had failed. By the time we got back to the house, I still hadn't come to terms with the doctor's prognosis. I went immediately to my room and sat on the edge of the bed. I tried to put everything in perspective, but my mind was a jumble. I heard my mother stirring in the kitchen. She was singing the old church hymn, *Blessed Assurance, Jesus Is Mine!* A moment later she came into the room.

"Herschel, I know that what the doctor said was hard to take, but you and I know a lot more about these things than he does. You know that if you put your mind to it, if you have a pure desire, you can do anything. Do you hear me, Bo? *A-n-y-t-h-i-n-g.* If you want it good enough, it will come true."

I always liked how my mother turned that phrase around; instead of saying if you want something bad enough, she said that you should want something good enough—again, that purity-of-heart concept. Then she recited the words from Psalm 18:32–33, words that I have found comfort and motivation in ever since:

It is God who arms me with strength
  and makes my way perfect.

He makes my feet like the feet of a deer;
  he enables me to stand on the heights.

Looking up at her, it was as if she'd wiped the slate clean and I had no memory of what that doctor had said. I smiled at her. I had a second chance to take that test.

"You want to run. Go run." She smiled back at me.

Breaking Free

I changed into my workout clothes. The railroad tracks seemed the best place for me to run. If I was out on the track, my mother or one of my siblings could have seen me. For this, I needed to be alone. I waited until my mother was busy hanging laundry on the line before I set out. The sun was angling from behind a stand of pine trees, and its light was filtered through a haze of dust. Just before I'd left the house, I'd heard a freight train rumble down the line. A chorus of insects was buzzing and from somewhere far off, a distant dog's bark echoed.

I'd estimated that each railroad tie was about two feet from the next, and I'd set rocks at various intervals—a starting line, forty yards, fifty yards, one hundred yards, and two hundred yards—to mark various distances. I was going to loosen up with a few easy fifty-yard sprints. My knees had been throbbing the entire time it took me to walk to the tracks, but as I dragged my foot across the parched earth to create a starting line and then toed it, I felt nothing. I mumbled an on-your-marks-get-set-go to myself and took off running. Almost before I knew it, I was past the first marker and then the second. I slowed and then jogged back to the fifty-yard mark and completed the round-trip. I may not have had the feet of a deer as in the psalm, but I sure felt more fleet of foot than I had before. A little bit of faith was working wonders for me.

A film of sweat soon coated my skin, and soon that was shel-lacked with the reddish orange clay dust of the railroad bed. I must have been out there for more than an hour chasing my shadows. A passenger train bound for Macon sped past me, and I only diverted my attention from the task at hand long enough to see a boy a few years younger wave at me. All I could do was raise my hand in salute and keep pumping.

For the next few weeks before school started, and then after when classes began, I ran and ran. Morning distance work—running into Wrightsville; more sprints when I got home. Everything I'd done before. Only when I lay in bed at night did

53

the pain set in, but when I closed my eyes, it seemed to go away.

Now that I know about DID, and based on later experiences, I'm pretty sure that I developed an alter who was more or less impervious to pain—someone who was simply able to erase both the pain itself and any lasting memory of it. I mean, I'd feel the discomfort at first, but then something else would kick in, the Erase would kick in and I was able to go again at full speed. Unlike before, with my alters who helped me with my fear of the dark or to endure the teasing, when it came to dealing with pain, my switching, for lack of a better word, was closer to a truly conscious effort. I was aware that I was in pain, and I'd say to myself, "Okay. It's time to go. We've got to go. This isn't going to stop us. Push. Just push on through it." And I would.

In preparing for my training, I'd read a great deal about the human body, any book I could find on the subject. I think that having a good idea of what the body's physiology is and what it's capable of doing really helped me to overcome Dr. Thomas's dire news about my future as a runner. I really don't know what else could explain how in time, the knots disappeared, the nosebleeds stopped, and I had the track and football careers that I did. Without a doubt, the disciplined approach I took to my training helped me, but I can't emphasize enough how much pain my knees caused me when I first began to run after seeing Dr. Thomas. Somehow I was able to block out that pain and keep up with my training.

Wanting it good enough also meant that I had to be pure of heart in regard to my intentions for succeeding. It would have been easy for me to be motivated by a desire to show up other people who had made fun of me, doubted me, thought of me as the untalented runt of the litter destined for mediocrity at best. I could have found an almost endless supply of anger and bitterness to fuel my efforts to succeed. And believe me,

I was sorely tempted sometimes to go down that road. A few years ago, I saw the movie *The Apostle* with Robert Duvall. In it, the veteran actor plays a preacher whose life spins out of control. He discovers his wife's infidelity, attacks the man who is involved with his wife, and sets out to establish a new life in Louisiana. There, he begins to preach again on the radio. He's more than a bit tormented, and his internal struggle with issues of good and evil, right and wrong, his past and his present struck a chord with me.

I hope that I haven't given you the impression that the foundation of good strong values and ethics always made it easy for me to do the right thing. I struggled with the idea of avenging myself on people who had done me wrong—my abundant imagination sometimes led to fantasies of whaling on my tormentors. It wasn't always an easy matter to simply say, "Jesus told us to turn the other cheek, so that's what I'm going to do." The alters I developed didn't insulate me completely from the cold I felt, the loneliness, and the isolation. Remember, they developed in response to the kind of spiritual and emotional pain I felt. They weren't preventive measures initially but defensive ones. It's like if someone slaps you in the face and then you put your hands up to block other blows, that doesn't mean you don't still feel the sting of that first impact. So, believe me, I was sorely tempted to succeed on the football field, in the classroom, and near about anywhere else I could as a way of putting other people in their place. Sorely tempted.

I found some comfort in St. Paul's letter to the Romans. He made me realize that I wasn't alone in battling my wicked thoughts of revenge. As he wrote in verses 21–25:

> So I find this law at work: When I want to do good, evil
> is right there with me. For in my inner being I delight in
> God's law; but I see another law at work in the members
> of my body, waging war against the law of my mind and

making me a prisoner of the law of sin at work within my members. What a wretched man I am! Who will rescue me from this body of death? Thanks be to God—through Jesus Christ our Lord!"

Today, I can see how DID was waging war with me; not only was my body battling my mind, my mind was battling itself. Back then I wasn't aware of the effects of DID, all I knew was that there were times when I really wanted to take on those kids who harassed and tormented me. I needed the Lord to give me the strength not just to transform my body and overcome the doctor's diagnosis but to give me the strength to transform my impure thoughts into acts of forgiveness. I had to ask God for forgiveness as well. I knew that even though I didn't act on my revenge fantasies, they were still a sin.

The faith I had in God, the training, instruction, and role modeling that my parents had provided helped show me the way. That's not to say that I didn't become a football and track star at my high school purely because I wanted to be the best that I could be. That was a part of it. I enjoyed testing myself, but I also wanted something that had escaped me for the first twelve years of so of my life. I wanted to be noticed. I didn't want people to adore me, idolize me, or anything like that. I just wanted to end the isolation that I felt. I didn't want to be that kid who was shuffled to the bottom of the deck, to the back corner of the classroom, to get whatever scrap of leftover attention my teachers had to give. I wanted to be recognized for what I could do and not pointed at and stared at and tormented because of what I couldn't do. My improvements in overcoming stuttering took place over a long period of time. I didn't see the same kind of relatively quick results that I did with my body's transformation through exercise. And the taunts continued. What I described earlier was the immature phase of the teasing. As my classmates and I got older and our vocabularies expanded, they were able to muster up a whole new set of insults.

I'm a Christian man, so I won't repeat some what was said to me, but let's just say that they not only took the Lord's name in vain, they took mine, my mother's, my father's, my sisters', and my brothers' names in vain as well. To that, they added every combination of swearword for body parts, things that come out of our bodies naturally, things that naturally shouldn't go into our bodies, and every variation on fat, stupid, and lazy you can think of and mixed them all together. It was like they had a salad bar of insults to pick and choose from, and every day, they'd pile them up on an all-you-can-*speak*-size tray and dump them over me. I largely (pun very much intended) ignored them and tried to let it slide off my back.

The physical abuse slacked off and then stopped completely after I defended myself and beat up one of the eighth graders who had seemed to make it his life's mission to make my sixth grade year miserable. We each threw a few punches, but the fight settled into a wrestling match, and I outweighed him by a good margin. Once I was able to get on top of him, he burrowed into a kind of tick mode and the blows I rained down on the back of his head didn't do a whole lot of damage—they just kind of smashed his face into the dirt and scuffed up his chin and forehead. I took no real pleasure in beating him up, and, of course, added a bit of fuel to the verbal fire by sitting on top of him and squashing him like a bug. It's a good thing the General was able to rein in the Angry alter who I've always had to keep tight reins on. I had a whole lot of injustice tallied in my ledgers, and I don't like to think about what I might have done if I had balanced the books by taking it all out on that eighth grader.

I still experienced a lot of frustration in the classroom and socially. I don't know if I can help you understand what it was like to have so much to say, so much to contribute, so much to share, and to be locked out, silenced in many ways by many people. Speech is the most important tool of establishing human connection that we have. I've already told you that my family wasn't very demonstrative about affection. Without that kind of intimacy and without being able to make real connections with classmates or friends, I felt alien, like I was living in a world whose customs and nuances I could understand intellectually but not share in or participate in. Exclusion is often another form of inclusion, but as I've said before, I felt like my situation was so unique, that even the other castoffs, underachievers, and fliers below the radar that populate most high school hallways and classrooms didn't seem to want to welcome me. As is true of many schools, one way out of that anonymity and isolation is by acting out negatively. Being the class clown, getting in trouble with the law, or any of those negative options didn't appeal to me, weren't a part of my nature.

The only avenue open to me seemed to be sports. Johnson County High School isn't much different from most schools in this way. Jocks, and I never liked that term, were at the top of the social ladder. They were the ones whose exploits were the talk of the school. I wanted that. I wanted the attention, and I got it. And it felt good. What felt better is that I not only got it for succeeding in football, basketball, and track, but eventually in the classroom as well.

While I said I didn't take much pleasure in beating up my nemesis in sixth grade, I don't want to leave you with the impression that I was completely meek and mild. As my physical transformation was taking place, and my muscles grew thicker and stronger, my heart hardened as well. I only allowed this coldness of spirit to govern my behavior when I was working out, and later on the football field or the track. Call it another alter, or another facet of my personality being revealed as a result of my physical metamorphosis, but I eventually learned that I loved physical contact—the harder, the more brutal, the better. This Warrior alter is the one most people who competed against me or alongside me would, I hope, most likely associate with me.

It would take me some more time to get to the point where I developed a taste for that kind of physical matchup. To this point, I could only live vicariously through the stories of the Roman, Greek, and Spartan soldiers and warriors, tales of heroic pilots in World War I and infantrymen in World War II. I was a keen student of military history, and had designs on a career as a soldier.

Before I could enlist, I had more immediate concerns. My seventh-grade year meant graduation. The Georgia school system is a little bit different from most other states. Grades one to four were primary school. Fifth through seventh were the elementary grades, and eighth through twelfth constituted high school. Seventh grade, then, was a graduation year for me. It meant moving on to another phase and in a sense another group of kids to deal with. By that I mean the high school kids had a sense of entitlement and maturity that the younger kids lacked. We all went to school with one another for twelve years and few kids ever moved into or out of the area, so it wasn't like a new crop of kids was coming in, it was more like the crop I'd been planted with was coming into season and about to be harvested.

I knew I had to be prepared for eighth grade and everything that new phase meant.

As a sign of my own maturation, I did something somewhat out of character for me. I asked for help. Truth be told, it was more like I accepted an invitation for help. Mr. Tom Jordan became my guide. Mr. Jordan was the high school's football and track coach and knew my family well. Willis and Renneth both ran track for Mr. Jordan, and both received college scholarship offers, one for football and the other for basketball. For various reasons, neither Willis nor Renneth ever competed in college or graduated. Sharon and Veronica were both good athletes as well, and Veronica would precede me at the University of Georgia on a track-and-field scholarship.

One day at school, Mr. Jordan approached me and asked me if I was working out, if I was going to be ready for high school and football. I'd not played at all yet—we didn't have a peewee football program—so I told him I was doing some running. We talked about what I was doing for a little while, and he told me that he could help me refine what I was doing. I hadn't shown much promise as an athlete yet, but Mr. Jordan had vision and a belief that DNA doesn't lie. I didn't commit to anything at that point, I just thanked him for talking to me. I still wasn't used to any adult outside my family showing any kind of interest in me, and I think I was a bit thrown off by his approaching me. At first I figured I was in some kind of trouble. I took a few days to consider his offer.

Later that week, I decided to approach Mr. Jordan on Sunday after church. I don't know exactly what I was thinking when I headed across town to Mr. Jordan's house to ask him for advice. After all, I was one of the least athletic kids at the school, and he was the head track-and-field and football coach. As a white man, he lived in the white part of town, a place I seldom ventured. I grew up in the South in the late sixties and early seventies and the Klu Klux Klan was still a force in our community and cast a long shadow. Fortunately, men like Tom Jordan didn't care about color and race. I know that caused him some grief, but later on, when the football team started winning, folks cut him some slack. I guess winning knows no color.

Mr. Johnson's father was in the navy and worked with their Underwater Demolitions Teams. That's noteworthy not only because of the invaluable contribution the man made, but because he passed many of the lessons on to his son. The UDT and the legendary Navy SEALS are both branches of the same strong limb, and they share many of the same philosophies about physical fitness and training. When I went to visit Coach Jordan that Sunday, I already had some idea of what he'd tell me, since I'd done some studying about physical fitness. I pressed the doorbell of Mr. Jordan's house eager to see him and learn other secrets of success from him firsthand.

When Mr. Jordan saw me standing on his doorstep, he smiled widely and ushered me in. We sat at his kitchen table and he told me a little bit about his father. His wife offered me a glass of iced tea, and I accepted it, but in the back of my mind I was wondering if maybe I should have declined it—if drinking iced tea was breaking training rules. I didn't stay for very long, and before I left, Mr. Jordan offered to coach me on weekends over the summer. School was out, but he still wanted to help me. That's the kind of man he is. We shook on an informal deal, and I was struck again by how powerful his grip was. Coach Jordan was then, and remains to this day, an athlete. He competes in age-group track-and-field meets. Age has slowed his times but not his spirit or his enthusiasm. He was the first in a long line of coaches I've been fortunate enough to have, men who've taken pride in molding the raw materials they have at hand into fine athletes.

On the advice of Coach Jordan, I began a daily physical fitness regimen of crunches, sit-ups, pull-ups, running, and jumping. Since there were no fancy gyms at my disposal, I set up my own training facility, and I must admit I came up with a pretty special base camp.

My improvised training equipment consisted of a large tree that I used for doing pull-ups. Since there were no fancy running tracks nearby, I used the next best thing. I ran along the old familiar railroad tracks to build and strengthen my ankles and leg muscles.

I had heard that running on sand at the beach was one of the best workouts; but, of course, there were no beaches in sight of my old home place. There were just tall Georgia pines and dirt.

One day my dad climbed onto his old tractor and plowed one continuous circle to break up the hard fallow ground and loosen the soil. Some say that a ring given from one person to another represents a circle of never-ending love. In my small world, my ring came in the form of a plowed earthen running track.

I did not have a beach with a cool breeze blowing and the smell of the ocean waters in my nostrils; I had a hot, dusty field of dirt. But in my mind, I could see and hear the seagulls beckoning me toward the imagined waters. Mentally absorbed in my private beach daydream, I ran that dirt track barefoot and with a lot of determination.

You may wonder why I ran barefoot. It certainly was not by design, and it was not my desire or choice. It was simply because I had no shoes that fit my feet. In those days, my shoes did not come from the shiny shelves of a store in a supermall. They came in the form of hand-me-downs either too small or too big. I could hardly walk in them, much less run. I was determined not to let this dissuade me from the challenge I had set for myself: to beat my sister in a race.

At first, the hard clumps of dirt hurt my feet as I ran over them. However, I trained my mind to imagine they were merely the finely ground seashells and rock that make up a sandy beach. When the hot Georgia sun baked the lumpy earth until it felt like hot coals of fire, I imagined waves of cold ocean water rushing ashore to cool my feet.

All my alters collaborated in getting me through those workouts. I've been in good physical shape for so long, and followed so devoutly the routines I established back in 1975 between my seventh and eighth grades, that it is hard for me to remember a time when I wasn't as driven and disciplined as I am now. I do know that without DID, I would probably not have been able to endure all the taunting and teasing from my classmates. With DID, I was able to find a safe space I could go. Through DID I was able to accomplish so much and remake myself, with God's guiding hand, into who I really wanted to be.

I'm struck all the time by people who come from so-called oblivion to emerge as stars in their field, whether they are athletes, musicians, movie stars, or whatever. Whenever the public first hears about their exploits, they get the impression that each of them has been on the same meteoric trajectory to overnight success and acclaim. Maybe there's something to that, but most successful people I know worked long and hard and had periods of struggle and doubt in their lives. A lot of people don't want to know about this, I guess. Maybe we'd all prefer to think that it could happen to us, that suddenly, overnight, we can have our lives transformed. The end of that last sentence is important: "have our lives transformed" is kind of incomplete. The unwritten thought is that it will be transformed by somebody else, by good fortune, by a "break."

That would be nice, and it's a comforting thought for some to think that all they have to do is to sit back and wait. Maybe that works for some people, but for me, my attitude during that summer of transition and since has been that it was time for me to go get it. No one was going to hand anything to me, I was going to have to take it. Yes, Coach Jordan helped me and advised me. Yes, my parents encouraged me and supported me, as did my siblings. Ultimately, though, it was my responsibility to do the work. I was the one out there on those scalding-hot Georgia days running wind sprints. I was the one who was doing pull-ups until it felt like so much blood was pumping into my biceps that they were going to burst like a too greedy tick. I gratefully acknowledge the help I've received from God, from family, friends, and rivals. They all contributed in some way to my success, but truth be told, ultimately it came down to me.

I guess that ultimately, the Coach/General got tired of sending the Consoler to rescue me. Enough was enough. No more defensive posture. Time to get on the offensive and take charge. My decision wasn't motivated by a desire to show those people who tormented me that I was better than they thought or better than they were. I'm a Christian man, and revenge wasn't a dish I wanted served hot or cold or any other way. I simply wanted to fulfill the potential that God had invested in me. As much as God controls my life, I certainly do believe in free will. God gave me the materials and the tools I needed to make something of myself. Let me repeat that: make something of myself. I know that pride is one of the Seven Deadly Sins, and I hope I don't come across as proud. I'm simply trying to relate to you the facts as I remember them and my beliefs and values as I've lived them. Something awoke in me, and I answered the call. I'd been reading about warriors and soldiers for most of my young life. I made a conscious choice to join that proud group. Having had those alters aid me for so many years gave me the tools and strength I needed to support the pain-ignoring Warrior.

I know that what I did on the football field, on the track, or anywhere else pales in comparison to what courageous men and women have done on the battlefield. I feel both blessed and cursed that I was never able to experience combat, to truly test myself as a warrior. I was in the process of tapping into a wellspring of strength and discipline that would change my life. I owe much of that to DID. Once I was able to endure and overcome the abuse I suffered as a kid, I knew that I could take on just about anything else. If I could endure pain that others inflicted on me, if my alters could marshal their forces to carry me to that goal line, then dealing with the physical pain I chose to inflict on myself through my exercise regimen was something I'd practiced for.

Just so you don't think that this occurred without a bit of

struggle and effort, here's what my typical day was like when the new Herschel was emerging. I told you that one of the reasons why I had decided I would go out for the football team as an eight grader was that I thought if I was busy with practices and games, I'd be relieved of some of my household chores. I thought that if I was busy doing other things, my mother would let me out of some of my chores. I was wrong then and later. I would still have to do my share of washing dishes, helping with kitchen prep and cleanup, laundry, and a whole host of other things. That meant that I'd have to find other time for my new exercise and running routines. I woke every morning and ran three to five miles before breakfast. Of course, during the summer, I didn't have to attend classes and I had a bit more time, but when school was in session, after school I had my chores, so I worked in my new exercise routine during the evening. So, on a typical Tuesday night, I'd be in the living room watching *Happy Days*. At every two-minute commercial break, I'd pump out as many push-ups and sit-ups as I could manage. After *Happy Days*, it was *Welcome Back, Kotter,* and the same routine, though I would substitute doing dips—I'd sit with my rear end on the edge of a chair and my hands grasping the arms and push myself to develop my triceps—in place of the push-ups. Following that, during the hour-long police drama *The Rookies,* I'd continue exercising. Most of the time, during the commercial breaks, I could manage to get in at least fifty of each exercise in the minute I allotted to each. With eight breaks per hour and two hours of TV watching, that came to nearly one thousand sit-ups and push-ups/dips each evening. That was in addition to the others I did at school during gym class, at football practice, and even in the morning as a warm-up for my run.

People are amazed that I've never lifted weights, and wondered how I could build the power in my legs without them. I believed that what the Spartans, Greeks, and Romans believed about using the body's weight instead of an artificial weight as a form of resistance is the most effective means to build muscle. I did do squats, thousands of them, but used only my own body weight or sometimes a log or something else heavy that I could find. I also became a master of the art of duckwalking. To duckwalk, you squat down so that your thighs are perfectly parallel to the ground or slightly below parallel. Staying in that position, you kick your feet and lower legs out in front in a walking motion. You can't help but waddle like a duck when you do it, but I eventually developed enough leg strength and coordination that I could move really fast. I'd do laps around the makeshift track on our property. I've probably duckwalked as many miles in my life as most people have run.

Now, I know that today's doctors will probably tell you that duckwalking and some of the other traditional forms of exercise that I did could hurt your joints in the long run by stressing them too much. I've always believed that the mind is a powerful tool, and I'm pretty sure that if you believe that a form of exercise or some method of stretching is bad for you, it will probably cause you some pain or even injury in the long run. I think it's your mind that's wrong in those cases and not the form of exercise that you're doing. I've done these old-school (well, actually *ancient school* is probably a better term for them) my whole life and I've not experienced the kind of deterioration or pain that others of my peers or younger players have. I don't think it's that I'm especially gifted; in my mind, my experiencing so few aches and complaints is because I was so strong of mind and spirit and believed so deeply in what I was doing and embraced these methods so wholeheartedly that my faith in them was rewarded. Believers achieve. Doubters don't.

I had another plan in mind besides eighth grade and football. I had worked all that year, and I was about to graduate. I wanted to go out with a bang. I wanted to announce to the world the presence of a new Herschel Walker. As part of the end-of-the-school-year festivities, Johnson County Junior High always held a one-mile fun run. While a fun run is supposed to be fun, boys being boys and girls being girls, some of the kids took it far more seriously than the others. I was going to be among the serious fun runners. I heard some of the kids in the cafeteria at the next table talking about the run, and when they saw me looking over at them, they all shook their heads and laughed. One of them piped up, "We don't want you running in this thing. Our house ain't too steady on its foundation!"

Undaunted, I said, "I'm running," and left it at that. I'd known about the race for a while, and I considered it the second of my three personal trials or final exams.

A rumor got spread around the school that I was bragging that I was going to win. I didn't say that, but it didn't matter. No one expected me to show up, and even if I did, they all knew that I could not possibly do well in the race. I can almost laugh thinking of it now, how my training sessions and Lorenza's pacing me and his cheerleading had me thinking big thoughts. None of the other kids noticed, or at least didn't comment on, how much weight I'd lost. That's understandable considering at that stage in my development, I'd gone from conveniently visible or invisible (depending upon whether or not they wanted to torture me) to only halfway visible. Also, it wasn't so much a question of me losing weight as it was redistributing what I had and growing a bit taller. Again, at this stage, the changes were subtle, and no one was looking very closely at me. I hoped to use that to my advantage.

The day of the fun run dawned hot and sunny, and I was eager for race time. I'm not one to daydream at all now about success—I'm more about putting a concrete plan into motion—but back then I was a little bit more of a dreamer. I remember sitting in class waiting for the noon dismissal bell and mentally rehearsing my victory speech. I'd grown up watching Jim McKay and the rest of the crew on *ABC's Wide World of*

Sports, so that veteran announcer was interviewing me. I was proud but humble.

Once we were let out of the building, all the students gathered on the school grounds for various activities. All of that was a blur to me. The race was the only thing I could think of. Finally, the start of the race was announced. The high school had a regulation one-quarter-mile six-lane track, and about thirty of us toed the chalk starting line. I was among those in the front row, and I looked down at that dirt track dusted with chalk and was reminded of my father's hands after a day of work. I knew that he worked hard every day to support us, and I was determined to honor that hard work with a strong effort of my own.

Mr. Jordan was the run's starter. He didn't want to use any of the charges from his starter's pistol, so he raised the device over his head and shouted "go." Thirty kids crowded onto a six-lane track meant there was a lot of jostling at the beginning of the race. Almost immediately, the pack broke up into two unequal size groups. The lead pack of competitive kids consisted of eight to ten kids, and the fun runners—the majority of the kids—ran in a laughing shouting amoeba-like shifting mass behind them.

I had always run barefoot since my school shoes and church shoes (the same pair) were something that had to be kept in good order. This was the first time I was running on a crushed cinder track in bare feet and the new sensation was both painful and pleasant. I didn't have to worry about large stones like I did near the railroad tracks, but I'd occasionally catch a sharp edge. I had to remind myself to stay focused on my stride and not worry about the pain. All around me kids in sneakers—Keds, Converse, one pair of three-striped Adidas—pounded along. My footfalls were nearly silent, and I imagined that I was invisible as well. To the other kids, I might as well have been. No one was really paying any attention to me until we passed the start/finish line of the first lap and I was still hanging with the leaders. On the second lap, I started hearing a voice in my head. It kept repeating over and over that I was going to lose. I tried to block it out, but it was insistent. "You're going to lose. You're going to lose."

Lap two was complete, and I was still among the leaders, and little changed through the third lap. The voice kept telling me I was going to lose, and I kept hanging in there. Finally, on the last lap, the voice changed, not its tune but its lyrics. In rhythm with every one of my strides, it started to tell me, "Just quit. Just quit. Just quit."

I looked around me, and realized that I was running alone in second place. The leader was a couple of strides ahead of me. Rounding the far turn just before the last curve and the home straightaway, I stopped.

I don't remember feeling totally exhausted or having any other physical sensation. I just remember stopping. I edged over to the inside lane and stepped over the little curb and into the infield. I didn't even watch the end of the race, just walked with my head down toward the elementary school. I have no idea if the rest of the kids in the school taunted me or sang my praises because I'd surprised them. The only thing I remember after stopping is seeing Lorenza's wide-eyed and questioning expression. He didn't even have to say the words.

"I hurt my leg. I had to quit."

Lorenza shook his head. "Dang, that's too bad. You would have had him. You'll get them next time." He draped his arm over my shoulder, and we walked back inside the school. I didn't want to have to look at him, so I immediately went to the water fountain to wash the taste of my lie out of my mouth. My leg was fine. I suspect that he knew that it was, too. I've never asked him, but I have a feeling that he knew something else was going on with me.

What was going on with me is difficult to pinpoint. I was

tired by the fourth lap, but I wasn't drop-dead tired. After all, I'd been running three to five miles every day for months. In looking back on it, I realize a couple of things. First, I'd never won much of anything before. I think it takes time to develop the habit of winning. Second, winning would have put me under a different kind of pressure than I was used to. Sure, I thought I wanted attention, but did I really? Wouldn't it have been safer and easier for me to remain the sometimes anonymous, sometimes outcast young man paraded in front of my peers as an example of a no-good nothing? The unknown is a very scary thing, and as much as my alters had prepared me to survive the siege I was under, I don't think they'd prepared me to triumph. A large gulf exists between survival and triumph, and I wasn't prepared physically or mentally to make that leap yet.

What troubles me equally about the incident is both the quitting and the lying. I guess that it's understandable that a recently turned fourteen-year-old boy would lie and fake an injury to avoid embarrassment, but that doesn't make it okay to have done so. If there's one thing that I've believed—and was raised to believe—it is that you do the right thing regardless of the consequences. Right and wrong matter as much to me as anything else in this world—that Judge alter has worked really hard to refine this sense. Lying was wrong. Quitting was wrong. I didn't like how I felt about myself after that race, but instead of going home and sulking, I did something that has characterized my life since that day. I went home and worked out. I vowed to myself that I would never quit at anything again. I swore a solemn oath to myself that I was going to succeed on the track and on the football field. I wasn't going to do it for personal glory, though glorifying God was something I was happy to do. I was going to do it because succeeding and competing and not quitting were the right things to do. God had shown me the way, and I was to follow His lead.

Breaking Free

I was hoping to get to the Promised Land, but it was going to take some more time, and I had one more test to take. I did make the football squad my freshmen year of high school. We only had two teams, the B team and the varsity. We had such a small enrollment that we could play on the varsity team as eighth graders, whereas at most other schools freshmen could not. I wasn't good enough to play on the varsity team, nor was I good enough to play regularly on the B squad. Just as I'd endured the teasing by telling myself that it was okay, that I was going to be fine, an alter stepped in and told me to be patient and to keep working.

Even though I was a B-team scrub player, Mr. Jordan continued to take a special interest in me. After and sometimes before practice, he would set aside some time to work with me. One of the things he did that I think is responsible for a lot of my success is to continually focus on my fitness and strength. A lot of times after practice, he'd take me onto the track to have me run with a homemade contraption he'd devised. He'd taken an old car tire and put in a few ten-pound shots—the ones used in the track-and-field event—along with a bunch of dirt. He attached a rope to the tire and created a loop kind of like a draft horse's harness. He'd drape that end over my head and shoulders, and I'd have to run sprints—anywhere from forty to four hundred yards dragging that old tire behind me. Talk about getting tired!

All the time I was dragging that thing behind me, Mr. Jordan would be right beside me, talking to me. He'd tell me about other players who were tough and how they did things. He was planting a seed in my head, trying to measure how competitive I was. He'd tell me about guys he knew who could do so many push-ups, guys who could run the forty in less than 4.5 seconds, the hundred in under ten seconds. He was pushing me while I was pulling that weighted tire. When I got to the point where the tire wasn't holding me back enough, he'd add

71

more weight. He'd lead me to the point just before I'd achieve a time or a distance that he'd set as a goal and then knock my time down again with that additional weight. He was testing me, and I knew it. And I loved it.

I had biology my freshmen year, and I had learned about the three stages of an insect's development—larva, pupa, and adult. I'd entered eighth grade a larva, and by the end of it I was a pupa. I still had a ways to go, and along with Mr. Jordan's series of tests, I faced one other.

Just after school let out, I was sitting on the porch. It was a steaming hot Georgia day, more like a day in July than late May, so I sat sipping a cold glass of water. Beads of perspiration popped out on my forehead as I watched the water droplets forming on the glass. I set down the book I was reading, one of the *You Are There* . . . series of historical novels, and looked at the pad on which I'd been absentmindedly sketching out the first few lines of a poem. My focus was elsewhere, and when I heard footsteps pounding down the road, I knew my final test was near. I looked up and saw my sister Veronica, chest forward and high, her head perfectly still, while below, her arms and legs pumped and churned furiously. After she passed by me, I watched as the cloud of dust she'd kicked up glittered in the late-afternoon sun and then settled. The dirt didn't stay still for very long. A moment later, Veronica sprinted past the house again.

I took a last sip of my water and stepped off the porch like a gunslinger about to challenge the town's reigning fighter. I walked to the side of the road and stood staring as she whizzed past me again. Veronica had stopped about twenty-five yards past me, so I jogged over to where she was standing, hands on hips, her face twisted from the exertion, and rivulets of sweat running off her and spotting the reddish soil.

She didn't notice me at first, then squinted at me with one eye shut against the salt sting of her perspiration.

"What's up, Bo?"

"I want to r-race." By this time, thanks to my mother's efforts and years of reading aloud in front of a mirror, only a trace of my stuttering remained.

Veronica laughed and threw her hands in the air. "You! Bo, the only way you'll run is to chase the boy who stole your lunch." She smiled to take the sting out of her comment.

The trap was set. She was still thinking she was going to be racing the other Herschel. She was in for a surprise. The other Herschel would have likely just gone back and sat down.

"I can beat you."

"Oh, okay then, Bo. Then in that case, I can see I've got no choice but to dust you. I'll give you one more chance to go on back to the house and lie down with the other porch dogs." She stabbed the toe of her school-issued track shoe into the dust and flicked some of it onto my bare feet.

I walked out onto the road and got down in the starting position. I relaxed and sat on my haunches and looked up at Veronica; her head was haloed in sunlight and I couldn't see her facial expression clearly, but I heard the seriousness in her voice. "Don't expect no mercy. To the mailboxes."

We'd be racing about a hundred yards. I raised myself again into the starting position, listened for her countdown, and as the first sound wave from the letter *g* in "Go" reached my ear, I took off, pumping my arms legs like a madman. Veronica had her track shoes on, she got out of the gate faster than me. By thirty yards, she'd built a few lengths' lead on me. I remembered the fun run and being in a similar position. This time I wasn't going to quit. I dug deep and found another gear, and by the time we'd reached the mailboxes, I had drawn even with her. Out of the corner of my eye, I saw her leaning for the imaginary tape. I did the same, and in doing so, lost my balance and fell into a tumbling tornado of limbs and dust. I rolled and bounced right up onto my feet and jogged alongside her until she stopped.

"Nice try," she said. She held out her hand.

"What do you mean?"

"I got you."

"Did not."

The did-not-did-so debate continued for a bit. I knew in my heart that I'd outleaned her and won. I also knew that she wasn't about to admit defeat and neither was I. We started walking back toward the house, still exchanging verbal jabs. Out of the corner of my eye, I recognized the look on my sister's face—a mix of mischief and mission. We both took off running. In our desire to best the other we were equals. I'll leave who really won up for debate, but you have to know I never back down from a challenge—and seldom don't come out on top. You should also know that by the end of that upcoming school year, I'd establish myself as one of the fastest runners in the state of Georgia.

If my experiences in ninth grade added up to that school year being one long coming-out party, then the first full-contact practice of the football season was my alters and me sending out invitations to my debutante ball. We had lined up in a one-on-one tackling drill in which one of the offensive players took the ball and ran toward a defensive player. One of the coaches stood between the defensive player and the offensive player holding a tackling dummy in front of him like a shield. Facing the defensive player, he'd jab that shield at you to try to keep you off balance and to teach you to keep your head up and your eyes on the runner. I was among the first of the defensive players in line, the first underclassman, and I'm sure my decision to move toward the head of the line instead of my usual back-of-the-pack position drew a few laughing *oohs* and *aahs*. Nobody was laughing after I got through with that first back I faced.

It's hard for me to describe exactly what was going through my mind and my heart, but it was similar to what I had experienced in the doctor's office. I was calm, but more than that, I was confident. Gone were any whisperings of self-doubt. I was definitely in "Time to Get It Done" mode. When the coach blew the whistle, instead of sidestepping or backpedaling to get a better angle on the runner or to avoid the coach's blocks, I took one step forward, pivoted, spun around the coach, and met the runner head-on. The Warrior in me was on the prowl.

There's no other sound like the one that occurs when one football player makes solid pad-to-pad contact with another. There's the thunderclap of the plastic meeting plastic. Some people enjoy that sound. For fans, that's most of what they get to hear sitting in the stands or watching on TV. For me, there's another part of that symphony that is sweeter music, sweeter than that timpani. When you're driving forward and you hit another player as hard as I hit that junior fullback in that first drill, you hear a kind of sucking exhalation. I know that's contradictory, but that's what it sounds like. First you hear their sharp intake of breath—like they've been surprised—and then a wheezing sound like when an air mattress is being solidly pressed down. The final notes are a grunt and then a clattering thud as the runner is knocked onto his back.

I myself was never one for making noises, shouting, whooping, or anything like that. Maybe that was because of my stutter, but it was mostly because I didn't want my own sounds to interfere with the sound of my brute force overcoming the force of another man. When I was on offense, I tried to remain as quiet as possible as well, not wanting to give my tacklers a chance to hear the same sweet music that I craved.

When I leveled that running back in that drill, it wasn't just the sound of the air being forced out of his chest that I heard, it was almost as if I could hear the collective intake and exhalation of the entire staff and roster of the team simultaneously. I'd landed on the chest of my teammate, and I thought for a moment that I should pull him to his feet, and then I did—it was the right thing to do, after all. More than the hit, more than the transformation of my body, that gesture spoke volumes about how far I had come. There was a part of me that I could call on when necessary to exact the physical toll on an opponent that I needed in order to dominate him. I would go no further than that. I didn't want to hurt someone—not in the sense of causing an injury—but I wanted to inflict pain on them so they would remember me and the encounter we had. Also, in giving him a hand up, I was saying, not so subtly, "I can knock you down, I can pick you up again—I have that kind of control over you."

I don't think you can play football without having the desire to dominate someone physically—with your arm, your legs, your mind, or your heart. It's kind of cliché and an oxymoron, but controlled aggression is what I strove for and what I achieved. I didn't have a dark place in my heart or my soul from which I could extract anger and rage and revenge. But I did have an alter who could go there on my behalf for that fuel. In a kind of intricate mental dance, he could do that dirty work behind the scenes, then just as quickly step aside. He was a kind of silent and invisible assassin—the most effective kind there is—and he served me well. This was the Shadow of the Warrior, an alter ego of an alter, I suppose. I don't know who summoned him or how, all I know is that the display I put on that first practice set the tone for the rest of my high school career. I still experienced some down times, but for the most part they were brief and served to inspire me rather than hold me back.

My first year on the varsity as a sophomore, I was mostly restricted to playing outside linebacker. In some ways, that was fine because I loved to tackle people. In another, it was not so fine but taught me a little bit about the ways of the world. Along with playing linebacker, I was also the fullback on offense. I never got a chance to carry the ball; instead, I blocked for the tailback—a senior. About halfway through the season, he got hurt in the first quarter of a game. I got put at tailback, and by game's end, I had rushed for almost two hundred yards. I was looking forward to another start at tailback the next week, but the senior healed up and Coach Jordan put him back in even though I'd gained more yards in three quarters than he had in any single game. A few weeks later, the same thing happened with him getting injured and me substituting for him and having a great game. Still, I didn't get to start the next week.

I learned a little bit about patience and a little bit about the politics that goes into sports. I was clearly the better runner, but his seniority carried the day. I swore to myself that if I was ever in the position of holding back another player, and he'd clearly outdone me and won the job, I would step aside. After all, that was the right thing to do. In my black-and-white view of the world, the best man should get the job regardless of the circumstance. The rest of my high school, college, and professional days, I motivated myself by thinking that the guy behind me on the depth chart had the same kind of mentality that I did as a sophomore—that he was better than me and he was coming for my job.

By the time I was through competing at Johnson County High School, no one could ever say that my job was in jeopardy. We would win two state championships—one in football and the other in track. In football, I scored eighty-five touchdowns, rushed for 3,167 yards in my senior season alone (averaging 211 yards a game) and was named *Parade* magazine's national high school running back of the year in 1980. At the state track meet, I won titles in the hundred- and two-hundred-yard dashes, and in the shot put. That tells you a lot, doesn't it?

People say that numbers don't lie. I agree, but only because numbers don't tell you much of anything—fact or fiction—about a person. I could go on and tell you stories about some of the games I played or meets I ran in, but that's only one part of my life and it's been pretty well documented already. You've probably seen football fields as the season progresses and you know how the middle of the field between the hash marks gets trod down and turns brown or gets chewed up completely and turns to bare dirt. I kind of feel like that's what happened in my life. The sports stuff gets run over and over again. I know that if it weren't for that, you'd likely never even have heard my name. I'd like to think otherwise, though. I'd like to think that I would have made something exceptional of myself in any case. I don't know why; maybe its because I believe that God has a big plan for me. There's no real evidence to support that conclusion—if you've read only what has mostly been written about me. I remember being interviewed once, and the interviewer was focusing on my childhood and things.

Of course, I didn't say anything at all about DID since I'd not been diagnosed with it yet. I came across the interview not too long ago, and I was amazed. I was asked what kind of dreams I had as a young kid. I replied that I was from a small town in Georgia, an area that was primarily agricultural with some light industry like the clothing factory my mother worked at and the chalk factory that employed my father. I didn't dream of being a football player or an actor or anything like that. That's probably why my desire to play football had to do with being noticed but not to be the big man on campus. In that interview, I went on to say that my dream at that age was to go to Atlanta. If you still like numbers and think they matter so much, that's a hundred and thirty miles, give or take. Hard to believe, isn't it? That maybe you can measure a man's dreams in miles? Or that his reality only stretches that far from him? How did I manage to get so far beyond that?

Running in a high school All-Star football game. When I started playing football, I learned to control and focus any aggression on the field, which made me a better player.

Accepting a trophy at a track meet. Watching my brothers and sisters run track motivated me to exercise and get stronger and faster, particularly so I could beat my sister Veronica in a race.

With the Trans Am my parents bought me in 1980 before I started college. There were quite a few times when I found myself at either the university in Athens or at home with no memory of the drive. I later discovered this loss of time was one symptom of Dissociative Identity Disorder.

I didn't like school much at the start because of the isolation I experienced due to my stutter, but I loved learning. By the time I graduated from high school, I had traded the "stupid" label for the titles of Beta Club President and Class Valedictorian.
Photo courtesy of Kimball Studios, Inc., Dublin, Georgia

At my older brother Willis's wedding with my family in 1985. From left to right: Carol, Veronica and Tasha, Sharon, my mother, my father, Willis Jr., Renneth, me, and Lorenza. Photo courtesy of Kimball Studios, Inc., Dublin, Georgia

Running for the University of Georgia during my freshman year, 1980. When the stadium was deafening, I was able to ignore the crowds and distractions and narrow my focus to the action on the field. Photo courtesy of Georgia Athletic Association

Leaping over a defender for a touchdown in a game at Georgia. Photo by Richard Fowlkes

I ran track for Georgia during the football off-season instead of training with the football team. This kept me in shape, but also helped make me what a friend of mine called a "tweener"—a person in between groups, not fully a part of either. Photo by Tim Gentry

At the Heisman Trophy ceremony in 1982. ©Bettmann/ Corbis

Running in a game for the New Jersey Generals. Instead of staying at UGA for a fourth year I decided to go pro, and by the end of my first year with the Generals I had earned Most Valuable Player honors and set a single-season rushing record of 2,411 yards.
Focus on Sport/ Getty Images

On the Cowboys sidelines with my coach, Tom Landry, and teammates Victor Scott (#22) and Vince Albritton (#36) during a game against the Washington Redskins in 1987. I deeply admired Coach Landry's military-inspired discipline and respect for his players. Ronald C. Modra/ Sports Imagery/ Getty Images Sport/ Getty Images

I pushed the two-man bobsled with driver Brian Shimer (right) in the 1992 Winter Olympics in Albertville, France. My friend Willie Gault and I both wanted to represent the U.S. in the Olympics, and he came up with the idea to compete in bobsled, rather than in track events. Tom G. Lynn/ Time & Life Pictures/ Getty Images

Here I am with another #34, the legendary Chicago Bears running back Walter Payton. I never watched football when I was growing up, but when Walter and I were at the same benefit and I was playing football, of course, I knew who he was, and people asked us to stand together for a photo. He was a great guy, and I'm glad I had the chance to meet him.

Pregame warm-ups with the Minnesota Vikings. "The Trade," as it came to be known, was the largest player trade in NFL history, sending me to Minneapolis and several Vikings players and future draft picks to Dallas.

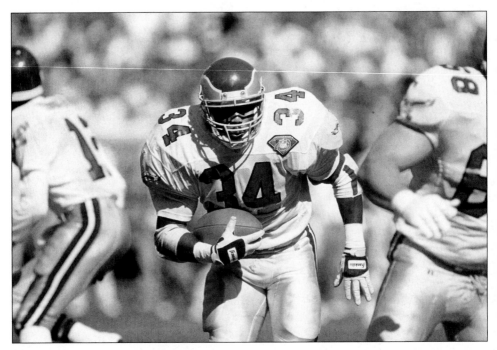

Finding daylight in the San Francisco 49ers defense. It was good to be back east, closer to family and friends, when I signed with the Philadelphia Eagles in 1992. George Rose/ Getty Images Sport/ Getty Images

If I'm proud of anything I did in my high school career, it's what I did in the classroom that I reflect on and relish the most. I did more than just shed the "stupid" label placed on me as a result of my speech impediment. I shed it, erased it, and rewrote it with the titles: Beta Club president and class valedictorian. My grades had been steadily improving, and I applied some of the same structure and discipline to my studies that I brought to my workouts. I used time efficiently, completing most of my homework in study halls, leaving special projects and papers to be done at home and on weekends. I'd become a voracious reader well before high school, and I can recall sitting and reading the Sears Roebuck catalog, learning about sewing patterns and things, and wondering why I was even reading those pages. I was interested in anything and everything at that point in my life, a trait I retain even today.

Earning all A's and becoming the president of the Beta Club was a real achievement, particularly since I was the first African-American student to earn that honor. I wrote earlier that I wanted to get attention, and my achievements on and off the athletic field earned me exactly what I was hoping for— and a little more.

My parents taught us that race and color weren't characteristics that defined who you were. They preferred to think the way that Dr. Martin Luther King, Jr. did in his famous "I Have a Dream" speech. They believed that we should be judged on the "content of our character." Unfortunately, not everyone in Wrightsville, or the country for that matter, felt the same way as they did. Also, the content of my character was to be tested a number of times, especially when it came to the divisive subject of race.

During my senior year, 1979–80, Johnson County High School was still predominantly white. That has changed in the last twenty years of so, with African-Americans now being in the majority. Racial tensions were always present, a lot of the time percolating under the surface, and sometimes bubbling up and making their presence visible to everyone. One of those visible instances was in the fall of my junior year. One of my African-American classmates got involved in a verbal altercation with the principal. This happened in a hallway, and many students witnessed it. I did not. From what I was told by both African-American and white classmates is that the student had just been goofing off in the hallway, teasing another student and taking his ball cap and running with it. The principal happened to be in the area, saw the student running, and yelled at him to stop. When the principal tried to escort the student to his office, the student said he wasn't going to go, he was just messing around and "it ain't no big thang."

The principal then said—and here's the source of the controversy—that it was a "big thang" and imitated the student's voice and gestures. The student then went off about being "disrespected" and the two of them jawed at each other for a minute, before the principal and other teachers could get kids to clear the hallway and on to their next class. Of course, the way things typically go in high school, the accounts of the incident varied from the two of them going three rounds until the principal TKO'd the student late in the third round to the student going berserk and the calm, cool, and collected principal being a model of civility, to the principal putting on blackface and doing a minstrel routine.

Regardless of what really happened between the two, and because of the long-simmering racial tensions at the school, this became a really big deal. As one of the most visible African-American students at the school, and one of the student body's leaders, I was put in a tough position. Almost all the African-American students at the school expected me to side with them in their belief that the principal, in imitating the student, had crossed a line. He was mocking not just the belligerent student, but all of the African-American students at the

80

school. According to them, while the principal hadn't used the N-word, he might as well have. The white students cited this as just another example of the overly sensitive African-American students looking for ghosts where there were none. I didn't agree with that position, but I also didn't want to look at this as a racial issue at all. In my mind, if you took out the issue of race, then the student was in the wrong. He was the one who was being disrespectful. He was running in the hallway and messing around, and if the principal, the highest authority fig-ure at the school, asked him to knock it off and to just go about his business, then that's what he should have done. To me, ev-erything that happened after that was a result of the student's lack of respect.

I couldn't get many people to see my line of reasoning, and when I didn't come out and publicly support the allegations that the principal was bigoted, a lot of African-American stu-dents were upset with me and felt I'd turned my back on my people. I never really liked the idea that I was to represent my people. My parents raised me to believe that I represented humanity—people—and not black people, white people, yel-low people, or any other color or type of person. I know that sounds idealistic and maybe even a little naive, and later on, my consciousness would be raised about just how much a part race played in Wrightsville specifically and the rest of the world generally. I also know that my desire to look at the issue from a logical point of view wasn't going to satisfy anyone on either side of the divide. Though I was more popular than I had ever been, by not taking sides in that dispute my junior year, I was further isolated. I could never really be fully accepted by white students and the African-American students either resented me or dis-trusted me for what they perceived as my failure to stand united with them—regardless of whether they were right or wrong. That separation would continue throughout my life with only the reasons for it differing from situation to situation.

What complicates my memory of these events and further tested my character and the character of every other African-American at the school was the presence of the Klu Klux Klan. If some African-Americans were prone to seeing ghosts, it was because we'd had visions, real and imagined, of white sheets parading in our heads since the time we were young children. You couldn't be alive in the United States in the sixties and seventies and not be exposed to racial issues and the civil rights movement and the protests against Jim Crow laws. You couldn't watch the news and not be horrified, as an African-American, as fire hoses and attack dogs were turned on peaceful protesters, or watch in shock as cities like Chicago, Detroit, Baltimore, and many, many others endured fiery riots. Those images were stored in our brains in the same way our name, address, and phone number were. They were part of our life, our history, and terrifyingly, our present.

The legacy of lynching in the South will never go away—and I don't think it should. Those memories should be preserved as a reminder so that our society won't ever go there again. When my parents talked about those events, it was with that concept of preservation and reminder in mind. As I've said before, my mother worked for a white family and cared for the children of that family. The clothing factory she worked in was owned by that same family. My mother and father had no ax to grind against white people. I never heard them utter a derogatory word about another person based on color. They did tell us stories of African-Americans who had been lynched, beaten, etc. While it may seem as though most of the racial turmoil in this country happened long, long ago, consider that in my lifetime, in 1969, when I was seven, the U.S. Department of Justice filed a lawsuit against the state of Georgia requiring complete integration of all public schools, restaurants, and other public places. Many business owners chose to close rather than comply.

I have vivid memories of being a young child going with my family into Dublin shortly after that ruling. The Klan was marching through the streets, shouting slogans and making threats against us. Even though I'd heard stories, I was still extremely frightened. Their presence alone was enough to have me overcome by fear. If I was afraid of the dark, I was equally afraid of what the KKK could do to me and my family.

As much as anything else, that was what the Klan wanted to spread—fear. Their tactics of intimidation were pretty well refined by the time I was growing up. One of the so-called games the Klan liked to play in Wrightsville was to follow some of the black children home from school. Even though most of us rode the bus home, we still had to walk a considerable distance to get to our houses. Much of the land we had to walk through was farmland, but there were still wooded areas. On a number of occasions, Klansmen would stalk a black child and then grab him (there may have been young girls grabbed but I don't know for sure) and bring him into the woods. Once hidden in the trees, they would carry out a mock lynching, complete with a noose slung over a branch. They would put the noose around the hysterically frightened child's neck, force him—often at gunpoint—to climb up on a stool. They would kick at the stool and make it wobble, all the time saying the most horrible things to these kids.

I was never grabbed, but once when I was six years old, as I was walking with my cousin and one his friends in the woods, we witnessed firsthand one of these fake lynchings. Even though I developed a courageous alter who was able to not turn tail and run or pass out at the sight of the Klan in our town, I can still never erase those images from my mind. A young boy, not much older than I was at the time, standing wide-eyed and sobbing, his pants stained with his urine, his thin arms and hands helplessly tugging at the coil of rope around his neck, while all around him a group of white men poked at him and prodded him, knocking him off balance and off the stool. They'd catch him in their arms and swing him around and then set him back on the stool. The boy shivered in fear and begged and pleaded.

As fearful as I was while watching those events unfold, I also remember the tremendous feelings of anger and powerlessness that nearly blinded me and erased my memories. I wanted to do something to help that boy, to rush into that circle and rescue him. But what could I do? I didn't have the verbal skills to deliver any kind of speech, was too fat and too slow to whisk him to safety. Worse, what would they have done to me, a stuttering, frightened kid?

Why didn't we report this incident? To whom could we go? The police were white men, and what good was the word of three young African-American boys against grown men?

What we witnessed was horrifying, and did have the effect the Klan wanted—for years, we all walked around with our heads on a pivot, wondering who might be coming up behind us. I know for certain that the young boy we saw being tortured survived his attack. I also know the rationale these men gave for their wrongdoing—it was all just in good fun. A "good ol' boys will be boys" stunt that meant no harm really.

I had to develop an alter in order to face that fear. In time, I discovered that I was terrified of crowds. I hated being in large groups of people, mostly because of, I realize now, my experiences growing up and hearing about the Klan and wondering what they could do to me. Crowds are anonymous, and unknown, and who was to say that any one of those people in that crowd could be a Klansman? Who's to say that someone could have snatched me up, fired a shot at me, or any one of a hundred other things. I hated being in crowds when bodies pressed against me and faces swam in front of me like kaleidoscope shapes. I developed that Hero alter to help me deal with crowds. I'd start to feel myself gasping for air, and the next thing I knew all was fine, and I could make my way among the people smiling and chatting.

The Klan itself seemed to be making its last gasp in 1979 when it held another rally at its ancestral home on Stone Mountain outside of Atlanta. The site was significant because that was where the "second" Klan, the Klan of the nineteenth century reborn, rose from its ashes in 1915. Membership in the Klan and the amount of its virulent activities declined since the early and mid 1960s, but as a part of that last-ditch effort to remain in the public eye, they seized on my success on the football field as a kind of launching pad to distract attention from all the good I was doing.

I've never understood the Klan's mentality—how can anyone, really?—and I'm at a loss to explain why it is that some people seem offended by something good and want to tear it down. That's true of the Klan's efforts to capitalize on the media attention I was receiving and the public's fascination with finding out dirt about celebrities. That drag-down-the-celebrity's-reputation part of the equation didn't happen to me while in high school—quite the opposite. People did start to treat me much differently than they had when I was a "nobody." Instead of being made fun of or ignored, I had kids coming up to me all the time and congratulating me. I didn't let that kind of attention get to me. I just blocked it out like I had the taunts and insults earlier. I had transformed myself, and I was not about to let anyone else influence me to change. I was in total control.

There were many distractions, and I kept my eyes firmly planted on the direction I wanted to go in. Later on, I learned to ride a motorcycle, and still enjoy doing this. One thing I learned from those experiences as well as in driver's education at school was that your vehicle will travel in the direction you are looking. If you allow yourself to focus on something on the side of the road, you'll end up going off your intended path in that direction. I'd come too far to let myself take any kind of detours, stop at any rest areas, or, worst of all, have to double back for something I'd forgotten to bring with me. Because my focus was so totally and completely on my schoolwork and on football, basketball, and track, I allowed myself time for little else. I didn't socialize at all, and I did not date. Johnson County High School had plenty of attractive girls, but when I walked down the hallway they might as well have just been a locker; in the classroom, they were bookcases; and in the stands at football games, they were just another part of the nameless, faceless blurry images and white noise that were orbiting somewhere outside the center of my universe. My family and my faith remained central to my existence. They were the elements present during the bad times and I wasn't about to discard them in favor of some Johnny-come-latelies who wanted to know Herschel the Athlete but didn't care before about Herschel the Young Man.

The way I like to describe my attitude back then is this. I had been privileged to get a glimpse of what my future might be. It was as if a door had been cracked open and a sliver of light was angling into the darkness I lived in. I wanted to throw that door wide open to let the light come flooding in—both because of what it could do for me and for my family and loved ones. I wasn't giving thought to pro football and financial rewards at that time; what I was thinking of was being able to go to college. My sister Veronica was well on her way at the University of Georgia, having earned a scholarship in track and field. I wanted to produce the same look of pride that was on my parents' faces when Veronica had formally accepted her offer. My parents had worked long and hard, and to now see one of their children going to college was a thrill and an accomplishment we all shared in. Of course, being the Walkers, we kept our emotions tightly held to our chests and didn't say a whole lot about it, but you could tell. We still lived in the same house and dressed the same and all of that, but there was something different about us all. The house smelled of success and accomplishment—each of my older siblings had been offered scholarships and now it was my turn. But I had to keep my eyes on the prize.

Once again, I had to turn inward, circle the wagons, so to speak, to insulate myself from outside influences. Among those were the hundreds of college coaches who were recruiting me. I have to admit that at first I enjoyed the attention I was getting—from my classmates and from the colleges and universities and their football programs. In time, that attention got excessive. Every day I would come from school and the phone would be ringing, a stack of mail would be on the kitchen table, and all I wanted to do was to sit down to dinner, watch TV, do my exercises, read, and go to bed. I have to admit that the attention I was getting from Ivy League schools did penetrate my defenses. Because of league rules, they couldn't offer me an athletic scholarship, but they could put together attractive financial-aid packages. With my A average and good test scores, I was an ideal candidate. I had heard of Harvard, Yale, and Princeton, and knew of their outstanding reputations, and boy, did it feel good for a stupid stutterer to have been offered an opportunity to go there. I persevered and was going to be rewarded.

That reminds me of one of my favorite stories, one I use frequently when I give speeches. There was this kid who used to be a goof-off at football practice. He was a third-string running back, and he never got to play. His team was really good and they made it all the way to the state championship game. The starting running back got hurt in a car accident during the week before the game. The second-string guy started the game, and he got hurt halfway through the first quarter. A bunch of coaches had come to the game to see the first stringer. They were disappointed that they didn't get to see him, but they stuck around. Then they saw the second stringer get hurt. Still they stayed.

The third-string player ended up playing phenomenally well and his team won the state championship game. He rushed for two hundred yards. All the coaches were deeply impressed. The recruiters came up to the coach after the game and said, "Coach, why didn't you tell us about this guy? We haven't heard a thing about him."

The coach said, "I haven't ever seen him play like this. He was always just goofing off." So the college recruiters asked the kid about his transformation.

"You know what?" he answered. "My father was blind. He died last night. This game was the first chance he got to see me play."

To me, that story is all about the power of faith. I had faith in God for a long time before I really developed faith in myself, before I was able to really see the light that God had placed in me. There's that old Negro spiritual we used to sing that goes along with Jesus' saying that we shouldn't hide our faith under a bushel basket. Over time, I learned that lesson. My physical transformation was just an outward manifestation of what had gone on inside of me. I decided that I was going to let it shine, let it shine. Nothing was going to dim that light that God first sparked in me. I was on a mission, and as far as I was concerned, my rockets were firing, but I was just beginning to creep up off the launching pad. I was using my feet, and the distances I was going to cover would take me far beyond the boundaries of my original dream of going to Atlanta.

Chapter Five

The Harvard of the South

Even though I was a relatively late bloomer and I played football for one of the smallest schools in the state of Georgia, I managed to attract a lot of attention from college recruiters. As I mentioned before, piles of mail accumulated each week. I tried not to pay too much attention to it all, but that was nearly impossible. Truth be told, I wasn't all that excited about the prospect of playing college football. Don't get me wrong, I liked the game, especially the physical contact, but my heart was really elsewhere, on another field of battle.

Growing up where I did in the small-town South, opportunities were generally limited. It was like we lived in a valley and our horizons were limited by what we could see. Unless you were someone who was extraordinarily gifted academically, musically, athletically, or in some other way, college wasn't really something you considered. First, it was expensive. Second, you didn't have many role models who could show you what opportunities were available to you. Sure, we had some good teachers and all, but we didn't have college and career counselors who could expose us to all the options out there.

I said that my failure to stand up for the African-American students in the dispute over the school's principal had isolated me from many of my fellow black students during my junior year. That carried over into my senior year. Racial boundaries had been firmly established in Wrightsville and the surrounding area, so I wasn't going to be socializing with white students. Regardless of race, there was the long history of them treating me so harshly, my own focus on sports and academics created another kind of barrier between me and the rest of my peers. I wasn't invited to any parties, didn't go to the school dances or even hang out with anyone after school, on weekends, or in the evenings. I led a fairly solitary existence but didn't really mind it—or at least that's what the Consoler had me believe. And the Watch Dog was also on full alert, identifying those who hadn't been there for me when I was a less desirable friend and who suddenly saw the light once I became successful. "I don't need anyone" was just one of the mantras I repeated to myself.

That said, I got along well with my classmates, for the most part. I would have casual conversations with them in the hallways, before classes, and in the cafeteria. I can honestly say, none of them really got to know me and I didn't get to know them. To them, I was Herschel the football player or Herschel the Beta Club president. In a lot of ways, I was like a celestial object they might have studied in a science class. They knew what I looked like—some from up close, others from a distance. They knew what some of my major characteristics were, knew the locations at which I could generally be found, the frequency and territory of my orbit, but that's about it. They could never know where I was.

Some of that separation and distance I attribute to my personality, my past experiences, and to my circumstances. Despite the simile above, I think of myself as a down-to-earth and approachable person. I don't think I ever put on airs or consider myself better than other people. Unfortunately, when you attain a certain level of success, people automatically apply certain traits to you. They saw me receiving what they probably considered preferential treatment. I missed days of school because I went on visits to college campuses. I was pulled out of some classes when college recruiters came for visits. I can't deny those things took place and they further separated my high school experiences from most of my classmates. Success on the football field had brought me the attention I'd wanted, but just like my stuttering did, it set me apart from my peers.

One thing I did have in common with many of them is that I really, really wanted to go into the military. Quite a few of my classmates enlisted and served right out of high school, and I really wished I could have joined them. With all my reading of military history and my disciplined ways, I thought I would be a natural as a United States Marine. In most people's minds, the Marines were the toughest, most tenacious, most disciplined outfit there was. They were frequently the first to enter a field of battle, and even though it would be a few years after I graduated from high school that the recruiting slogan "The few, the proud, the Marines" became so popular, that's how I viewed them all along.

I had another reason for wanting to join the military. As I Peter 2: 21 tells us, "To this you were called, because Christ suffered for you, leaving you an example, that you should follow in his steps." I had no fear of sacrificing my life for my country or my fellow soldiers. Christ's example was all I needed to understand the deep and abiding responsibility we all have for one another's welfare. John 3:16 is often quoted and with good reason. "This is how we know what love is: Jesus Christ laid down his life for us. And we ought to lay down our lives for our brothers." Though I was never graced with the opportunity to do so literally, I applied the same mentality to my role in sports with my teammates.

I've said that I had a highly developed sense of right and wrong that came from my mother and father and the Christian upbringing I had. That translated into a keen sense that enabled me to sniff out injustice. I wanted to go to war to right wrongs. I know that sounds highly idealistic and perhaps naive, but I still hold that fundamental belief close to my heart.

One appeal of the soldier's life was that all of my needs would be taken care of. I would be fed, housed, clothed, educated, and socialized all in a very contained environment. I had visions of sending most of my money home to my parents. I could very easily have accepted the idea of dying on the battlefield. I would have felt fulfilled, like my life had purpose and meaning well beyond yards gained and touchdowns scored. I have sometimes had conversations with other men of my generation, those who didn't serve, weren't drafted, and many of them share a similar feeling with me. Something has been missing in our lives because we didn't serve in the military. We don't have the sense of duty and sacrifice, we have to look for other outlets to experience the kind of camaraderie that soldiers enjoy. Football fed some of that need, but in reality, it was a very poor substitute.

Ironically, even though I was being recruited by so many schools, including the Ivy League schools, I never heard a word from one of the military academies. I would have loved to have attended West Point. The same is true of any of the historically black colleges and universities. Specifically, Grambling University and its legendary football coach Eddie Robinson

had an amazingly successful program, and I'd have been honored and felt privileged to attend such a prestigious university.
Again, I don't know why I was never contacted by any of those
schools, especially ones in the state of Georgia like Morehouse
and Clark Atlanta University. I realize now that I could have
contacted them or had someone do it on my behalf, but at the
time, I really didn't understand everything about recruiting. I
guess I felt about those schools and they felt about me the way
my classmates and I did about one another. They didn't bother
to invite because they figured I wouldn't go, and I didn't spend
time with them because they didn't seem to want me.

A host of other schools did want me, and I took trips to
visit the campuses of the University of Alabama, the University
of Southern California, the University of Southern California
at Los Angeles, Clemson University, and Georgia Tech, along
with the University of Georgia. I have to admit that a part of
me wanted to go to Georgia Tech just because of the legend of
the "Ramblin' Wrecks of Georgia Tech." The poet in me loved
that, but their football program at the time wasn't really on a
par with the other schools I was looking at.

Those recruiting trips were my first real ventures from
home. I'd done some travel in state for football games and
track meets, but this was a whole different experience. USC
really wanted me to sign with them, and they had a great
tradition of tailbacks. They flew my mother and me from
Atlanta to Los Angeles for the Rose Bowl game at the end
of the 1979 season. A lot of people remember USC's victory
over Ohio State because of Charles White's touchdown near
the end of the game, which capped a comeback from being
down 16–0, but I remember it because I was standing on
the sidelines surrounded by more than a hundred thousand
screaming fans. I also remember being impressed by Ohio
State's marching band and the guy who strutted to the center of the field to do the *I* in the famous script Ohio forma-

tion. My mother had been escorted around by O. J. Simpson, and I felt like I'd traveled to another world and not simply left the state of Georgia. Everything in Southern California seemed alien to me. I experienced that same sensation when I went to visit UCLA. Their great tailback, Freeman McNeil, showed me around the campus. I was used to warm weather as a Georgia boy, but there was something different about the Los Angeles area. I'd seen pictures of palm trees, and they always looked so neat and clean. The pictures didn't show the gnarled, twisted, and dirty bases of the trees, the dried cornhusk-looking leaves that fell and rasped along in the winds. They say it never rains in Southern California, but it did on my visit, and the sidewalks were invaded by slugs. The air smelled fresh and fragrant, then fog rolled in from the ocean, the temperature dropped a few degrees, and a few minutes later it was sunny again.

None of that really influenced my decision about where to go to school, but I didn't feel comfortable there. The thought of being so far from home didn't really influence me that much either. The first time I flew in an airplane was a bit surreal, but I kind of enjoyed it and kind of thought it was boring—a bus ride in the air. To be honest, it would have been hard to really impress me. So much of what I was experiencing was new and potentially frightening that my alters took over completely. I don't know what my prospective teammates and coaches thought of me on those trips. I was kind of a robot, I think. I didn't say a whole lot, didn't register much emotion that I recall. I definitely turned inward and let my public alter do all the work. He was the one who wasn't weirded out by the crowd at the Rose Bowl, who chatted politely with coaches, players, university representatives, and anyone else who I was paraded in front of. He took in whatever sights were arranged for me to see, nodded knowingly when some fact about the school or the team's history was recited, accepted the offer to sit on a bench in the weight room, a bed in a dormitory, or a seat at a restaurant.

In the face of all the attention I was getting and the kind of frenzy that accompanies the recruiting of a running back who ran for 3,167 yards, scored forty-five touchdowns, and was named National High School Back of the Year by *Parade* magazine, I must have appeared to many people to be sphinx-like. In college recruiting, schools like to have players commit verbally sometime in the fall of their senior year at the latest, and earlier if possible. According to NCAA rules, schools can't officially sign a player to a letter of intent—one that more or less binds them to a school—until the early signing period in November. If you don't sign a letter of intent at that point, you usually sign up in February of the following year—during your last semester in high school. I was under a lot of pressure to commit early, but I wasn't about to, and if I went to the Rose Bowl, in January, it's clear that I didn't sign with anyone early. I also didn't sign with anyone during the regular initial signing period in February. I was in no hurry, and I could block out all of the phone calls, letters, and pleas from coaches. A lot of them told me that if I didn't sign early or in that initial phase, they might run out of scholarships. They didn't want to do that, they really wanted me, but they had to be fair to other players and not deny them the opportunity to live out a dream.

I understood all of that, and if I didn't get to sign with the school I really wanted because they ran out of scholarships, that would be okay. I was still stuck in that invited/not invited/ would go/wouldn't go mind-set. I'm sure I came across as another arrogant athlete who thinks that he can string along a bunch of coaches and schools because he's the best. The truth is, I really didn't understand how my holding off until the last date would affect the entire scheme of a school's program. I was still thinking that it was just me, Herschel Walker, and where I went wasn't really that big of a deal to me, so why should it be to anyone else? My attitude was partly based on humility and partly based on ignorance. I've always said that I may not be smart and I may be naive, but because I have a pure heart, Jesus looks out for me.

Now, I'm not one of those people who believes that Jesus really has a stake in deciding who's going to win a football game or what school I ultimately chose to attend. I do believe that He wants what's best for me, but I didn't ever ask Him to send me a sign showing me which scholarship offer I should accept. That would be excessively proud of me to believe that He'd intercede on my behalf in making that decision. He'd look out for me, but He wouldn't decide for me.

I had narrowed the candidates down to a couple of schools, and in April of 1980, I tossed a coin and the University of Georgia came up a winner. I notified Coach Jordan and he got in contact with Coach Dooley and his staff at UGA, and I signed my letter of intent. Why did I flip a coin to make a decision that many people consider to be one of the most important ones that a student athlete can make? A lot of it is because I trusted in God and in myself. I knew that I would be okay no matter where I went to school—God would be there to protect and to guide me. Now, in the light of my DID diagnosis, I wonder about my decision to flip a coin. I don't think I was afraid to make a commitment and to have to live with the consequences of making a conscious choice. I think that a little bit of the daredevil in me was coming out. This was a way of testing fate a little bit. I'd also been so tightly in control of myself and everything about my life, had been so disciplined, that this was a way of breaking loose from those strictures and making a kind of reckless gesture. (I wasn't going to be a rambling wreck, but I could still be reckless.) I'd had a few episodes with out-of-control behavior—particularly with an old Yamaha motorcycle that I wrecked when my Daredevil was driving. I always loved speed and what better way to get a taste of it than on a motorcycle?

If all this sounds a bit contradictory, that's because it is. I'm a human being, after all. So if I take a bit of faith in God, mix that in with a desire to tempt the fates, add in some naïveté, a pinch of pure uncertainty, confusion, humility, and a real sense that in the grand scheme of things none of this really matters, you get a kind of spicy gumbo of good intentions and mixed messages.

I did flip a coin, but given how things turned out, and what the University of Georgia had to offer me, it almost seems like my "choice" was divinely inspired. A lot of schools think of themselves as the Harvard of the (fill in the blank). Well, the University of Georgia is truly the Yale of the South. It was incorporated in 1785 and is the first state land-grant university in the country. That same year, the state of Georgia gave its trustees forty thousand acres. The first president of the university, Abraham Baldwin, was a Connecticut native and a Yale graduate. He very much hoped to create an institution of higher learning like the one from which he'd graduated. He even modeled the design and layout of what is now known as the Old Campus after his alma mater. If you can't tell, I'm a big fan of the university and don't mind bragging about it at every opportunity—including here.

When I first visited the campus, I was, of course, taken to the football stadium. Sanford Stadium seats ninety-two thousand-plus fans, but its probably best known for the privet hedge that encircles the playing field. It was first planted in 1929, and has remained a distinctive feature of the place ever since. Games at the University of Georgia are said to be played "Between the Hedges" and unless you've lived in the South and attended one of its schools, I don't think you can fully appreciate the sense of history and tradition that goes along with Saturday afternoon and football games. There's nothing like a game at Sanford Stadium anywhere in the world. I know, I know what you're thinking about where you went to school or your home state, but trust me on this one.

As impressed as I was by the athletic facilities, I was even more impressed by the architecture of the North Campus—the Chapel, Old College, New College, and Demosthenian and Phi Kappa halls are a mix of Federal, classical, and antebellum styles. For a kid who loved reading about ancient history, I felt very much at home there. My tour of the campus, like most tours there, included the Arch. It sits on the border of the campus and downtown Athens, and its three pillars stand for Wisdom, Justice, and Moderation—the state motto of Georgia. In time I'd learn a few more things about the Arch, mostly about the legends that are associated with it. One is that if an undergraduate walks through the Arch, he or she will never graduate from UGA. The other is that if you walk through the Arch as a freshman, you will become sterile. The school's motto is *Et docere et rerum exquiere causas* (To teach and to inquire into the nature of things), but I never put the nature of those two legends to a personal test, so I can't say for sure if they are true or not.

I also can't say I felt an enormous sense of relief when I signed, but I was glad to have that task out of the way. Only after I'd attended UGA did I fall under its spell. I wasn't the only one who kept an even keel through the whole process. Rumor had it that someone, upon hearing I had chosen Georgia, asked Coach Dooley if the news prompted him to do hand flips. He answered no, paused briefly for effect, and continued, "I don't know how to do hand flips." I suppose that meant he was glad I was going to play for the Bulldogs.

After signing my letter of intent and getting all the paperwork done so I could enroll in classes, I still had to finish out my senior year. Along with class valedictorian, another honor was bestowed on me that year. I was one of two hundred students nationwide who was selected by the Academy of Achievement as an "Honor Student." The academy is a not-for-profit organization that not only recognizes the achievement of high school students like me, but honors adults who have made significant contributions in the fields of business, entertainment and the arts, science, public service, and scientific exploration. One of its main programs is an annual summit meeting at which the members of the academy meet with a select group of highly regarded graduate students from around the world. The list of the academy members is a who's who of American life, from Rosa Parks to Oprah Winfrey, Jimmy Carter to Willie Mays. It also honors leaders in their field from around the world like Benazir Bhutto, Desmond Tutu, and Lech Walesa. Later on, I was selected to be a member of the academy and was the first person who was a high school honoree to be inducted into the academy as an adult. Of all the things I've accomplished, this is one of which I'm the most proud.

One of the reasons why I mention this now is that it fits into a pattern that can in some ways help you better understand my life and why I think that DID has been a positive force. So far, I've talked a lot about the isolation I experienced. I've always had a sense that I was different. It wasn't until a few years ago that someone pointed out something to me that I hadn't recognized myself. My friend told me that I was a "tweener." He explained that I was always between things. He said that I was a good athlete and a good student but didn't "belong" with either group. I was a football player and a track athlete. I was a jock and a devout Christian. I played against guys like Tony Dorsett and lasted long enough in the NFL to play against his son.

Either I never quite fit into a category or I defied categorization and actively worked to not fit into any one slot. I'm not saying that I was a rebel and tried to break every rule and be a big shot who wouldn't go along with society's conventions. I did some things my own way—primarily when it came to my approach to training—but in most other areas of my life I've played almost boringly by the rules. I'll admit, I didn't like it when people tried to tell me what I could and couldn't do—like not ride motorcycles when I was in the NFL—but I wasn't way out on the fringes of what society considers acceptable. I wasn't a rebel without a cause. I was just doing what interested me, being who I was, and somehow I slipped through the cracks, I guess.

I don't know what people expected of me, but I wonder if, as you've been reading this, you've been thinking that if I was going to talk about my time at the University of Georgia, you'd be hearing mostly about my exploits on the football field or my dorm-room conquests of various coeds. You probably didn't think I'd be mentioning Demosthenian Hall, or that when I was on the tour of the campus, I didn't need anyone to explain to me who Demosthenes was. I already knew he was a famous Athenian orator who led an ill-fated political struggle against the Macedonians and their creeping expansionism. While I didn't necessarily admire him, I did admire Alexander the Great, who opposed him and squashed the rebellion against the Macedonians that Demosthenes helped lead.

I do know that people make judgments based on assumptions all the time. I didn't understand this fact as well when I was a senior in high school as I do now. A lot of these things I had to learn the hard way. I've never been afraid of hard work or hard lessons—especially when the rewards have been so great. One reward I earned that turned into a lesson about assumptions much later on was the car my parents bought for me as a graduation present. My parents saw how far I'd come and were very proud of me. They were pleased that I was going to school in Athens, about a two- to two-and-a-half-hour drive from Wrightsville. They knew that I'd be doing a lot of driving back and forth between home and school, and with Veronica already there and running track, they wanted to make it easier for her and me.

This car-buying decision wasn't all about practicality, though. They wanted to reward me for my hard work, and I guess I did edge them in a certain direction. Like soon-to-be freshmen everywhere, I had to buy some clothes and other supplies. I was able to afford a few things because of the generosity of Mr. Robert Newsome. Like Coach Jordan, he was a white man who took me under his wing. He owned a service station in Wrightsville, and I worked there after school my last semester as a mechanic's assistant. I enjoyed the work and being around mechanical things, and I enjoyed Mr. Newsome's company. He helped my family and me out whenever we needed something, and he never expected anything in return. That's why it bothered me that other whites in town gave him a hard time. He was simply a good Christian man who saw folks in need—and not just my family—and tried to help them. His cured hams couldn't cure everything, but they sure were tasty and made a lot of folks' holidays a little brighter.

One day while on my break, I strolled over to the Pontiac dealership in Wrightsville. I saw a brand-spanking-new 1980 Pontiac Firebird Trans Am gleaming in the sun. Its grille seemed to alternately smile at me to beckon me to come close, and to snarl to let me know what its real intentions were—high speeds and thrills. Now, you already know about my motorcycle exploits and my need for speed, but that was a puppy-love crush compared to the lustful feelings I had trembling through me when I saw that Trans Am sitting there looking all black and enticing.

I made a casual mention of the car I'd seen later that night when we all sat down to dinner. I knew it was a dream, but I could still talk about what I'd seen, right? My parents were both still working their full-time jobs. My dad had been working double shifts for a while now, and my mother was still laboring at the clothing factory as hard as ever. When I mentioned the car, my father rested his elbows on the table and folded his hands in front of his face. I could see the chalk zebra-ing the creases in his hands. It was hard to see around his hands, but I thought I saw his eyebrows twitch and his eyes dart over to my mother. I couldn't tell if he was irritated with me or what. He unfolded his hands and scratched at the corner of his eye and then leaned back in his seat to stretch. "Sounds nice, Bo."

My mother rolled her eyes and picked up the plate of corn bread and offered it to my father and then to me.

"Willis, don't torture the boy. Go on and tell him."

My father took a big bite out of his piece of corn bread, and I could see the grin spreading around the yellow edges. After a few thoughtful, painfully slow chews and a long sip of tea, he told me that they'd decided to get me a car. They were going to take a second mortgage out on the house to pay for it, and if that Trans Am was what I wanted, well, that's what I was going to be getting.

I didn't know what to say. My parents were very frugal, and taking from Peter to pay Paul wasn't their usual mode of operation. I started to say something in protest, but my mother gave me one of her looks to let me know that discussion was neither necessary nor desired.

Two days later, we went down to the dealer with cash in hand, a little more than $7,500 after taxes, and I was handed the keys to that amazing car. It wasn't until only recently that Dominique Wilkins, the legendary UGA basketball player, let me know how it looked for an aggressively recruited freshman running back to show up on campus driving a brand-new muscle car. Everyone assumed that a booster or someone else had illegally helped me to obtain it. As Dominique laughingly put it, "The first time I saw you on campus driving that Trans Am, I wanted to go to my coach and say, 'Where's my darn car!'"

At the risk of protesting too much, let me tell you that three years later when I signed my first professional contract with the USFL, one of the very first things I did was get some of my money, go to the Bank in Dublin that held the note on my parents' second mortgage, and pay off that car. While an amateur and playing NCAA football, I wasn't about to do anything illegal to risk my eligibility. I say that as someone who believes so strongly in doing the right thing that he decided to major in criminal justice.

When I look back on those days, I'm struck by another kind of "tweenness." In some ways, I see that I possessed the kind of intellectual sophistication that allowed me to expound on Demonsthenes. In other ways, I was as dumb as dirt. A few weeks before I was to leave for Athens, I got a letter from Coach Dooley and his staff telling me when and where to report on our first day in August of 1980. I read the letter, noted the location of the first meeting and the time. Now, I'm a country boy born and bred, and I'm used to getting up early and working hard. I also believe in being punctual to the point of being overearly, but not even I could have purposely gotten to that first meeting *twelve hours* early.

I was ready to go and get started on this new phase of my life. Along with driving my new car all around the back roads of Johnson County, I did little else except think about the day I was going to leave. I knew that I had to be at the cafeteria attached to the athletic dormitory, McQuarter Hall, by five o'clock. I didn't need to set an alarm clock the night before I left because I knew my mind would not let me oversleep. I got up at about 2:30 A.M. I had packed everything in the days before, and most of what I was taking was already in the car. The house was dark, and I crept around trying to be as quiet as I could. My mother came out of her bedroom in a robe and slippers.

"You be careful out on those roads this time of the morning."

"I will." There is no interstate that connects Wrightsville and Athens. I'd be on Route 441 most of the way, and there was likely to be a lot of critters running around. My mother always worried about them.

"You got everything?"

We'd checked over my list at least three times, so I nodded and assured her I'd been thorough.

"Let me get your father."

I stood in the dark waiting for a moment. I could hear my father saying that he'd said his good-byes last night. Then he added, "He's gonna be a hundred miles away, not on the moon. We'll see him again."

I smiled. My father was nothing if not a practical man. I knew how he felt about me, and getting up early to see me off wouldn't have made a difference one way or the other.

My mother came back smiling and shaking her head. "You know your father. He says to go on and get on the road. Don't be late." My mother looped her arm around my elbow and escorted me to the porch. She hugged me and told me to be good.

Hours later, I pulled onto campus and wound my way around to McQuarter Hall. The first pale light of day was leaking between the buildings and spilling out onto the parking lot. I wondered why it was empty. I checked my watch and saw that it was only five minutes after four. I figured I was a little earlier than most would be, but that was okay. I was used to that. I didn't want to run the battery down on the car, so I switched it off and didn't play the radio. I could only sit for so long, so periodically I would get out of the car and walk around the parking lot, pacing. I didn't want to wander too far, figuring that someone else was sure to arrive shortly. At about four-thirty, it seemed as though every bird on campus decided to join in when the Chapel's bell tolled the half hour. The sound was amazing, like the voices of a choir of a thousand warming up and chatting.

By this time, I was getting a bit more antsy. Somebody else had to be pulling up any minute. I walked over to the cafeteria to peek through the window to see if maybe there was another parking lot and other guys on the team were already inside laughing at me. All I saw was row after row of tables with chairs sitting on their tops, legs poking up like petals on a flower. I looked to my left and saw that a piece of paper was taped to the door a few feet down from where I stood. I walked over and read it. It was the same letter as the one that had been sent to me. I looked closely and saw that the meeting was scheduled for five o'clock. What I'd failed to notice, as is probably obvious to you, was that it was scheduled for five o'clock in the after-noon.

If this was the Yale of the South and I was to succeed here, then I was already behind for failing my first test in basic read-ing comprehension. I didn't dwell on that fact for too long. I had a little more than twelve hours to kill. I could easily have gotten back into the car, driven home, gotten eight hours of sleep, and then driven back in time for the meeting. I didn't even consider that option. I was here, and I was going to stay. I've never been one to dwell on my mistakes, figuring that this is counterproductive. You've already wasted time in making the mistake; why compound it by wasting time thinking about it or beating yourself up over it? Better to spend the time doing something positive to make up for it. So that's what I did. In between sessions of sitting in the car, I walked over to a grassy area near the dorm and did sit-ups and push-ups.

I said before that Jesus especially looks out for me in my moments of stupidity (and at all other times) because I am pure of heart. I believe that is why He chose to have the first person I met on my first official day on campus be Frank Ros. At the time I didn't think much of God's selection, and I'm sure that Frank had some interesting thoughts about me. I was sitting in my car with my legs out of the open driver's-side door. I heard the sound of a vehicle coming up behind me, and I immediately jumped to my feet and took off at a jog toward this car. Even before Frank could come to a stop, I was running and yapping at him like I was a little puppy. I was so relieved to see another person there that I couldn't contain myself. I'm usually not like that, but my emotions got the better of me—the Sentry and Watch Dog must have fallen asleep after getting up so early.

I knew immediately that this guy had to be one of the football players; he had the thick neck characteristic of nearly every football player I knew. Frank had a dense shock of curly dark hair and a square head and jawline that reminded me of a Rock'em Sock'em Robot. He also had a pair of thick eyebrows that sat above a pair of bright dancing eyes. I couldn't tell if he was shocked or amused by this crazy kid jogging along beside his car. When he stopped his vehicle and put it into park, it was like he was shifting the gears of his attitude and expression as well. He leaned back in his seat and squinted at me like I was bird droppings on his windshield. "Rook, get my bags."

I was busy trying to introduce myself and this guy was already ordering me around. I don't know if it was because I sensed something about him or because I'm a polite Georgia boy, but I immediately said, "Yes, sir. I'll get your bags."

I stepped back from his car and let him out. He walked to the trunk and popped it open. Inside were four large suitcases and a trunk. I glanced at them and then into the car's interior. It was stuffed to the gills with milk crates, boxes, and an odd assortment of things.

"Let's go, rook. You're burning daylight."

I grabbed a couple of the bags and followed Frank along the sidewalk to the dormitory entrance. Frank and I exchanged names, but that was the extent of our conversation. For the rest of the time, he addressed me disdainfully as "rook." I knew that as a rookie I was low man on the totem pole and figured I was going to be subjected to my teammates' wrath at some point. I didn't realize how soon, though.

Frank stood waiting in front of an elevator. I drew up along-side of him and stood staring at the lighted arrow.

Frank emitted a low guttural laugh that turned into a snarl. "Stairs, rook. Third floor." He pointed down the hallway where an exit sign hung. "And hustle it up, you got a lot of stuff to get."

Frank had arrived shortly before two o'clock, and I spent the next half hour to forty-five minutes going up and down those stairs carrying his things. By the time I was about finished, a few other players had shown up. I didn't stop to introduce myself; Frank's orders to double-time it and their mocking laughter let me know what was up and where my place in the universe of Georgia football was.

When I got the last of Frank's things in his room, he tossed me a set of keys. "Bring it around back." He jerked his head to the right. Through the dorm-room window, I could see another parking lot.

I trotted down the stairs and got into Frank's car and moved it as he'd asked. When I got back to the room, he glanced out the window and shook his head. "Under a tree, rook. Under a tree. It's hot, you know. I don't want my seats to get too hot."

"Birds. I didn't think you'd want the birds—"

"That's your first mistake. Don't think. Do." He flicked his hand at me as if to shoo me away.

I moved the car as he'd asked. When I got back to his room to return the keys, he was standing at the window. We talked for a few minutes. He told me a bit about himself. He was originally from Barcelona, Spain, and had come here with his family when he was fairly young. His dad was a brilliant man who had graduated from college at thirteen; Frank's brother graduated at sixteen. He speaks five languages and, I was later to learn, was an academic All Southeastern Conference performer. He played middle linebacker and was one team's captain. After a few minutes, he stood up again and looked out the window.

"Damn birds." He beckoned me over with a finger. "See that, rook. That's why you don't ever park under the trees."

I looked down and saw that in the few minutes we'd spent talking, my friends the birds had done their thing on his car.

Frank held out his keys. "Wash it, rook. There's a bucket and some rags and things around here somewhere."

By the time I was done washing the car, and moving it to a spot in the shade of the building and not under a tree, it was a quarter to five in the afternoon. I still hadn't moved any of my things into my room, and I dashed out to my car. I got a few catcalls and yelps about the car, but I buried my head inside the trunk or the interior and started grabbing things and running to my room. My roommate, Barry Young, was already in the room, sitting on the bed. We barely exchanged a couple of words before heading down to the cafeteria. We walked into the room, where a lot of the guys stood in clusters, lingering far from the coaches. I'd expected them all to be seated in orderly rows already. I would encounter another surprise.

It may surprise you to know that when it comes to attending meetings and classes, I'm not like that nerdy guy you remember who came in, sat down right in front, had all his pencils sharpened, and his notebook out. I'm not like him, I *am* him. I sat right in front of the position that had been set up for Coach Dooley and his staff. I paid attention to everything they had to say as they went over our daily schedule, team rules, campus policies, and a whole lot more. They had prepared handouts for us, distributed a handbook, and generally tried to make us do as little thinking as possible, but I still took notes.

An hour into the meeting, Coach announced that we were going to break up into smaller groups based on whether we were on offense or defense and then later still into smaller group meetings based on our positions. He asked if anyone had anything to say before we began. I think he expected no one to speak up because he had already started putting all his papers into a kind of satchel when I heard a familiar voice.

"Coach Dooley. I have an announcement." Everyone turned around to look at Frank Ros.

Coach set his things back down and said, "Go ahead, Frank." All of us knew who he was because all the captains had stood and been introduced a bit earlier.

"Coach, I'd like to declare that Herschel Walker is my little brother."

With the exception of the freshmen, all of the other players started hooting and hollering. I couldn't really figure out what was going on, but it was clear that all these other guys were mad. They weren't shy about voicing their displeasure either.

After a few moments of shouting and accusations and boo-ing, Coach Dooley raised his hands and quieted the room.

"Rules are rules, gentleman. You all know that. If Mr. Ros wants Herschel Walker to be his little brother, then that is what is going to happen. End of discussion. Report to your assigned meeting rooms."

Coach Dooley had established a rule that an upperclassman could take a freshman as a little brother. That sounds kind of nice, but in practice it's usually anything but. What Frank had done to me when we first met was typical of how freshmen were treated. We were expected to do anything and everything the veterans on the squad told us to do. When I was selected as Frank's little brother, from that point forward, I only had to do what he told me and no one else could tell me to do anything without asking Frank's permission. Of course, most of the time that was just a formality, and your big brother let you get abused at will. I didn't know a thing about this until I got to that first meeting.

Georgia football had a couple of other traditions that served as initiation rites for the "rooks." One of them involved wearing calf-high athletic socks with your shorts when working out.

That was supposed to humiliate us because it was so unfashionable. Back in the fifties and sixties, players might have worn high socks like that, but when I entered the University of Georgia, you would have looked like some gym-class geek if you walked around dressed like that. The other thing we had to do was to carry the water and Gatorade out to practices. Those five- and ten-gallon drums are pretty heavy, even for a football player, so when you figure in the additional factor of people harassing you and trying to trip you up and things, you can see how it was a kind of punishment.

Fortunately for me, Frank Ros wasn't the typical football player as most imagine such a figure to be at his stereotypical worst. Frank later told me that when we first met and I was so nice and polite and did everything he asked of me without comment or complaint, he knew that he had to protect me. He knew that other guys on the team were going to take advantage of my respectfulness. I truly believe that Frank saved my life, but not for the reason you think or he thought. I'm pretty certain that if I had been hassled and abused to the degree that some of my fellow freshmen were, I would have seriously hurt or even killed someone. Frank didn't see the simmering anger that I carried around with me. On the surface, I was this really nice, shy, quiet guy, but underneath that was a very powerful and aggressive person. Couple that with my strong sense of right and wrong, my desire to be in the military, and my past as a person who was taunted and beat on unmercifully, and you can probably understand why I say I wouldn't have taken too much abuse from anyone. I wouldn't just walk away from it, like I did with some minor incidents, but would have gone on the attack.

I did reveal that ferocious side of my personality only once around my teammates. One day I was coming back to the athletic dorm after class. Eddie "the Meat Cleaver" Weaver was my teammate and he was sitting around outside with a few of his friends. Eddie was from Florida, where he was a great, if you believed his stories, wrestler as well as football player. He was always bragging about himself and cutting up. I liked him despite how opposite we were. One of the guys he was hanging around with wasn't on the team or even an athlete in another sport. I don't know what got into this guy, but he cut me off in front of the doorway and challenged me to a fight. One second I was walking along innocently, and the next, I snapped at him, loud enough for everybody else to hear, "You don't want any part of me. I can and will rip your head off."

I could tell by the way his eyes widened and his face went gray that he believed me. And he should have. The Watch Dog in me had summoned the angry Shadow side of the Warrior. The guy immediately backed away. I even shut up "The Meat Cleaver." He looked at me with a puzzled expression. He'd never seen that side of me before.

I didn't like to be challenged, and maybe my alters were responding to all the teasing and beatings I'd endured as a kid. No way was I going to let someone, especially not someone as weak as this guy, believe that he could harm me. Also, my sense of right and wrong had been violated. I was due some respect if only because I was physically so much larger and more fit than he was. I didn't think much of the incident at the time, but I can see how someone else might have recognized the Jekyll and Hyde sides of me coming out. I don't remember any other real incidents like that, but I know I put the fear of God into all those guys that day. They'd crossed a line they wouldn't dare approach again.

Frank was smart enough to sense that there were some lines I wouldn't cross, and like a good blocking back, he created some holes for me. A tradition that the University of Georgia football program had when I was playing was something called Sea Graves.

Sea Graves was a relatively mild initiation thing during which the veterans broke eggs over rookies' heads, had us bow down before them, and recite things. Harmless stuff. But there was another ritual that I didn't have to go through that was potentially harmful. Like fraternity hazing rituals (and the University of Georgia has one of the largest number of memberships in Greek societies in the country) and other things of that sort, it has since been eliminated. This second ritual took place in the spring, and during it, the upperclassmen on the team would take the freshmen off campus to a wooded site near a pond. The freshmen could only wear their shorts and T-shirts. Once in the woods, the freshmen were forced to down alcohol, large quantities of alcohol, usually in single shots. The point was to get enough alcohol into their system that they vomited. If you vomited up bits of meat, you'd be thrown into a shallow pond and your torment would essentially be over. If you didn't vomit, you'd get more alcohol. If you vomited but no meat came up, then you got still more alcohol.

It's a stupid and potentially dangerous ritual and thank God no one was ever seriously injured as a result of it. I know that if it hadn't been for Frank telling me that I didn't have to go through it, I would have torn up anybody who tried to pour alcohol down my throat. To this day, I have not had a single sip of alcohol, have never taken an illegal drug, and have used very few if any prescription or over-the-counter medications. I'm all for solidarity and being a team, but I would not have put up with being forced to get drunk.

Fortunately or unfortunately for me, depending upon how I look at it, I was running track in the spring and wasn't participating in spring practice when the second ritual took place. Once again, I found myself in a situation in which I was a tweener. A lot would happen that first football season, before I traded in one pair of spikes for another and really enlarged my view of the world.

Chapter Six

Caught in Between

One of the things I loved about sports is that they offer someone like me who had this black-and-white worldview a great deal of comfort. For the most part, football, and to a far greater degree, track and field, offered clear-cut answers. Either you gained enough yardage for a first down or not; either you crossed the goal line or you didn't; either you outraced your opponent to the tape or you didn't; either your time was a world record or it wasn't. One of the main reasons why I loved track and field, besides the sense of freedom running gave me, is that it was especially black-and-white. I also loved the idea that, even though at meets team scores are kept and I sometimes participated in relays, running and the field events are essentially solo activities. Your time is literally your own. In football, other people contribute directly to your success and failures. If someone missed a block, I could have been tackled for a loss. In track, if I didn't win my event, it wasn't because another sprinter failed to hold back my opponent.

On the playing field and on the track, the rules are subject to less interpretation than they are in life. Simply put, life on the playing field or track is, well, simple compared to the rest of life. So many other things in my life were complicated, but sports never really were for me. Despite my experiences as a high school sophomore and my feeling that I didn't get to play tailback even though I was clearly better than the senior who played the position ahead of me, I really believed, and still do, that effort equals results. Along with that, I believe that effort overcomes every other factor.

Living in that world offered me a sense of comfort and ease that I couldn't really find anywhere else. When I think of my years at UGA, I'm struck by an overwhelming sense of comfort and security. I don't know exactly why that is, but a part of it must be because I was starting fresh someplace. The old Herschel, the stuttering overweight country boy, wasn't a part of the memories of anyone on campus. I take that back. He was a part of my sister's memories, but any regret I might have felt about that was more than offset by having her around on campus. She was family, and she and her teammates on the track team became my extended family.

My first collegiate game kicked off on September 6, 1980. We faced the Tennessee Volunteers at Neyland Stadium in Knoxville, Tennessee. I was psyched about the opportunity to play in a place with as much history as the University of Tennessee. At the time, Neyland Stadium was the second largest in the country—second only to the University of Michigan's. It held nearly a hundred thousand people, and the interstate rivalry between Georgia and Tennessee was fierce. When we came out of the locker room and through the tunnel out onto that field, it was like I'd traveled through a wormhole to another universe. That many people can make a lot of noise. I felt like I'd stepped into a jet engine. I couldn't make out much of what was being said as we sprinted onto that green expanse, but I could tell that these folks weren't wishing us a nice day. You know I don't like crowds, but my alter kicked in immediately, and I ran out there and immediately felt calm. After all, given all of my teammates, the fact that I was just a freshman and a nonstarter meant that I was truly anonymous to these people. It didn't matter that I was appearing in front of as many people on that one day as I had in all of my career—both in football and track.

With my Hero alter in firm control, I could concentrate on our pregame drills, calisthenics, and stretching. We still had an hour and a half before game time, and once we'd loosened up a bit, we were back in the locker room. Some players received last-minute adjustments to their tape, others sat on their stools, their feet bouncing up and down with nervous energy. I just sat and looked straight ahead, trying just to take in as much of the atmosphere as I could. I finished dressing—we didn't wear our full uniform and pads for our first round of warming up—and looked over at Frank Ros. With eye black underscoring each of his prominent cheekbones, he looked even more fierce than usual. He walked up to my locker and said, "Think that was something, rook? That noise? Half the SOBs are still in the parking lot getting liquored up. Block it out."

I nodded and Frank moved on, saying something to every player.

Frank was right. Going through that tunnel the first time was like a whisper in a well. When we came out for the kickoff, I felt like a pack of people had put me in a metal garbage can, rolled me down a rocky hill, and run alongside me beating on the can with two-by-fours while screaming at me at the top of their lungs. I could feel my helmet vibrating. I put my mouth guard in just to keep from clenching my jaws too tight.

The first part of the game was a disaster, and both teams struggled. Standing on the sidelines and watching my team was one of the most frustrating and exasperating experiences of my life. We were down fifteen to two by the time the second quarter was only half over. Our offense wasn't moving the ball at all, and the defense had scored our only points on a safety. So much for our veteran leadership. I was trying to remain positive, but I hated feeling so helpless. That feeling wouldn't last long. The adjunct members of "Team Herschel" were about to make themselves known.

I noticed a faint sound coming from the bleachers. With all the noise the Tennessee fans were making, it was a wonder I could hear it all. Amid a sea of Tennessee orange, I could see a small splotch of red in a corner of the end zone on our side of the field. The Georgia contingent who'd made the trip to Knoxville were on their feet and waving and shouting. Tennessee had the ball, so I couldn't figure out at first what they were doing. Then, during a time-out and a lull in the roar, I could hear what they were saying:

"WE WANT HERSCHEL!"

"WE WANT HERSCHEL!"

There were only six minutes left in the first half when we got the ball back. I suppose at that point Coach Dooley figured he had nothing to lose, that things couldn't get any worse. I don't think his decision was influenced by those fans, however. Our running-backs coach called my name and waved me onto the field with the offense. I snapped my chin strap and trotted to the huddle. When the fans saw me entering the game, they let out a big roar. I'm sure the Tennessee fans were thinking, "Yeah, right. Whatever."

The ball was on the Georgia twenty-yard line. We took our places in the huddle. Our quarterback, Buck Belue, called the play. He didn't take his eyes off me the whole time, making sure that this rook knew that his number had been called. I held his gaze, and when we broke the huddle and lined up in formation, I could feel my chest beating against my shoulder pads. I scanned the defense for a moment, and what I'd been told was true. College players were a lot bigger than the ones I'd faced in high school. I'd have to rise a little higher to meet this challenge head-on.

I listened to the snap count, and fired off as soon I heard the right number. The play was designed to go off tackle to the right. Instead of seeing a gaping hole and running for daylight, all I saw was a line of orange. I dropped my shoulder and plunged forward for two yards. While this wasn't Hannibal's march across the Alps in the Second Punic War, I didn't have any elephants as blockers. Rome wasn't built in a day, but some people say the legend and reputation of Herschel Walker was made during that first game.

I finished it with eighty-four yards on twenty-four carries. I scored two touchdowns, and we came back to win 16–15. I scored my first touchdown, and landing on the orange-and-white-checked pattern painted on the artificial surface of Neyland Stadium was deeply gratifying. I had only played half of the game, but it was enough to earn me Southeast Conference Back of the Week honors from both the Associated Press and United Press International.

To me, those honors hardly mattered. They announced to the rest of the teams we'd faced that year that I was someone to be taken seriously. I didn't need to have the UPI or the AP tell me that was so. I could sense it in the eyes of the Tennessee defenders. If that first play wasn't significant in terms of yards gained, it was important in letting my teammates and opponents know what kind of player I was going to be. I could easily have been thrown for a loss on that play, done something foolish like try to reverse my field and gotten run down from behind when a cornerback kept containment and a speedy linebacker pounced on me like a big cat on a wildebeest. That wasn't going to be my style. That first run was a signature play, one that revealed my personality on and off the field. Straightforward, giving out as much punishment as I was going to take. Sure, I was elusive, and I had breakaway speed, but the runs I remember aren't those open-field ones; instead, I remember being in the trenches and digging and scratching and clawing my way forward. Georgia Bulldogs always *hunker down,* and that was what I was going to do.

I'm not the only one who remembers those other runs, the ones that may not be on anyone else's highlight reel. A friend of mine recently told me about a Web-site owner who has collected some of the broadcasts and transcripts of games that the University of Georgia radio network's legendary announcer Larry Munson called. One of Larry's signature lines was "Glory, glory to ol' Georgia." My friend told me that there was a clip of Larry doing the play-by-play of one play from that first game against Tennessee, and I looked it up and I think it sums up nicely what I've been trying to say:

> Tennessee leading 15–2, the crowd roaring against
> Georgia trying to make them drop it so they can't hear.
> We hand it off to Herschel, there's a hole, five, ten, twelve,
> he's running over people! Oh, you Herschel Walker! My
> God almighty, he ran right through two men, Herschel
> ran right over two men, they had him dead away inside
> the nine. Herschel Walker went sixteen yards, he drove
> right over those orange shirts, just driving and running
> with those big thighs. My God, a freshman!

I like that and think it truly represents what my experience was like. Notice that on that play, there was a hole I could run through. That was the case the vast majority of the more than one thousand times I carried the ball. I said earlier that I liked track so much because it was an individual sport. That's true, and I sometimes didn't like being dependent on someone else doing his job for me to succeed. Most the time, though, I loved football because of the team aspect, the camaraderie, the pulling in one direction to get a job done.

That day our team had worked hard together, and it paid off. We'd won, and I felt good about being able to contribute. I also feel good as I look back on those days now, seeing how my DID helped me to overcome my fear of crowds. That helped me on the field and off.

As any good Dawg can tell you, the team and I enjoyed a lot of success in 1980. I'm not sure how much was expected of us that year. The previous season, we'd finished with a record of six wins and five losses, so when we opened the season with a victory, it wasn't like everyone across the nation took notice. The Southeastern Conference is a football powerhouse, and 1980 was no exception. We rolled over our nonconference opponents, but nearly every conference game was a close one, but we managed to pull out victories on the road in Jacksonville, Florida, and Auburn to defeat our biggest rivals. With only one game remaining, we stood a chance of having an undefeated regular season and a shot at the national championship. When we beat Georgia Tech at home to end the season, all we could do was wait to see who we'd face in the Sugar Bowl. We were the number-one-ranked team in the country since the eighth week in the season, and as we saw it, the championship was ours to win or lose. The University of Pittsburgh was also undefeated, but they hadn't played the type of competitive schedule we'd played.

The Sugar Bowl committee selected the Fighting Irish of Notre Dame. This was in the days before the Bowl Championship Series and the "play-off" for the national championship between the two top-ranked teams. Notre Dame had finished

119

the regular season with nine wins, one loss, and a tie. Even though we had a better record and were the number one team in the nation, outside of Bulldog territory, not many people gave us a chance to win. That was fine with us, we were Dawgs after all, and being an underdog was something I'd been most of my life.

One of the great things about bowl games was the chance to go to new places. Since I'm a lover of history, New Orleans really appealed to me. On one of our free days, I set out with a group of teammates for the French Quarter. As we explored, we rounded a corner and spotted a brass band we had seen earlier. What had been a mournful procession had become a joyful festival. We watched as the musicians danced in the street while playing their instruments—this time, no floating coffin in sight. Apparently, the mourners had buried their dead, and now it was time to celebrate life. Their black umbrellas had been replaced by white flags to accompany "When the Saints Go Marching In."

When the celebrants had passed by, we continued along Bourbon Street until we encountered a group of children break dancing. They had an old top hat lying in front of them, but the tourists hadn't been very generous. My Daredevil alter kicked in, and the next thing I knew, I was out there dancing along with the kids. I loved music and dancing, so with my teammates staring drop-jawed at me, I spent the next half hour in front of a growing throng of tourists. I guess it isn't every day that you see someone six feet two inches tall and 210 pounds busting moves alongside some scrawny street performers. Maybe it was the Georgia Bulldogs T-shirt I was wearing that drew their attention. Whatever the reason, I was glad to see the hat filling up.

Just when I really had my feet moving and felt at ease, I noticed that the kids were giving one another the eye. One of them snatched the money and took off running. The others followed, and all were out of sight in an instant. I guess they had assumed I wanted a cut of the proceeds I had helped to generate and they weren't about to give it to me. They had no way of knowing who I was, or that I had no intention of taking the money they collected. All I wanted was to help them.

I didn't have much time to think about any of that. I realized I was standing there alone in front an expectant crowd. Some of them started to applaud. I took a quick bow and darted away, joining my teammates. They were all laughing and gave me a hard time, asking if they could get electric boogie lessons from me. One guy said that I had seemed like the Six-Million-Dollar Man and now that he saw my robot dance moves, he figured I was the $9.95 man.

No one knew how difficult it would be for me to regain *my* composure; since it had really been my uninhibited and fun-loving alter who performed. Although Herschel loved to dance, his shyness prevented him from doing anything to draw attention to himself. Maybe it was because we were out of our usual element, maybe it was just the spirit of New Orleans, but that giddy expression of joy wasn't all that typical of me.

On game day, it didn't matter to me where we were. We could have played the game in Mozambique, Mauritania, or on Mars. I was that focused on what we needed to do. I'd heard and read about Notre Dame and us being an underdog. I knew that several of Notre Dame's players were expected to be taken in the first round of the next NFL draft, and had heard the generally accepted prognosis that the Fighting Irish would crush Georgia. None of that mattered.

I often wondered myself if it was an alter who took over for me on game days. I don't think, at least not all of the time and at every moment during that day. I know I have a disciplined mind, and I can block out distractions very easily. In some ways, the ability I have to focus is like one of the hallmarks of DID, the ability to go somewhere else, to a safe place. I know that everyone who has the ability doesn't have DID. I believe that my powers of concentration worked hand in hand with my alters, that the condition enhanced my ability to focus but wasn't the source of it. I wasn't conscious of it, but when the whistle blew for a game to begin, I changed. Former teammates and opponents have commented on that to me over the years. They've said that I got a look in my eye, what one of them said he would have considered the "lights on but nobody's home look" characteristic of people who have "spaced out" or "checked out." In reality, I was doing anything but checking out—I was totally in tune with what was going on. The only thing that could check me out of a game was an injury. And that's exactly what happened in the Sugar Bowl.

On our second play from scrimmage, we ran a tailback sweep to the right, toward our bench. A Notre Dame player hit me from behind, just a glancing blow to push me out of bounds. I'd been hit thousands of times much harder than that, but something happened that I can't explain. My arm went numb, and I felt like it was paralyzed. It just dangled there, and felt like somebody had taken jumper cables and run them from their car to my shoulder and neck and started cranking the starter. Excruciating, unbearable pain shot through my body. I made it to the sidelines and fell to one knee. No one could understand what had happened. It wasn't like I'd been leveled by a vicious tackle.

Dr. Mulherin, the team doctor, rushed to my side, and my teammates gathered around as he examined me. I told him what happened and where the pain was, and his expression went grim. Dr. Mulherin explained that I had a classic anterior shoulder dislocation. He said it was the most common type of shoulder dislocation. I could feel the pain radiating from my shoulder up into my neck and the side of my head.

"Sorry, Herschel, you're done for tonight."

I sat there speechless. At first, hundreds of thoughts raced through my head. I knew that they weren't going to do me any good, so I quieted my mind. I took a few deep breaths and just stared at a patch of turf in front of me. A small ball of athletic tape lay there next to a flattened paper cup.

Together, the Hero and Warrior alters chimed in, "They don't know me. This ain't no big deal. I've come too far to let this stop me."

I walked along the sideline until I could find Dr. Mulherin. "If my shoulder is dislocated, doesn't that mean you can pop it back into place?"

He looked me in the eye, and then looked away. "Herschel, I can't do that now. That's the course of treatment we'll follow, but not here. Reducing the shoulder on-site like this would be too painful. There could be complications. You'd need to be under anesthesia . . ."

I didn't even hear the rest. Only later did I learn about the possibility of torn ligaments and permanent damage.

I persisted. "Sir, don't worry about the pain. Put my shoulder back into place. It's no big deal."

The doctor looked at our head athletic trainer, who shrugged his shoulders. "It's your call." Dr. Mulherin nodded. The trainer had me laid down on a table. He was joined by another trainer. One of them put his weight on my shoulder close to my neck, the other grabbed my injured arm by the wrist. I don't remember anything after that until I was strapping my shoulder pads back on. I wasn't in pain, and I had my usual range of motion. I was back on the field a few moments later.

We took advantage of some Notre Dame mental and physical errors and went on to win 17–10. I gained 97 yards in the first half, nearly all of them after the injury, but our defense really made the difference. Notre Dame outgained us in yardage, 328 to 127. I had 150 yards total in rushing and a couple of other backs combined for 4 more, but because Buck Belue lost 34 yards as a result of sacks and tackles behind the line of scrimmage (and passed for 7), our net yardage was that low. Once we had the lead, we played pretty conservatively, grinding it out to the tune of me carrying the ball thirty-six times. We weren't so buttoned up on offense that we didn't try at least one trick play—my only pass attempt of the game fell incomplete. Despite that incompletion, I was named the game's most valuable player. More important, we had an undefeated season and were voted the number one team in the nation.

The postgame celebration was amazing. My teammates and I jumped all over one another, and I know that fans of the Dawgs stayed up dancing all night on Bourbon Street. The one thing I remember most is that in celebrating after the game, we were hugging one another and thumping one another on the head and shoulders. That's when the pain came back to me. I'd made it through the game okay, but I was somewhat sore that next morning. The pain and stiffness didn't keep me from my routine, however. I got up early and did my sit-ups and push-ups.

Ever since that game, I've had people ask me how I was able to go back in after hurting my shoulder. The answer is twofold. First, the alter who takes on all of my pain came into play. Second, my faith in God allowed me to endure the pain. I've been fortunate not to have suffered any major injuries and I played through a lot of pain simply because I gave it up to God. Whenever I had a nagging little pain, I thought about what Jesus suffered on the cross for me, and I was able to go on. Nothing I've ever endured can compare to what the Lord Jesus went through on my behalf. To this day, each time I read the account of Jesus' crucifixion, I am filled with awe and wonder and gratitude. How petty and small my sufferings are in comparison to that great sacrifice. I was pleased that I could offer up my pain and help UGA win the game but I managed to keep things in perspective. I would continue to use Jesus' suffering on the cross as means to motivate myself when things got tough during the rest of my life.

I was thrilled that we'd won, but it wasn't like my life was changed forever by the outcome. I'm as competitive as anyone, and during a game I'm determined and focused, but once the game is over, I don't really dwell on the results. I hate to lose, but I can put losses behind me really easily by focusing on doing even more the next time to win. The same is true with winning. I knew that as the number one team in the nation, as an undefeated national champion, we'd set the bar really high for ourselves. Nothing short of perfection would be enough from that point forward. I was more than fine with that. We'd have to face the supreme challenge, and I was going to do as much as I could to be sure that I was ready.

I took no time off between the football and track seasons. The rest of the track athletes had already been competing indoors and were in the middle of that season when I joined them. That was just a part of being a tweener. Just as I did in football, I got along with my track teammates. Just as in football, we had teams within the larger team. I spent most of my time with the sprinters, while the middle-distance and long-distance runners had their own clique. I would have liked to hang out with the weight guys—the shot-putters, the discus and hammer throwers, even the javelin guys—but I had to give up the field events in college. I think that because those events had their roots in the ancient world and combat, I identified most with them. These guys were the real warriors, but since I was only running sprints, I really didn't fit in with them anymore. I took that warrior mentality to the starting blocks, though. I also took some of the practices that the middle- and long-distance runners used to the sprint events as well. Though my coaches didn't have me run long distance as a part of my regular training—for some of the sprinters, doing a four hundred, eight hundred, or a mile was a "long" run—I kept up my own routine of running upward of five miles every day. My fellow sprinters thought I was nuts for doing that, but "if it ain't broke don't fix it" applied here.

I enjoyed running track, but I'm sure that in some ways I missed out by not working out with the football team during the off-season and not participating in spring or summer drills with them. I never considered myself privileged or deserving of preferential treatment, but I sensed during my freshman year and even more strongly later on that some people were envious of me. Coach Dooley was a man of high integrity, and if he had rules, they applied to everyone. Now, I know I said that I didn't have to endure some of the initiation rituals that my teammates were subjected to, but those were unofficial, off-the-record, not endorsed by the coach kinds of things. Maybe some of the resentment I felt toward myself sprang from my not participating in those things, maybe it was my car, maybe it was me getting to go to New York City after the regular season was over for the Heisman Trophy presentation, maybe it was that I didn't follow the same weight-training regimen that the rest of them did. But I had that same experience of being a part of but apart from the team that I had experienced in almost all areas of my life.

As a student, I got the same impression from my classmates. Given the success we had on the field, I became fairly recognizable. I'd be walking to class on campus, and I could see some people looking at me and then quickly looking away. I could tell they recognized me, but they didn't want to be too obvious in staring at me. Other people would acknowledge me and wave and say my name or stop and talk with me, some acting like we were best buddies. I wanted to be just another student going to class or sitting in class, but it was impossible. The only way I can think of to explain how I felt sometimes is to compare my existence to that of a zoo animal. Some people go to the zoo and view the animals and just look at them and move on. Others try to interact with them, and still others try to do something stupid or show-offy to deflect attention from the animal to themselves. I had people do all of those things, along the spectrum that runs from casually indifferent to rude and obnoxious. I have to say, though, that the rude and obnoxious stuff was extremely rare and mostly confined to opposing team's players and fans. Maybe I was overly sensitive to the impression that many people had about athletes. That we were one-dimensional and none too interested in getting an education. That wasn't the case with me, and I could make the distinction between Herschel Walker, football player, and Herschel Walker, student. Lots of other folks couldn't.

I'm not sure if that was more their loss or mine. I have to admit that there were times when I wanted to be just a normal everyday student. Playing sports while going to college was like having a full-time job while attending classes. I had to schedule my courses around practice times; as a freshman, I had to attend a mandatory study hall with all the other freshmen athletes; I lived in a segregated dormitory away from the general student population. So both time and space issues kept me from really being a full-fledged member of the student body. I'd grown accustomed to life on the periphery, but that didn't mean that I really enjoyed it. I'm not blaming anybody for what I experienced, and believe me, I know that a lot of people had things far worse to deal with than I did. I wonder sometimes what role DID played in shaping those experiences.

I do know for a fact that the alter who could deal with physical pain played a dominant role in another episode from my Georgia days. During my sophomore year, I went into the school's medical center for a mandatory physical exam. The doctors did a pretty thorough work-up, and during one part of the exam, the doctor wanted to examine my throat. He put his hands on each side of my lower jaw and asked me to open wide. I winced a bit at his touch. He asked me what hurt, and I told him my lower jaw was a bit sensitive. He fiddled with it a

127

bit and said that nothing seemed structurally wrong, but suggested that I go see a dentist.

At first I wasn't going to do anything about it, but the doctor must have notified someone in the athletic office or Coach Dooley's office because I got a phone call a day later telling me that I had an appointment scheduled for the next day at three-thirty. This was during our usual weight-room session, but I was told I'd be excused from it and I had to go. I didn't spend much time in Athens itself usually, so it took me a while to find the dentist's office. My siblings and I didn't go too regularly as kids, but I'd not had any cavities or anything to that point, so I'd never had to undergo any kind of procedure. I'd had only that one bad experience with Dr. Thomas when he examined my knees, but that wasn't painful or anything, just bad news. I knew that a lot of people hated going to the dentist, but I was pretty much okay with it. I sat in the waiting room and could hear the high-pitched whine of the drill and smell the minty-antiseptic odor of the place. Before I saw the doctor, one of his assistants took me to another room and took a series of X-rays.

The doctor took one quick look in my mouth and then pointed to the sheet of X-rays, "Your wisdom teeth are coming in. Looks like they have been for a while. They're not coming in straight and they're crowding the other teeth—especially the lowers. I recommend you get them pulled right away."

"Yes, sir. Can you go ahead and do that?"

Turns out an oral surgeon would have to do it, but he recommended one that worked with the athletic department. His office was just a few blocks away and he could take me. The dentist asked me if anyone was with me who could drive me home. I told him I'd be fine. He then went on to explain that I'd be administered a general anesthetic and it wouldn't be safe for me to operate a vehicle afterward. I told him not to worry and left the office.

I had to fill out some forms in the oral surgeon's office, and when it came to the part about what kind of pain relief/block I had had administered in the past and preferred, I printed in big block letters NONE. I handed the forms back to the dental assistant and she scanned the pages and looked up at me with a puzzled expression. She told me the doctor would be with me in a few minutes.

When the surgeon came in, he sat down and explained to me what he was going to do, what wisdom teeth were, and showed me the X-rays. He launched into his explanation about anesthetics, asking me if I'd ever had a local or a general before. He pointed to the sheet I'd filled out and said he wanted to be certain that I understood all of this since I'd never had any administered before.

"No, sir, I've never had anything like that before, and I don't want to now."

"There's nothing to be afraid of. Going under the first time is an unknown, but you'll be fine. Many of my patients find nitrous oxide enjoyable, in fact."

"I'm not afraid, sir."

"If you really feel that strongly about a general, I can administer a local. I don't recommend it usually with first-time patients because a lot of them don't like needles."

"It's not that I don't like needles. I don't want any kind of anesthetic."

We went back and forth for a few more minutes, until I finally told him that he either did it my way or I was leaving and would find someone who would do what I asked. I told him I had a right to be treated the way I wanted to be treated and the athletic department had told me so. I think that last bit about the athletic department convinced him. He made me sign some kind of waiver and consent form, which I gladly did. I could tell he wasn't happy, and he had a couple of his assistants come into the room and made me repeat that I was requesting that the procedure be done without any kind of anesthesia. He also asked that the other assistants remain in the room to help him out in case he needed to take emergency action or hold me down.

By that point, I was getting pretty angry. I just wanted this thing done, and I told him that. He tugged his mask over his mouth and nose, tilted me back in the chair so that it was like I was lying on a lounge chair, and started in. The only thing I really remember of the procedure is the salty, coppery taste of blood in my mouth.

It wasn't until many years later when I was diagnosed with DID that I understood the connection between my Sugar Bowl shoulder injury and my wisdom teeth being extracted. The alters I'd developed had a strong sense of self-preservation. They also exerted a lot of control. What they feared is that under the influence of anesthesia, they would lose some of the control over me or be obliterated as identities entirely. So my refusal to receive anesthesia and my ability to endure pain were two separate things. The self-preservation alters took control and refused the medication, and another alter endured the pain. Through my alters, I was able to "go there," a place far removed from the dentist's chair. Just as victims of abuse can endure the pain through that kind of escape, I was also able to endure that oral surgery. DID is both remarkable and awful. To this day, I have not taken any kind of medication in my life with the exception of a few mild over-the-counter pain relievers—less than a handful of them.

Just as I didn't remember much of Dr. M placing my shoulder back in joint, I don't remember much of the extraction procedure. I don't even really remember how I got back to my dorm room. All I can recall is waking up the next morning and seeing a package of gauze pads and a set of postoperative instructions on my desk. I could feel some stitches in my mouth and a kind of dull throbbing, but that was it. I got up and went to class and did my usual workout routine. A few days later, I got a call from the oral surgeon's office reminding me of my follow-up appointment for stitch removal. I went in and was out within a few minutes, and never gave the incident much thought.

The mind is a very powerful and mysterious thing. I'm not necessarily proud of having gone through what many consider a really painful procedure without the benefit of anesthesia. My desire to do without it wasn't an example of macho posturing. I didn't drink a bunch of whiskey and bite on a bullet; instead, I was overpowered by a side of me that I didn't really understand and certainly couldn't have explained to anyone at that time. In my own head, I was as much of a tweener socially as I was athletically. There was me, there were the alters, and there was some other part of me that acted as a mediator between us—another part of my identity whom I wasn't conscious of, but must have been conscious of me and those other sides of me. He was the one who was in control, I guess. I'm fortunate that he never did anything to truly put me in danger; that darker side was to express itself later on. For now, and for at least the next ten or so years, I'd walk and run in his good graces.

Chapter Seven

Sugar and Spice

Our victory over Notre Dame and my performance in the Sugar Bowl catapulted the Bulldogs and me to national prominence. As I told you, however, I had little time to celebrate since I had to start running track right away. That was fine because I am the type of person who always has to be busy. I also had little tolerance for life in the spotlight, and by being involved in a second sport, I could avoid some of the attention. I really don't know what I would have done if I hadn't been involved in sports. I never looked at my fellow students with envy. They had plenty of free time, but not many of them used it productively, from what I could tell. The way I figured it, if I had a course load of sixteen to eighteen hours, that meant that I was in a classroom less than twenty hours a week. That averages out to four hours a day. I'll be generous and say that it takes a typical student an hour a day to get to and from those classes. That puts us at five hours a day. Another hour and a half for meals each day, and you are left with seventeen and a half hours a day to sleep, study, and spend at your leisure.

Since I lived in the athletic dorm and spent most of my time around other athletes who had at least a three- to four-hour-per-day additional time commitment, the amount of wasted/ unproductive time they spent was lower than the typical undergraduate. I don't know if I could have handled having the number of unregimented hours that most college students have. I'd be willing to bet, though I have no hard and fast evidence to back this up, that one of the leading causes of students failing or performing poorly in their classes is that they have too much free time on their hands.

Since I've been diagnosed with DID, I've looked on this issue of busy-ness or activity in another light. We all know the old saying about idle hands being the devil's workshop and all that. But what about the idle mind? What happens to it? In the wake of my diagnosis, I read psychiatrist Kay Redfield Jamison's memoir, *An Unquiet Mind*. In it, she describes what she experienced as a manic-depressive. Though I don't have that mood disorder, I found the book's description of hyper-activity helpful. I never thought of myself as hyperactive, but other people always commented on how packed my schedule was, how I could never just sit back and relax and always had to be on the go. I can't deny that it's the truth, but I always looked at those qualities as positives, as the benchmarks of someone who is an achiever. I still look at it that way, but I also understand that in trying to keep my hands and mind busy, I might also have been trying to run away from something. If I kept my focus all the time on achieving things, I had less time to let my mind wander to the past and things that caused me pain, or to the present and what I might or might not have been happy about. In the same way, by focusing on doing the things I'd always done—keeping to my exercise routine, for example—I could find comfort in the familiar. I sometimes wonder if maybe I felt so secure at Georgia because the routine I had wasn't that much different from what I experienced in high school and in Wrightsville.

After all, I had my sister Veronica there as a family member. If I wasn't in the library, in class, at practice, or working out, I was generally with Veronica. She became almost like my mother. Veronica had a lot of friends on the women's track team, and those young women became my friends, too. In fact, they became like surrogate sisters. With those young women and my teammates surrounding me, I didn't have to go outside of either of those two relatively small circles to do the very little socializing I did. When I showed up on campus my freshmen year, I had two built-in groups with whom I could spend my time. As I've pointed out many times before, I didn't really get that close to any of them, and felt somewhat distanced from them; they were there when I felt the need for companionship and camaraderie.

I also think it's interesting to look at one of the other activities I participated in during my last year of high school and ever since then—martial arts. Given my role of the overweight and stuttering victim of kids picking on me, it seems natural that I had some revenge fantasies to escape to. In my case, that meant Bruce Lee movies. Mr. Lee was the legendary martial artist and movie star whose father had been a star in a Chinese opera company. While still in China, Mr. Lee appeared in many movies, but it was after he came to the United States that he really became a star. I can still remember watching *Fists of Fury* and *Return of the Dragon*. I tried to copy some of his moves at home, but I was too awkward and clumsy and my kicks usually ended up with me on my butt instead of my imaginary attacker on his. In the twelfth grade, I started to study the martial arts with an instructor in Dublin. I would eventually learn, though

I suspected it even then, that he wasn't particularly good himself and wasn't a great teacher either.

When I arrived in Athens, one of the first things I did was find a program to enroll in. Whenever I had the time, I'd take a tae kwan do class under the guidance of Lawrence Huff. He ran a karate dojo, and was truly a martial artist in many senses of the word. Today, he lives in Japan and is a printmaker and a *shakuhachi* (traditional Japanese bamboo flute) player. The hero of the television show *Kung Fu*, David Carradine, played that instrument as well, and I watched that show as often as I could. Like most kids who develop an interest in the marital arts, I was originally drawn to its physicality. Simply put, I wanted to be able to kick people's butts. I think that God was looking out for me in this case also. The martial arts are as much about controlling your mind and that of your opponent as they are about the physical actions. I think that either deep in my subconscious or through God's intervention, I was led to this interest. Deep down, I think I knew that I needed some way to master all the anger, frustration, and desire to hurt someone I had buried deep inside me. I had to figure out a way to still my unquiet mind. In a very real way, looking back on it now, I think that Herschel, the essential me, realized that I needed help in controlling all of the alters in me. Somebody needed to be the Commander in Chief, the one monitoring the General's behavior. If I didn't develop a disciplined routine, if I didn't follow a regimented schedule, if I didn't learn the self-mastery so essential to the martial arts, those other sides of me could have easily run riot and destroyed my life. Just as my alters expressed their need for self-preservation when faced with possible obliteration through anesthesia, my essential self expressed its desire to not be exterminated or dominated by those alters by resorting to what some people might view as an almost obsessive need to be ordered, organized, and occupied.

In keeping with the theme of good thing/bad thing, my interest in the martial arts further set me apart from my teammates. After a game, a lot of them would go out drinking and celebrating. I wouldn't, for a number of reasons, including the fact that I had a martial-arts or kickboxing tournament to compete in on Sunday. I think that Coach Dooley tried to impose some kind of control over his players' carousing by instituting a rule that we all had to attend brunch on campus on Sundays. I'm sure that he saw his fair share of guys racing in just before the meal service began, looking and smelling like something the cat had dragged through a beer puddle. I remember one morning during my sophomore year, when I was running late for the meal. I had competed in a tournament that morning, and it had gone on longer than I'd expected. I won my division and received a healthy-size trophy. I didn't have time to go home to drop it off, so there I was running through Athens on my way to the athletic dorm's cafeteria carrying this trophy slung over my shoulder like a sack of cement. As I got closer to the building, I could see Coach Dooley and his family on the steps, standing and talking with a small group of people. I raced to the doorway, and came to quick stop when I heard Coach Dooley say, "Morning, Herschel."

I turned and watched surprise register on the faces of everyone gathered there as they viewed me in full splendor, still in the sweatpants and sweatshirt I'd pulled over the *kara-tegi* I'd worn in competition, my face dripping with perspiration, and a waist-high trophy now resting at my feet. Forgetting for a moment where I was at, I bowed and said, *"Kyong Ne!"* I wasn't so shook up that I addressed him as *Sabumnim*—that was a form of address reserved only for our head teachers.

Coach Dooley nodded back: "I take it congratulations are in order?"

"Thank you, sir." I was feeling a bit embarrassed, and I think Coach Dooley recognized that.

"Good to see you, son."

I took a lot of crud from the guys on the team when they saw me toting that trophy in there. I heard someone, I think it was the wide receiver Amp Arnold, shout, "Hey, Herschel, you run all the way to Carolina to steal that from George Rogers!" Everyone busted up laughing, hollering, and catcalling, but I just set the thing down next to me, acting like I didn't hear him. Finishing third in the Heisman voting my freshmen year was a real honor, and George Rogers was a great back. I knew I'd have to work hard to get my turn, but I could do it. Besides, if I wanted to, I could hand Amp Arnold his brunch and put my fist or foot through a whole stack of cafeteria trays just to show him what was what. I liked Amp and we had no grudge against each other, but all the same, I took comfort in knowing that when or if I needed it, I could use my martial-arts training to come to the aid of someone in need or defend myself.

I can see now that the idea of self-defense has a lot more than one meaning in my life. Again, I don't know how conscious I was of keeping people at a safe distance from me, if I knew that my ability on the football field set me apart, erected barriers, and that my as-yet-undiagnosed DID and alters were working to keep people from digging too deep or getting too close. All I know is that I kept myself real busy, loved to read Dante and Shakespeare (particularly the Saint Crispin's Day speech before the battle of Agincourt in *Henry V*), and kept my mind focused on whatever task was at hand. Though I'd made the trip from Wrightsville to Athens, I hadn't really traveled very far in my social development. I may have been lonely, but my alters shielded me from feeling any pain as a result of that loneliness.

Sometimes my desire to do whatever it took to win and to better myself took me down some curved roads to unexpected destinations. One day I was walking through a campus building and passed by an open doorway through which I heard music—a piano and nothing else. I looked in the doorway and saw a long narrow room with a mirrored wall at the far end. At that end of the room, dressed in leotards or T-shirts and tights, were a group of women. They had one leg on a railing that ran the length of the mirrored wall, and they were stretching in ways that made my hamstring muscles tighten up just looking at them. I stood there for a minute or two watching them, and I was amazed by their range of motion and the ease with which they moved. I knew I'd found something that could give me a much-needed edge.

I'd spent so much of my training time working on strength and endurance. I'd not spent nearly enough time on flexibility. My martial-arts training had helped in that regard—I could kick a board that was held up head-high but not with the ease that many of my classmates did. *Sabumnim* Huff told me that if anything would hold me back in progressing as a martial artist, it would be my less-than-ideal flexibility. I didn't do anything about my newly discovered source of flexibility training for a while, but the seed had been planted. I had to recruit some cohorts, however; this was one mission I couldn't undertake alone. That I even considered taking the class and talking teammates into it was an indication that another alter was at work. I don't know if labeling this alter's attitude as indifferent is accurate because that word has negative connotations. This personality didn't care a whole lot about what other people thought of him. This was equal parts a lack of self-consciousness, confidence, and a feeling that I'd been teased so much in the past that nothing could get to me now. This alter enabled me to do positive things and not be so concerned about appearances and the judgments of others, but it had a darker side as well—a callous, sometimes selfish alter who really didn't care about what anyone else thought or wanted. More on him later.

I told some of my teammates I believed that ballet could really help us with our flexibility and our moves on the football field. For that reason, I chose mostly receivers, backs (offensive and defensive), and a couple of linebackers to pitch my scheme to. None of them seemed too excited about the idea of taking something as unmanly as ballet. When I pointed out that most of the rest of the students would be young women, and young, reasonably fit women at that, I made a few converts. About seven or eight of us decided to give it a try.

I think we were all a little bit nervous at first, but the instructor seemed glad to have us and went out of her way to make us feel comfortable—no leotards or tutus for us. We just had to wear comfortable clothes and shoes. At first she led us through the history of ballet and the seven basic categories of ballet movement: *plier,* to bend; *étendre,* to stretch; *relever,* to rise; *sauter,* to leap; *élancer,* to dart; *glisser,* to glide; and *tourner,* to turn. If all we had to do was take a written test over those terms, we might have all done well, but this was a dance class, and well, we had to dance. I was already comfortable with moving on the dance floor—at least that show-off Daredevil of an alter was—so the first few weeks of basic ballet training were not too tough. I sometimes got to class a little bit early, just as a more advanced class was winding down. I was mesmerized by how well these people moved, the kind of air they got on their leaps, the balance and strength it took when the men and women paired off in a duet and the guy carried someone around with a single arm. That was all really cool and made the little leaps and turns of my class look silly. And *silly* doesn't do justice to how many of us looked.

It was when we started to put those seven basic moves and positions together into little routines that the defections began—first our coordination, balance, and self-esteem took a hike, then some of my teammates did. During class exercises, I could hear guys saying, to a sprightly piano accompaniment, "I can't believe I let you talk me into this. This is so stupid."

"Herschel, we're out of here. We're football players, not ballerinas."

By the time the semester was winding down, our gang of seven had been reduced to three. All the three of us needed to do was get through a recital that ended the semester and we'd be done, we'd receive our course credit, and we could resume our nonballet lives. Of course, we would never live down the ignominy of having taken the course; our teammates were sure to step in and remind us of our little venture if one of the seven of us should ever forget.

The day of the recital arrived, and I marched off to class like the dutiful soldier I am. I was enjoying the class as much as I could, and I felt a sense of obligation to finish something once I'd begun it. That resolve crumbled when I came face-to-face with this reality. Not only was the recital being attended by students from other classes and some of the dance majors, I was going to be the only guy out there performing. My little gang of three had mysteriously turned into a gang of one. Now, maybe my show-off alter had pushed me into street dancing in New Orleans and concocted this idea of the ballet class, but even he had abandoned me. I went up to the instructor and told her that I couldn't do it. I couldn't go out there as the only guy and perform. I can't remember the instructor's name, but I liked her. She was a very kind and patient young woman who, if you hadn't known she was the instructor, would easily have passed for another student. And I believe that's exactly what she was—a graduate student in the MFA dance program. She couldn't have been more that three or four years older than me.

When I told her how I felt, you'd have thought I'd told her that her puppy had run off and hadn't come back. The rest of the women in the class had gathered around and were either staring daggers at me or giving me the same pouty disappointed look as the instructor. I don't like disappointing anyone, and now here I was on the verge of disappointing a group of twenty women. I'd gotten to know a few of them, and they'd gotten to know me—not just as Herschel Walker, tailback, but as Herschel Walker, the sophomore from Wrightsville.

"Herschel." One young woman stepped out of the group and stood in front of me. She couldn't have been more than five foot two and ninety pounds. She looked up at me with eyes as wide as coffee cups. "Some of us have worked real hard, and so have you. We're supposed to do a few partner moves and now we don't have one. We need you."

The "conversation" continued in this vein for a few more minutes, until finally I caved in. I went out there and did the best I could. I was strong enough that I could hold a rock-steady *developpé* that earned me some applause. We also had to run across the stage in formation and perform a stag leap, like a deer bounding over some brush, and I think my landing nearly brought the house down—literally. Every time I'd done it in class, I'd been told to hold my abdominal muscles in as a way to soften the thud of my landing. Well, when you're as big as I am, softly is a relative term. When we did it in recital, it was as if the six women and I were a half-dozen mosquitoes and a crippled Learjet landing in unison.

By the end of the recital and the class, I was glad that I'd decided to hang in there. I'd been saying to myself that I wanted to do things to help out other people, and in the case of the recital at least, that's what I was able to do. I also benefited in terms of flexibility—physically and mentally. Stepping out of my comfort zone and doing something new and innovative—at least as far as football players are concerned—and dancing to my own drummer are all things I've tried to continue to do. I think that they balance out the discipline and the regimentation that govern so much else of my life. I like to keep people guessing, and I don't want to be labeled and slotted into a prescribed nook. Venturing beyond the "boundary" of my personality or what is expected of me resulted in my learning something, helping a few people out, and taking a chunk out of some stereotypes, so it was a good experience.

One of the best experiences I had at the University of Georgia was meeting my future wife, Cindy. One late afternoon following practice, the trainers insisted I report to the treatment room. I had tweaked an ankle just a bit making a cut, nothing serious, but they wanted to be sure that I had an ice treatment to prevent any swelling or inflammation. I didn't like going into the training room at all, even for being taped and untaped, much less being treated. Don't get me wrong, the head trainer and his staff of assistant trainers and student volunteers were great people and performed an invaluable service. I just didn't like being around weakness. That's what I thought injuries were. If your mind stayed strong, and you didn't allow yourself to think of the pain, you wouldn't be hurt. I know you may be thinking I'm crazy, but studies have shown that players are more susceptible to injuries when they have something else on their minds besides their performance on the field. Those studies show that when athletes are under stress—troubles with interpersonal relationships, finances, classes—they are more prone to injury. Distractions can cause trouble and I'd been dedicated to eliminating them whenever and wherever possible. My martial-arts training was definitely a part of that, but not even a Dan Gun tae kwan do move could have blocked Cindy DeAngelis, the half-miler out of Cocoa Beach High School in Cocoa Beach, Florida, from getting past my Sentry and Watch Dog.

I first saw Cindy that late afternoon in early October of my freshman year. I was sitting with my entire right foot and lower leg in a tub of ice and water. She was on a treatment table across from me, with a thermal heat pad on her right quadriceps. I was just sitting there minding my own business when I looked up. She smiled and waved at me, and I thought she looked

familiar. Then I realized I'd seen her in Veronica's room a couple of times. If this was a fairy tale, I'd tell you that it was love
at first sight, but it wasn't. Not that Cindy wasn't worthy of such
a reaction, it's just that old Herschel was so involved in football
and his studies, he wasn't thinking about women that much.
She said, "You're Veronica's brother, right?"

I do remember liking her voice. She had a distinctive accent, and when I found out later that she was originally from
New York, I understood why that voice had stuck with me.
She didn't have one of those really harsh Brooklyn accents or
anything like that, but you could tell she wasn't from Down
South, where people's vowel sounds come out sounding like
they're being poured through molasses. Her voice was quick
and sharp, and I especially liked that she thought of me as
Veronica's brother and not as Herschel Walker, freshman sensation. That said something about her right there, and I took
note of it. In classes, I was a quick learner, but in the ways
of love and romance, I am definitely slow. Cindy and I didn't
begin to date until the middle of our sophomore year—more
than a year after we first "met" in the training room.

Even our getting to the point where I would say that we
were dating took some time. For the longest while, Cindy was
just another of my surrogate sisters. After our freshman year,
she became more of a regular, or at least I noticed her presence
more than I had before. As beautiful as she is, she was hard not
to notice. I liked that she treated me like I was no big thing,
as did most of the women on the track team, and for a long
time I thought maybe she was mocking me. There's nothing I
can point to exactly to substantiate that claim, I just had a feeling that she didn't think I was all that I was cracked up to be.
Whenever she spoke to me, it was like her words were laughing at me. She could be saying something completely straight-
faced and serious, but it was like there was a smile peeking
around the corner of her expression and words. According to

my sister Veronica, a woman would have to hit me over the head with a frying pan and announce that she was flirting with me to get me to understand her intentions, but I truly don't think Cindy was flirting with me.

Cindy was a very smart woman, still is, and now I think that back then she was just assessing me, probing me, taking notes. She was shrewd about that, too, because I don't ever remember feeling like I was a slice of a muscle cell on a slide under a microscope. I know my Sentry would have noticed that, but maybe my focus was so intent I wouldn't have. Anyway, Cindy was around and I was around, and Veronica was around, and so were all these other teammates of Veronica's. They were like my sisters and all, and that was fine. I wasn't particularly close with any one of them—the Sentry let them on the grounds, but they weren't allowed inside the building, and they certainly weren't allowed to look inside any of the file drawers and the confidential information I'd stored there.

At the end of the first semester of my second year at Georgia, I was done with all of my final exams. I was waiting for Veronica to finish up hers so that we could go back to Wrightsville for a few days. We'd had a pretty good year, finishing with ten wins and one loss in the regular season. We finished at the top of the Southeastern Conference again, and the only blemish on our record was a 13–3 loss to Clemson. That was a tough one, but we were headed back to the Sugar Bowl, this time to play the University of Pittsburgh—the only other major college team like us who had been undefeated the year before. We were the number-two-ranked team in the nation, and if things went our way and Clemson lost, we'd have a chance to repeat as national champions.

I was done with my tests, and I didn't feel like sitting around and just waiting for Veronica. One of the things I did a lot of with what little free time I had was to go to the movies. Athens had several movie theaters, but as the season progressed and I became better known around the campus and the surrounding community, it got harder for me to go anywhere anonymously. Being recognized wasn't a big problem at first, but I was still not real comfortable around crowds anyway, so I tended to go to movies that were shown on campus. That particular evening in December, I was hanging around Veronica's room. She had to study but a few of her friends were over just after dinner. I kept bugging her about going to see *Time Bandits* with me. Finally, exasperated, she said, "Bo, just go to your movie and leave me alone."

"I don't want to go by myself."

"I'll go." Cindy had been sitting on the bed leafing through a magazine. She tossed it aside and stood up and stretched. She could barely get her hands down below her knees. This was just before I enrolled in the ballet class, and her demonstration of inflexibility reminded me of my latest goal. It was a cold night for Athens, and a light drizzle fell as Cindy and I made our way along the campus walkways. The streetlights seemed to set our words on fire as we walked in the cool damp air. When we got to where the movie was to be shown, we bought our tickets and entered the lecture hall. Cindy checked her watch. "What time is this thing supposed to start?"

"Eight."

"Well, it's five to eight and nobody's here."

"Maybe the bandits stole all the time."

Cindy's face curled into a puzzled look, then she looped her arm through mine and laughed as she led me down the aisle to our seats. I liked the feeling of warmth she transferred from her arm to mine. I felt myself relax a bit, and the Sentry stopped standing at attention.

Maybe a half dozen other people were in the hall with us, and it felt kind of funny to be sitting in the dark watching a movie with so few people. Cindy told me that the director, Terry Gilliam, had been a member of Monty Python's Flying

Circus. I'd never heard of them, but wisely kept my mouth shut and didn't ask if this Python guy had been a trapeze artist or something. Cindy picked up on my silence and explained about the BBC television show and seeing it on her local Public Broadcasting Service station. I settled in to watch the film. It was funny and strange and loaded with interesting bits of history and little people and giants.

Ten minutes into the movie, Cindy decided it was silly to stay seated in one of the wooden chairs. She sat down on one of the landings, bunched her jacket up behind her like a pillow, and using the step behind her head as another cushion, lay down with her head propped up. She patted the floor, and at first I didn't want to join her, but the seats were hard and I didn't have a lot of legroom, so I joined her. We laughed and whispered comments back and forth throughout the rest of the film, both of us cracking up when the little people got into all kinds of trouble and a godlike character has to intervene and destroy a devil-like character by turning him into chunks of molten rock and charcoal. The big boss tells all the little people in a very proper English accent, "Pick up all this evil. Every bit of it." Of course, they don't get every bit of it, and according to this screenwriter, that's how evil got into the world. Cindy and I didn't discuss the allegorical implications of the movie, but we did like to use that quote a lot, both of us struggling to employ an upper-crust British accent when we said, "Pick up all this evil."

By the time the show ended, the rain had stopped, but a low fog swirled around our ankles and calves. I commented that it was like London.

Cindy replied, "No. France."

"Why France?"

Cindy shook her head. "C'mon. Play the game. You were supposed to say something about underpants."

I liked this girl. She was fun and energetic and funny, and

she had me doing things I wouldn't normally have done. Variety is the spice of life, so they say, and I'd been on a bland diet for a long time. Being with Cindy didn't exactly break up my usual routine. She became another dimension of it, and I was glad about that. Being an athlete herself, she seemed to understand what I was about. Even though she had hamstrings as tight as cello strings and I had to work with her constantly to loosen them up, she stretched me in other ways, made me a little more flexible and exposed me to ideas and ways of seeing things I might not have otherwise.

As simple as it sounds, that first movie we saw got me out of my usual comfort zone. If I had gone to the movie by myself, I would likely have just walked out of the theater if I saw so few people there, and I certainly wouldn't have lain down on the floor like I was at home watching television. I was comfortable around Cindy. I felt like I could be myself, whichever self it was who could claim to be the essential Herschel. It took a long while before I got up the courage to ask her out on a real date—another few months. I had other matters to attend to, going to New York for the Heisman Trophy presentation, for one. I finished second in the balloting, losing out this time to the great Marcus Allen of the University of Southern California. Just about a month later, I would be disappointed again. The University of Pittsburgh and its future NFL Hall of Fame quarterback Dan Marino beat us in the Sugar Bowl, 24–20. It was a great game, and the lead changed hands six times before Marino sealed the victory with a long touchdown pass. I was held to eighty-four yards rushing by a Pittsburgh defense that was keyed to stopping me. For my first two years, I'd only experienced two losses, so I had high hopes for my junior year—for a lot of reasons.

In time, Cindy and I were as inseparable as it's possible for two people who were as busy as we both were to be. Cindy was the first woman I ever dated, and truth be told, she scared me a little bit. Maybe she didn't frighten the essential Herschel, but some of the alters felt threatened by her. For that reason, I don't think I let her get too close to me. Closer than anyone else in my life, but not as close, as I've come to learn today, as couples should be or can be. If I held the rest of the world at arm's length, then Cindy was allowed to stand right beside me, our arms grazing each other's like they had as we lay on that landing watching *Time Bandits*. It makes me sad to think that even though we were together for many years after that, had a child together, lived as man and wife, and in almost every way were supremely happy together, I probably only let her inch incrementally closer to me but never really let her in. But that's a story for another chapter.

One issue that didn't keep us apart but some folks thought would have was race. Cindy is Italian-American. Our difference in skin color made no difference to the two of us, but even though we were in the enlightened 1980s, this was still Georgia. I don't recall that we were ever harassed, and if we were stared at on campus, I generally attributed that to people spotting me and not them gawking at a biracial couple. Maybe I was just hoping that was the case, but among our close-knit group, no one ever raised it as an issue. In looking back on it, I know that my choice of girlfriend further separated me, made me more of a tweener than I already was. I didn't care, though. Just like I had done in high school in the dispute about the principal's comments, I chose not to view who I dated as a racial matter. It was just a pure and simple question of right and wrong. Cindy was the right person for me to be with, and I never considered her to be the wrong color. I've said it before many times, but it bears repeating. I may be naive, but I'm pure of heart, and God amply rewarded me for that by bringing Cindy DeAngelis into my life.

Among the people who weren't happy about our being together, we were most stung by her parents' reaction. When they found out she was dating me, they confronted her and a big blowup ensued. The result was that for a year after that Cindy was estranged from her family. She was definitely welcome in Wrightsville. My mother and father embraced her, keeping to their belief that color was just a wrapper that some folks saw, while others looked at what was inside. I didn't get a chance to spend a whole lot of time in Wrightsville with track and all and traveling to Europe for the summer, so I don't know what people back home had to say about me dating a white woman, nor did I care. I was too busy focusing on what I had to do to finish up another semester of school, my budding "dance career," and my upcoming trip abroad.

I remember coming across Mark Twain's *Innocents Abroad* and sitting in the library reading that funny account of his world travels. I don't think the term *ugly American* had been coined when it was written, and Twain certainly wouldn't have qualified as one. If he had been around in my day, I think he would have had me in mind as someone he could profile as a true innocent. Back when I was running track and competing on the European circuit, it was still an "amateur" sport. Any NCAA athlete who accepted money to play or to perform in any sport including but not limited to the one for which they received a scholarship and competed in while at college would lose their amateur standing and be banned from competing. You're probably all familiar with the case of the legendary Native American athlete Jim Thorpe, who was stripped of his Olympic medals because he had received a few dollars for playing semipro baseball one summer. I'd read about Mr. Thorpe and lived in fear that I could suffer the same fate—maybe not having my Olympic medals taken from me, but being involved in a scandal, embarrassing myself, my family, my team, and my school.

I don't like telling tales out of school, but I think that by now most people realize that back then track was an amateur sport in name but not in spirit. Many, many athletes received appearance money from meet organizers and promoters. These individuals wanted to attract the best athletes, so they had to fork over money to get them to come. Track was a big business in Europe and the number of people who attended meets was almost on a par with our crowds at football and baseball games. So there was money to be made for the promoters and the athletes. I was approached a few times with offers of money, and every time I nearly jumped out of my skin and said, "No. No. No." I'd practically run as fast as I could from whoever had approached me. Today, I think back on those days and laugh, and I wonder what those representatives thought of me. I was just a big dumb unsophisticated country boy in their minds, and the truth isn't very far from that.

Athletic apparel companies also competed for our services. Any number of times, a representative from Adidas, Asics, or Nike came to me and tried me to get to wear their shoes. I always refused the money they offered, but I did accept free clothes. I don't know what the specifics are of the NCAA rules and what monetary level I was allowed to receive before something could be considered a violation, but I didn't ever abuse the privilege like a lot of athletes did. In recent years, there's been a call to give student athletes on scholarship a stipend. The thinking goes that the school derives enormous financial benefits from our "services." Nonathletes can work during the school year, but we can't. A scholarship covers tuition, fees, housing, and books, but doesn't provide us with money to socialize, pay phone bills, and such. It's a complicated issue, but I know that a lot of my teammates and I came from poor backgrounds and the temptation was always great to accept what people were offering. It was wrong, so I didn't do it, but it didn't seem fair that the guys on the team often didn't have enough money to pay for a pizza, and that our fellow classmates, who didn't generate millions of dollars in revenue, could work to earn spending money while we couldn't. So, if I got a few T-shirts, warm-up suits, and running shoes, I didn't see the harm in it.

One time I didn't even get a chance to say no when I was presented with something that the NCAA calls an "illegal inducement." Again, I don't know if this qualifies, but I felt guilty about it for years. This is as good a time as any to bare my soul. As an athlete, you get interviewed a lot, and every now and then someone will ask you a question that comes totally out of left field. That happened once at the tail end of my sophomore season, just before the Sugar Bowl. I was being interviewed by a group of reporters and dealing with the usual questions by firing off clichés one after the other. Toward the end I heard a voice coming from somewhere behind the group clustered in front of me: "What's your favorite candy bar?"

I wish I had said something funny like, "This is the Sugar Bowl, right? So of course it's Sugar Babies."

Instead, I just said the first thing that came to mind. "Snickers."

I didn't think much of it until I got back from the Sugar Bowl and began the second semester. Coming back from classes one day, I found a box sitting outside my dorm-room door. It was a box filled with a dozen cases of Snickers bars. Now, I don't know if the people at M&M Mars who make them sent me the box or if some fan who read that interview stepped up and did it; all I know is that I had more Snickers bars in my possession than I'd ever eaten in my whole life. Ever since my physical transformation, I'd become—how do I put this?—an unconventional eater. Your image of a football player is probably one of a guy who sits down at every meal, on his own or at the training table, with a pile of food fit to feed a family of five. That wasn't me. I didn't, and haven't, eaten breakfast in years. I generally eat only one small meal a day. My teammates used to think I hated the food at the athletic dorm and always went out to eat or ate on the sly or something. Truth is, I just don't eat that much.

For a long time after that box came, I ate Snickers bars exclusively. Now, I don't want anybody sending me boxes of them, but they are good and they do sustain you. I don't recommend the Snickers bar diet to anyone, but it is possible to live off them and to compete at a high level while doing it. Just another way that I was a tweener, I guess. Now, if the folks at Wendy's want to work out some deal for their hamburgers, maybe we could talk. If I ever indulged myself, it was by going to a franchise of that fast-food chain.

I can remember sitting at our required brunch watching my teammates going back and forth to the food line, trays piled high with mounds of scrambled eggs, leaning towers of sausage patties, biscuits, stacks of ham slices as thick as coffee tables. They'd look at me like I was some alien as I just sat there, sipping a glass of water or maybe some orange juice.

"Herschel," they'd say, "where are you from, dude?"

I wouldn't answer, and it wasn't until recently that I think I understood a reason why I didn't eat much then or now. When you grow up hearing all the time about how fat you are and you finally break out of that, you don't ever want to go back. I'm pretty certain that one of my alters took control of the food consumption for the rest of us. He was trying to protect us from harm, I suppose, and even after the threat was gone, the habit remained. Someone needed to be in control of what I ate, exert some discipline and order. Truth is, though, that even today I don't ever feel really hungry or starved by my one-meal-a-day diet. I've got too many other things to do, too many other things to keep my mind occupied, to think about eating. I know now that there are lots of ways a person can be starving, but back then I didn't have much of a clue about that.

Chapter Eight

King of the Hill

I've always viewed life as being like a game of king of the hill. Back when I was a kid, we used to play it all the time. I liked playing it because of the rush of adrenaline I got from it. Whenever you got to the top of that dirt pile, you had to be on the alert because someone was gunning for you—in fact, a lot of "someones" were coming after you and you had to be prepared. If you didn't believe you belonged up there, you wouldn't last long. When I was young and pudgy, I could sometimes get to the top of the pile—especially if two or three or four other kids were all waging their own battle. I could sneak up there and set myself in place, hoping that my weight and girth could keep me there. I figured if I sat there and let gravity do its work, they wouldn't be able to move me. Unfortunately, I didn't have enough faith in myself to last. As soon as a kid came up to me,

I'd start to squirm, lose my connection with the hill, and they'd tumble me down to the bottom. When I was real young, I'd just sit there, thinking about how stupid I was for letting them get the best of me. As I got older, I sat there and figured out ways to get back to the top. When I finally came into my own, I was so determined to not ever let anybody knock me from my perch that no one ever really did.

I learned another lesson from those king-of-the-hill games. You had to pay attention and stay focused on what was going on around you in your immediate environment all the time. If you stood up there thinking too much or were caught enjoying your lofty position and the view from the top, someone was sure to knock you off balance. You can be sure you'd be rolling down that hill enjoying the taste of dirt and not the fruit of your efforts in no time. For that reason, as was typical of me, whatever disappointment I felt at losing the Sugar Bowl and not repeating as national champions was soon a thing of the past. At that time I didn't have a personal rearview mirror even if I'd wanted to look back on those events. I had another track season to prepare for, and then I was off to Europe again to race.

I didn't get to see Cindy that much over the summer, but when I returned to campus at the start of my junior year in early August of 1982, we spent all of our free time together. Almost forgotten in all of that focusing on the present and looking ahead to the future was the fact that I'd set a world record in the sixty-yard dash with a time of 6.15 seconds. This was at the *Dallas Times Herald* meet the spring of my sophomore year, and it's mostly noteworthy because the legendary Carl Lewis came along in the next heat of that event and broke my record. So much for being king of the hill—I was world record holder for less than half an hour.

I guess that my brief reign reinforced what I already knew— the race really is to the swiftest and to the strongest, and that somebody was always out there hoping to knock you off your perch. Don't ever be a sitting duck. Clinging to the past isn't very wise either—the present can end up racing past you with the speed of Carl Lewis. I've always tried to keep my eye on what's immediately ahead of me, and at the time of which I'm writing, my focus was on avenging our loss to the Clemson Tigers the previous year. This would be a matchup of the last two national champions. I was looking forward to the challenge. Unfortunately, in a practice before the season opener, with just a few minutes before calling it quits, I was out on the field during a drill.

I collided with a teammate and broke my thumb. This time Dr. Mulherin and his staff couldn't just pop the injured part back into place. I had to have surgery, and I wore a cast for much of the year. I didn't let that affect me too much; in fact, having a big wrap over my hand made me concentrate on holding on to the ball even more than usual. Teams tried to strip the ball from me on lots of occasions, but by concentrating on the fundamentals of ball-carrying technique, I was able to do okay.

I agreed to the surgery only because it was the surest and quickest way to get back to being 100 percent. And I was determined to sit out the fewest minutes I could. In this case, the Coach alter overruled any objections the other alters had and the Consoler must have calmed their fears about being eliminated.

I wanted to be ready for the season opener. Unlike today, when a lot of big time teams open the season with nonconference games against cream-puff opponents, our season opener was at home against the Tigers—defending national champions and one of our biggest rivals. We had a lot of players from South Carolina on our squad, and it seemed that every school had pinned a bull's-eye on Georgia. I suspect a lot of it was envy. Folks in the South—from places other than Georgia, that is—think that because of Georgia's long history and outstanding reputation, those who go there are some kind of rich-kid elitists. Sure, UGA is expensive, but it is a state university and lots of students there were, like me, from anything but privileged backgrounds.

There was a whole lot at stake, and I didn't have to think about such foolishness—but knowing what I did made me want to win only that much more. We won in a hard-fought battle, 13–7. I didn't play the whole game, but did pretty well despite that. The next week, we squeaked past Brigham Young, 17–14, beating quarterback Steve Young. That was our last close battle for much of the season. One of our most dominant performances came at Jacksonville, Florida, against the Gators when we beat them 44–0. I was having a good year, but not a great one. Our annual big game with Auburn was the one very close game we had after we'd gotten over some beginning-of-the-year stumbles. Our defense bailed us out again, and we won at Auburn, 19–14, thanks to some good luck and staunch plays when Auburn drove deep into our territory late in the game. When the clock finally ticked down to zero, we had another SEC championship and a number one ranking. Auburn had a young man by the name of Bo Jackson, and I could relate to him. Like me, he was a gifted two-sport athlete, and he enjoyed a nice career in baseball and football, though his career was cut short by a hip injury.

Nike eventually did some advertisements based around the slogan "Bo knows," but I'm here to tell you that Herschel goes. And that year, I went to the tune of 1,752 yards. My number of yards and touchdowns were both lower than they had been the previous year, but Coach Dooley took me out of several games when we were well ahead of the opposition. That was good sportsmanship, and I didn't mind. I was in the game to win, not pile up records, and finishing that regular season undefeated meant accomplishing a goal we'd all had in mind. Family and friends who couldn't make it to the Auburn game recall good old Larry Munson announcing it over the radio and saying at the end of it, "Sugar is falling from the sky." That meant as regular-season champions of the Southeast Conference, we were headed back to New Orleans for the third straight year to play in the Sugar Bowl.

Before I would go to New Orleans, I had to travel to another place for the third year in a row—New York City—for the Heisman Trophy presentation. Finishing runner-up the previous year and third the year before had been, I have to admit, kind of frustrating. I'd lost out to some fine players, but in my mind I was the best player every year. I had to have that kind of mentality—that king-of-the-hill belief was what kept me humble and motivated. I also heeded the words of Proverbs 18–19: "Pride goes before destruction, a haughty spirit before a fall. Better to be lowly in spirit and among the oppressed than to share plunder with the proud."

New York City can keep anyone humble. I enjoyed traveling there for the Heisman presentation, and it felt about as different from Wrightsville as any place could possibly be. I told you I didn't like crowds, but the same alter who helped me cope with performing in front of thousands of fans helped deal with the crowded streets of New York. Unlike in New Orleans, where we had some free time to wander, the trips to New York were fairly brief and highly structured. I didn't get to do too much wandering, but even the few cab rides to various events around the city were thrilling.

Winning the Heisman Trophy was a new experience for me. I'd been in the national spotlight and come up short the previous two years, but this time I beat out a distinguished group of guys. John Elway of Stanford University was the runner-up. I had more than 500 first-place votes to John's 139. The other finalists that year were Eric Dickerson, Todd Blackledge (who would quarterback Penn State against us in the upcoming Sugar Bowl), and Anthony Carter of the University of Michigan. All of the guys who attended the award presentation ceremony were great, and we had an interesting time together. I would have liked to have met Dave Rimington of the University of Nebraska. He got a lot of votes, and that was unusual because he was a lineman. Most of the time the Heisman went to a player who was at one of the so-called skill positions—quarterbacks, wide receivers, and running backs. I consider blocking to be a skill like any other, and the fact that Mr. Rimington impressed enough writers to be in the top ten on the balloting—in what was considered to be the "Year of the Quarterback"—says a lot about him. Along with Elway and Blackledge, other quarterbacks who received votes that year were Tony Eason of the University of Illinois and Dan Marino of Pitt. All of us went on to have good NFL careers, and I'm proud to say I was in that group, and especially proud to be at the head of that pack of horses.

Prior to the Sugar Bowl, the Georgia coaches did a good job of keeping the team focused on what we wanted to do, and the media's access to us was strictly controlled. I understand that reporters have a job to do, and I tried to be as accessible as I could, but I was still struggling a bit with being myself when I was interviewed. As my time at UGA went on, I noticed that from time to time I would refer to myself in the third person— as Herschel Walker. This got to be even more common when I was in the pros. I know a lot of people think of that as arrogant, but I disagree. A part of the reason for making those kinds of self-referential statements was DID at work, but a lot of players who haven't been diagnosed with it employ the third-person singular pronoun when referring to themselves. I think that some of it is a defense mechanism, and some it is a product of being treated as one-dimensional.

I've already said that there was the essential Herschel and other satellite Herschels as well. The Herschel that everyone wanted to interview was Herschel the football player—he really was another alter, a more public self. So, referring to him in the third person was, in fact, logical.

In a lot of ways, I had no problem with being labeled a jock. In a lot of other ways, I resented it tremendously. I know that the reason reporters wanted to speak with me was a result of what I did on the football field. I got that. If I was just Herschel Walker, criminal justice major, from Wrightsville, Georgia, I know nobody in Fargo, South Dakota, would give a hoot about what I had to say about anything. And that's fair and understandable. It's also kind of offensive after a while. If nearly every day of your college career (and later on, your pro career) people are making assumptions based on what you do and not on who you are, you'd get frustrated. If you even made the smallest attempt to get people to understand that you were more than what you appeared to be on the field, and got shut down for it, you'd get angry. Only the thing was, we couldn't really get angry. We'd been instructed to be cooperative with the media, and for the most part, I had no problem with the media, particularly while in high school and college.

I just wish that I could have had the opportunity to have more people get to know the more complicated, layered person I am. Maybe I reacted the way I did to the media's inquiries because I didn't open up much except to Cindy. I take a lot of the responsibility for projecting the image that I did. I was growing up like most teens, trying to figure out who I was, and I didn't like being put in a slot labeled *football player* or *jock*. Some people will probably respond to this by saying, "Shut up and quit complaining. You got a free education. You got paid millions of dollars. You were playing a game. What did you contribute to society?" I can understand that attitude to a degree, but it's hardly a Christian one. I know it's not exactly as if we were gladiators sent into the arena against lions, but we did provide a lot of entertainment for people, and made a lot of money for owners and the universities and the cities in which we played.

The only lions I was really concerned about back then were the Nittany Lions of Penn State. There was a lot of buildup to our game against them, and all the hype about a shoot-out between number one and number two could have resulted in a dud of a game. Fortunately for the fans, it didn't. Unfortunately for the UGA football team, we lost. For all I've been saying about preparation and mental toughness, for all the times that Coach Dooley preached that we wouldn't make mistakes and beat ourselves, for all the countless hours of drilling we did on fundamentals, in my mind, we gave that game away. Just as we had done the previous year, we gave up a touchdown late in the fourth quarter, again on a touchdown pass, to go from leading 23–20 to losing 27–23. I can't blame the defense for that loss, we had plenty of chances on offense, but we just couldn't quite pull it out at the end.

What a lot of people don't know is that I almost didn't play football at all my junior year. It took that unlucky break of my thumb to convince me that I should keep on going. The summer between my second and third years at UGA, I'd pretty much decided to give up football and school to go into the Marines. I'd never let go of my dream of serving in the military. I loved being at Georgia, and I loved being on the football and track teams, but the reason for my desire to serve goes back to that statement I attributed to some sports fans a little while ago: What have you contributed? That question was always running through my mind. Sure, football was important to a lot of people, and it brought in a lot of revenue to the university, but back then I wasn't really aware of the financial impact of what I was doing. I still wanted to do something heroic, be somebody who made a real sacrifice, and really made a difference in people's lives. My Warrior alter, the ultracompetitive guy, joined forces with the Enforcer, the one with the highly pitched sense of right and wrong, to get me thinking I should enlist.

I've said before that God had a way of looking out for me. That broken thumb kept me in the game in one very real sense. I wouldn't have been able to enlist with an injured thumb. I mean, I was a day or so away from going in to talk to Coach Dooley about my decision. Once my thumb was messed up, I couldn't go to a recruiting office and sign up. As a result of the injury and my brief recuperation period, I got to see things from a different perspective. I would go to practice, but I couldn't participate in any of the drills. I basically sat on the sidelines under a covered bench to help me stay out of the hot sun and watched my teammates bust their butts. I hated having to sit there on the sidelines and see them working so hard. That was the same feeling I experienced when I thought about guys serving in the military while I was sitting all comfortable in my room. I'd gotten even more comfortable now that I'd rented an apartment off campus. One thing I realized is that teammates are like your comrades-in-arms. I don't mean to say that laying your life on the line in the military and playing a game are anything alike, but I did realize that when I'd signed up to play for Georgia, I'd signed up to play for GEOR-GIA. That meant that I'd been kind of selfish in thinking about leaving the team and all. It didn't matter what the reason was, I'd be hurting my team, my coaches, the fans—heck, all of the state of Georgia, by leaving.

I didn't enjoy feeling like I'd been self-centered, so sitting there on a hot steamy late August afternoon, I made a vow that I would do everything I could that year to make us successful. January of 1983 would be the big test. It's hard to say that a year in which you lose one game and fall four points short of a second national championship in three years is a failure, but that's what happens when you're playing a real serious game of king of the hill. We were number one, and we were on top.

I can't say we didn't see Penn State coming, because we knew that they were the number-two-ranked team in the country. Somehow, though, we got thrown off balance and slid down that hill. I didn't know it then, but that was to be the last time I ever played on that particular hill again.

Standing on the sidelines watching the clock wind down and seeing the Penn State players whooping it up in celebration of a national championship, I wasn't giving any thought to my future. I had no way of knowing it then, but I was watching the last seconds of my college career wind down. Regardless of the situation, I wasn't feeling nostalgic or angry, just kind of numb. My mentality was always to be as strong as possible, to never let any pain or disappointment or any other emotion show. I think I entered a state not too different from what I experienced in the Sugar Bowl my freshmen year when my shoulder got dislocated. It hurt. I was stunned, and then I thought of the job that lay ahead and what I wanted to do. I had no time for contemplation. Wishing that someone could come along and pop our season back into joint was unrealistic. It was over—simple as that. I had next year.

I did feel bad for some of the seniors. They knew it was going to be the last game of their college career, and for most of them, the last organized football game they were ever going to play. I saw a few of them shedding tears, and I knew I never wanted to experience what they were experiencing. I never wanted to have the knowledge as I stood on the sidelines or later in the locker room that what I was experiencing was finality. I always kept my eyes on what was ahead of me, and I needed to have something there. I couldn't imagine what it was like to be looking ahead and seeing nothing but emptiness. Eventually, I'd find out something of what that was like. Maybe it was one of my alters that had put blinders on me so that I could only look forward, I don't really know. I think sometimes people confused my absence of negative emotions—pain, regret, sadness—for a lack of caring. Nothing could be further from the truth. I cared, and I cared passionately. Somehow, the way my brain was wired or because of how I'd disciplined myself, that never showed as much as maybe it could have. All I know is that I played with a few guys in college and a few in the pros who were sideline "streeps"—as in Meryl Streep.

A lot of the time, these guys were the ones who didn't play much. They would be standing on the sidelines watching us play, and depending on how close they were to a coach, they were either chatting about their postgame plans or acting like a combination of a cheerleader, mascot, and lawyer for the defense (or offense depending on which team had the ball), pleading our case with the officials. When we won, they were ecstatic and would jump up and down and pound their fists and chests and give out war hollers so loud you could hear them all the way back in Wrightsville. When we lost, they'd go from being all fired up or completely indifferent to emotional wrecks. I always suspected that any flamboyant display of emotion couldn't be genuine, and I never liked being around guys who got too high or too low. Not only were they unreliable teammates because their overemoting caused them to lose focus, they would throw things and stomp around and they could hurt you. I steered clear of them as much as I steered clear of too strong an outward display of my own feelings.

Also, when I took off my uniform, my feelings and emotions stayed with it—back in the locker room. I'd go home and the last thing I wanted to do was to replay the whole game. I wouldn't let victory or defeat influence who I was or what I did. Most often, I would go home, and Cindy would come over, and maybe my sister Veronica and her boyfriend Bill Richards would join us. Bill was a high hurdler on the track team and eventually he and Veronica would marry. The four of us grew really tight, and we'd go to the movies together and just hang out. None of us was the partying type, so we got along really well. Bill was from Haines City, Florida, along with another teammate of mine who had one of the best nicknames ever, Eddie "The Meat Cleaver" Weaver. You may remember that I mentioned him before.

So after our loss and our return from New Orleans, I settled into my usual routine, switching over from football to track. I had no way of knowing then, that I'd played my last game for the University of Georgia, that a very different kind of meat cleaver was going to fall, and that my adventurous and defensive alters would work together to separate me from the familiar and the comfortable once again.

Chapter Nine

Running Till Empty

One evening, I got a call from a gentleman by the name of Chuck Fairbanks. He introduced himself and told me that he was the coach and general manager of the New Jersey Generals of the USFL. I told him that I knew who he was, but I wasn't so sure if I should be talking to him. At that point I was still so naive and paranoid about my amateur standing that I was thinking for sure I was going to get caught talking to a man in pro football and lose my eligibility. I remember sitting there, looking around the apartment, checking the phone, looking out the window, believing that someone had either bugged my apartment or was spying on me from somewhere. Mr. Fairbanks told me not to worry, he just wanted to speak with me and let me know a few things about the league and what they had planned.

Growing up, I had never really followed sports. Even when I was a freshman, I still didn't have much of a clue when I heard my teammates talking about pro football, basketball, or baseball. Along with talking about women, sports was about the only subject we discussed. As I had done all of my life, I decided it was important for me to know about a subject, so I set myself a goal of learning as much about the sports world as I could. I started to read the sports page, magazines like *Sports Illustrated,* and eventually I was able to join in on, instead of simply listening to, all those sports-related conversations. Thank goodness I had done that, because I would have been mighty embarrassed to have received that phone call and asked Mr. Fairbanks to explain who he was and what the USFL was. We'd all heard that another league was being formed to challenge the NFL, and in January of 1983, it had held its first draft of college seniors. Since I was only a junior, none of this seemed like it would have a direct impact on me until the next year.

Coach Fairbanks had been a head coach at the University of Oklahoma and then of the New England Patriots of the NFL. He returned to college to coach the University of Colorado before accepting the dual role of GM and coach with the Generals. We talked for a while, with him doing most of it. I hung up and didn't think a whole lot about it. At this point in my life, I pretty much knew that if I stayed healthy and continued to perform well, I would have a pro career. I wasn't that thrilled about it since I was still hung up on the idea of serving in the military. I sure didn't have dollar signs dancing in front of my eyes—I really had no idea at that point what kind of money players made. I'd only recently made the transition to sports fan, so I was still in that innocent stage when I knew about scores, yardage gained, wins and losses, and not things like salary caps, franchise player designations, collective-bargaining agreements, and all the other stuff that made pro sports a business. All that would come later; I still thought of all this as a game.

The USFL was started by a man named David Dixon. He was from New Orleans and an antiques dealer. The formation of the league was announced in May of 1982 at the "21" club in New York. It would have twelve teams, and because of their proximity of New York, the New Jersey Generals were considered to be its showcase franchise. The other eleven teams were scattered around the country, and many were in cities that already had NFL franchises—Los Angeles, Chicago, Detroit, Boston, Tampa, Oakland, Denver, Washington, Philadelphia, and San Diego. The lone exception was Birmingham. Even in the early days, there was a lot of turnover and switching of franchises, but I was only vaguely aware of any of that. All I really knew is that they wanted to challenge the NFL.

Even when Jerry Argovitz, who would eventually become the owner of the Houston Gamblers USFL franchise, called me a little while later to set up an appointment to speak with me in Athens, I was still just really being polite. I'd been so used to accommodating media requests and other things, I could hardly say no to this man. After all, who was I to say no to someone who owned a team? When he showed up, he was accompanied by a gentleman named Rod Blanding, who owned the Denver Gold. The two of them mostly talked about the USFL and what they hoped to accomplish with it. They talked about how the NFL wasn't really a players league and that the owners took advantage of the players and controlled a lot of the revenues and all kinds of things that, to be honest, went in one ear and out the other. This wasn't exactly like what I went through when I was recruited, but it was similar. The big difference was that college recruiters at least pretended they wanted to get to know me and were interested in my welfare—not just as a player but as a student. With these pro people, it was all about taking care of myself and my family financially and having an opportunity

167

to be a part of something new. With college coaches, it was all about the history and tradition of their program and the school. The USFL had no history.

After those first few phone calls and visits, things got quiet for a while. By Valentine's Day, I thought I was going to just keep running track and going to school. I was wrong. I got another call from the New Jersey Generals a day or two after Cindy and I celebrated Valentine's Day. This time, I was asked to meet with the team's owner, J. Walter Duncan. I had never heard of him, and when I got off the phone and told Cindy who was coming to visit me, she laughed and said, "Isn't he the guy on the Monopoly game? The one with the fancy suit and fistfuls of cash?"

As it turns out, Cindy was half right. Mr. Duncan showed up wearing a pair of slacks and a kind of cowboy shirt and a bolo tie. He was from Oklahoma and had made a lot of money in the oil business. He was the kind of man I was used to being around back home. He was extremely polite, soft-spoken, and had a slow easy drawl that immediately put me at ease. Cindy and I had been playing an Atari video game when he showed up, and he saw the controllers sitting on a chest I used as a coffee table and the images on the screen. He asked if he could see how the game worked, and Cindy and I resumed playing Space Invaders. Mr. Duncan seemed to get a real kick out of the marching pixels on the television screen and the relentless sound of their descent. He asked a lot of questions about my family and me, about Cindy and her family, and what kind of future we envisioned for ourselves. At that time, I hadn't given much thought to such matters, but Cindy talked about wanting to be secure, to do some work that was fulfilling. I thought of mentioning the military, but decided not to.

We had a nice talk, and after about an hour, Mr. Duncan stood up and shook my hand. He said they'd be in touch, and that he really enjoyed meeting me, and he hoped I'd consider coming to play for him in New Jersey. After he left, Cindy and I sat back down and started playing Space Invaders again. A few minutes into the game, Cindy asked, "Would you do it?"

I shrugged and winced as a shot just missed the purple mother ship floating above the top row of invaders. "I haven't thought about it much. None of this seems real. Just people talking."

"Everybody seems to really want you."

"But it would be wrong. Rules say that I can't." At that time, underclassmen were not eligible for the NFL draft.

"Those are the NFL rules. This is different. They wouldn't be here talking to you about money and opportunity if they couldn't do it. It's not illegal, Herschel. The NFL isn't the law of the land."

"It would be nice to be a part of something new. Do something different."

Our conversation went on for a while longer. The rest is history. I decided I'd consider going to the USFL, and once again, I took out a coin and flipped it. It came up tails, and that meant I'd listen to whatever offer I got. On February 23, 1983, I signed a $3.9-million three-year contract with the Generals. I also received a million-dollar signing bonus and part ownership in one of Mr. Duncan's wells. At the time, I didn't realize how much of a big deal it all was. Once I'd made the decision to go ahead and sign, I needed someone to represent me in the negotiations. Through my former teammate Frank Ros, who was now working, I was put in touch with the people at the International Management Group. I eventually signed on with them and worked with Peter Johnson as my agent. Cindy and my family were really ecstatic. I was essentially set for life financially if I didn't do anything stupid. And I wasn't about to. I also didn't have time to. I had a training camp to get to.

I think that the reality of what I'd done didn't really hit me until I was on the practice field at the University of Central Florida in Orlando. The guys on the team had greeted me pretty warmly. At the time, no one knew the details of the contract except my family, me, and the people in the Generals front office. Coach Fairbanks knew because in addition to being coach and general manager, he owned a 10 percent interest in the team. The rest of the Generals were glad to have me since they realized that I gave them a better chance of winning. Maurice Carthon, who would go on to have a good NFL career and was the fullback on that team, was another rookie, and we kind of hit it off right away. So there I was, stretching alongside Maurice on a quiet February day in Orlando when we hear a helicopter in the distance. It grew closer and we couldn't hear the coaches any longer. Then the helicopter came overhead and began circling above us. We had no idea what was going on. Next thing we knew the helicopter descended and disappeared behind the grandstands of the football field. A few moments later, a tall slim black man comes running through the tunnel entrance to the field trailed by a man lugging a camera. They made a beeline for me, and I recognized the guy with the microphone as Irv Cross of the CBS Sports show *The NFL Today*. I did the only thing I could think of. I started walking away from him, and when he kept following me, I broke into a jog. I didn't know it at the time, but the Generals had issued a press release letting everyone know that I'd been signed.

My deal was a big deal for two reasons—the money and the precedent it set. The NFL had its rule about underclassmen, and the USFL tromped all over it—at least that's how the NFL looked at it. I was also the first really big-name player to sign, and this was supposed to give the USFL some legitimacy, to let the fans and media know that it wasn't going to be a minor league. Their strategy worked, at least in the New York area, since in the days after my signing, the Generals sold more than half of their thirty-six thousand season tickets. What I didn't know until later was that the USFL had created its own version of a salary cap—each team had to abide by a maximum amount of money it could spend on players' salaries. At the time, there was also supposed to be a limit on how much money any one player on a team could receive—$500,000. This wasn't set in stone, but when everyone learned that I was going to be making more than twice that amount, it must have seemed to them that the maximum salary provision was set in Jell-O. The total salary per team was $1.8 million, so I was making the lion's share of the money. Not a great situation.

I'd had to deal with envious teammates and opponents while at UGA, but this was going to be different, and I knew it. Before, players could be jealous of the attention and what they might have perceived as special treatment I received; now it was all about the money. This wasn't a hobby for these guys anymore, something they were doing for the love of the game. That's not to say that they didn't love the game, but they had families to feed and clothe and house, and they all knew that they had a somewhat limited amount of time during which they could earn those needed dollars. Looking back, I can understand some of their reactions. Back then, I didn't even really try to understand it. I went into "Herschel mode" and just blocked a lot of the negative stuff out. I knew that the fans at Georgia, some of the players, the coaches, etc., viewed me as a traitor. I'd done something that, to that point, hadn't really been done before—leaving the team to pursue a pro career.

I don't feel the need to justify to anyone what I did. I do think it's interesting to look back on it in the light of my diagnosis with DID and just who I was back then and what that decision said about me. I've said before that I can't believe how naive and stupid I was about so many things. I was so incredibly worried about doing the right thing and living up to the letter of the law. In track, I told you that I had people offering me money left and right. I could have taken advantage of what I was doing on the football field as well. There are always shady people hanging around the fringes of college programs who are willing, for a variety of reasons, to "help you out." Some do it because they want to feel a part of something big and successful. I don't understand that mentality, and I never took anything from anyone (well, okay, those Snickers bars) both because it was wrong and because I was so afraid. So why did I do something that was considered by so many people to be so wrong? I don't have a single one-size-fits-all reason.

I think my decision was partly the reckless Daredevil and Different Drummer alter of mine sticking a hand up and saying, "You've been doing the right thing for so long, now it's time to do something to shock the world. You can be the first here." Signing with the USFL was a way to break out of the pattern of being a "do-gooder" I'd been in for my whole life. Second, I would be breaking out of the pattern of following the same routine and doing the same things all the time. I found a lot of comfort in that pattern and much of those regimented behaviors were self-imposed. Not having that pattern to rely on, doing something and going someplace completely unfamiliar to me, was frightening—but it was also a challenge. I liked challenges, and being scared fed some dark part of me that was to emerge and grow larger as I got older. Allowing a coin toss to decide my future was motivated by the need for some kind of thrill and for some kind of challenge, a way to break out of the mold, and the USFL gave me a chance to do all of those things.

There is also a part of me that has to be constantly moving forward. I'd accomplished quite a few things at UGA, and I could have gone back for my senior year (and if the coin had come up heads instead of tails, I gladly would have) and had new goals and challenges. I sometimes think that there's a part of me that doesn't want to say good-bye. I left the University of Georgia, my teammates, coaches, and friends, in a kind of whirlwind of activity. One day I was there, the next I was about to be a millionaire, I was off to Florida for training camp, I'd shortly be moving to New Jersey. I was gone. I didn't have time for farewell parties and emotional speeches and dramatic good-byes. It was all kind of emotionless. That's how I'd always been. In order to defend myself against the attacks I suffered as a kid, I'd kind of shut off emotions. When you're in a never-ending game of king of the hill, you can't afford to get too emotional. I never wanted to experience the kind of lows that I had known as a kid, so I became a kind of emotional bulldozer—a machine, a powerful force, something you turn the key on, fire up the ignition, throw into gear. The machine goes, almost always forward, leveling the highs and lows of the terrain it crosses into a smooth, flat, featureless plane. I truly didn't feel that my leaving Georgia was any big thing. The team would be okay, my teammates would be okay, my friends would be okay. I guess I didn't want to think they'd miss me because I didn't want to miss them. I wanted to get on with the USFL part of my life, because it allowed me to get involved in something immediately. No time for thinking, no time for tears, no time for second thoughts. Always in my mind, I kept hearing, "Time to get going, Herschel. Get moving."

I didn't realize it then, but I do realize it now, that all of this was part of a larger pattern. I had been trying to put distance between myself and other people my whole life. I've said before that I'd held people at arm's length and not let them get close to me. To use a football analogy, I'd used the stiff arm pretty effectively. It helped me to hold people off, to not get tackled, to continue to gain yards. I'd been running not so much from all those people who belittled me, didn't believe me, and who caused me physical and emotional pain, but I'd been running from the Herschel who put up with all that, allowed himself to be taken advantage of and beaten. I'd been trying to put distance between him and me. For the longest time, I didn't talk about him, didn't want any reminders of my weakness to penetrate my armor.

So, I got out of Georgia while the getting was good. No fanfare, no tearing of bonds, just getting out and moving along. I was simply going to trade one hill for another. I was going to do my best to be king of the new one as well. The thing is, and pardon me for mixing my metaphors, but all the king's horses and all the king's men wouldn't be able to put all the pieces of this Herschel back together again. He'd have to do it on his own—or so he thought.

That first year in New Jersey, I got a real taste of what it is like to lose—not a taste I'd ever hoped to acquire. We finished the year with a record of six wins and twelve losses. Those twelve losses represented more defeats than I'd experienced in three years in college and I didn't enjoy myself a whole lot. We were a success in one regard—we averaged 35,004 fans per home game. I started out slowly, but eventually picked up steam and rushed for 1,812 yards and scored seventeen touchdowns. I had enough to do in learning a new system and playing in unfamiliar cities and studying game film of new opponents, but behind the scenes a whole series of changes was going on that I would eventually become aware of.

When I first signed with New Jersey, I didn't realize that Donald Trump had originally wanted to own the franchise, but had backed out because he needed to focus more of his attention on his real estate business, and in particular on building Trump Tower in Manhattan. Mr. Duncan had stepped in, but by the end of the year, he was feeling torn, too. His business was in Oklahoma, and his team was in New Jersey. He decided to sell the team to Mr. Trump.

I didn't know a lot about Mr. Trump initially, but I would eventually get to know him quite well and spend a lot of time with him and his family. Back then, he was married to Ivana, and I had a lot of respect for him because he was truly a family-oriented man. I saw how he doted on his children and did so much of what he did in order to provide for them. Donald Jr. was only about six or seven when Mr. Trump took over the team; he and his family used to come to the games and I got to spend time with all of them. They were a lovely family and treated me and Cindy well. In a lot of ways, Mr. Trump became a mentor to me, and I modeled myself and my business practices after him.

I wouldn't have continued in pro football if it hadn't been for Mr. Trump. I had made a lot of money right away with my signing bonus and salary, and I was young and uncertain of what I wanted to do with my life. I still had dreams of being in the military. Football wasn't my only love, like it was for a lot of other players, and I could easily have walked away from it. I had at least a hundred other things I would have considered doing. I had some very honest conversations about my feelings with Mr. Trump—something unusual between an owner and a player. He told me that I was young, that I loved to compete, that I was so good at what I did, and that I should really just stick with what I did best. I'd have plenty of time later on to take on other things.

I'm glad I listened to him, and I am really glad that he became our owner. As soon as he took control of the team, he started to upgrade our talent. He signed away from the NFL players like Gary Barbaro and Kerry Justin and, in a great move, signed 1980 league MVP Brian Sipe of the Cleveland Browns to become our quarterback. We improved greatly in 1984 and finished the regular season with fourteen wins and four losses. That great turnaround was spoiled by a loss in the first round of the play-offs to the eventual league-champion Philadelphia Stars. We'd beaten them twice in the regular season, and as any football fan knows, it's hard to beat a team three times in one year. Why we were matched up against them in the first round always mystified us, but there wasn't a thing we could do about it.

During the 1984 season, Maurice Carthon and I both rushed for more than a thousand yards. Quite an accomplishment for a fullback/tailback duo. Though my yardage was down and my number of carries decreased by more than a hundred, I was still happy to be winning and never voiced a single complaint—mostly because I had none and also because I was just a soldier doing what my general told me to do. I also continued to catch the ball quite a bit, and once again was the leading receiver for the team, just as I had been in 1983—though I was tied with a wide receiver for that honor my second season.

Not content to let us rest on our laurels, Mr. Trump made another bold move. He signed the 1984 Heisman Trophy winner, Doug Flutie, to be our quarterback. Fresh out of Boston College, Doug was a tough competitor who went on to have a great career in both the NFL and the Canadian Football League. I admired Doug because everyone told him he was too small at five feet ten inches to succeed at that critical position. He won nearly every major award coming out of Boston College—the Heisman, the Maxwell, the Davey O'Brien, the Walter Camp—and he deserved every one of them. Many people consider his "Hail Mary" pass against a heavily favored University of Miami team to be one of the greatest moments in sports history.

That said, what Doug Flutie was lacking was experience. He was going to get as much of it as he could handle in 1985 because we traded away Brian Sipe and installed Flutie as our starting quarterback. In some ways, I benefited personally from that lack of experience. I rushed 438 times that year, an average of nearly 25 carries per game. I also led the team in receiving again. Unfortunately, the results weren't that great. We finished with a record of 11–7 and once again were eliminated in the first round of the play-offs by the Stars—who had relocated from Philadelphia to Baltimore.

I remember one game from that year with a particular

fondness. We were facing the Jacksonville Bulls, and I was riding a wave of nine consecutive games in which I'd rushed for more than a hundred yards. Sixteen games into the season, I had gained 1,961 yards and needed 144 more to break the great Eric Dickerson's season record for most yards rushed in professional football. More important, we were in a battle for a play-off spot with the Birmingham Dragons and really needed a win. Doug Flutie had injured his shoulder the week before and he was out. That meant that more of the burden for our team's success fell on me. I was happy to take up whatever slack was necessary to get us a win. At halftime we were up by only four points, 14–10. I'm told that I was just 51 yards shy of breaking the all-time single-season rushing record, but I didn't know that then. All I knew was that we were in a dogfight, and I was top dog and I had to show it. Shortly after halftime, I took a handoff, cut back to the middle, shed a couple of tackles, and sprinted 55 yards into the end zone. We would eventually win the game by a touchdown and go on to make the play-offs with another win the following week.

The record was also mine. I'm pleased now to say that I did it in the same number of games as an NFL season. More important, all those yards got us wins and a shot at the play-offs.

Little did I know then that those 2,411 would fade into oblivion and become little more than a footnote in my career. I also didn't fully understand that our 1985 season was being played against a backdrop of a legal battle that eventually resulted in a major victory for the USFL that led to its collapse. Mr. Trump led a group of owners who wanted to really challenge the NFL by playing at the same time of year as the more established league. The owners also filed suit in the Southern District of New York following the 1984 season against the NFL for violation of the Sherman Antitrust Act. The main argument was that because the NFL had contracts with the three major television networks, they had exerted pressure on them not to televise our fall-season games. They also alleged that the NFL had conspired to do damage to two franchises—the Oakland Invaders and the New Jersey Generals. Interestingly, Al Davis, the so-called maverick owner of the NFL's Oakland Raiders, had agreed to testify on the USFL's behalf in exchange for not being named as a defendant.

After forty-eight days of testimony, in July of 1986, the jury convened and eventually arrived at a verdict that sided with the USFL's claim that the NFL was a monopoly. It ruled against the rest of the claims, and awarded the USFL owners a single dollar.

Only eight teams were left in the league, and all were in difficult positions financially. They had been counting on the award money to keep them afloat. Even though that one-dollar award was tripled to three dollars, it wasn't going to be enough to keep the league in operation. The NFL had to pay the USFL's court costs, but even with that, there was no way the league could be kept alive.

At first the USFL announced that it was going to suspend the 1986 season, but eventually we were all let out of our contracts and told to look for employment in the NFL or CFL. I had another one of those talks with Mr. Trump, and he advised me once again to keep at it and join the NFL.

I couldn't really understand the jury's verdict, and the alter in me who was so wrapped up in right and wrong and fair and unfair was working overtime to make sense of it. How could the NFL be guilty and still only have to pay that three-dollar fine? None of this made sense to me, and we later learned that there was a lot of confusion on the part of the jurors regarding just what it was they were supposed to be doing. None of that mattered once they'd rendered their verdict. Though the USFL asked for a new trial based on the damage award, their request was rejected, as were other later appeals.

I suppose in some ways it is true what some people have

said—that the USFL's worst enemy was itself. Instead of sticking to the plan of keeping salaries low, owners started to spend a lot more money in the hope of being merged into the NFL at some point. They had a model for that kind of thinking. The NFL of 1985 was made up of teams from another so-called renegade league—the American Football League—which had merged with the NFL in 1970. Why the NFL didn't want to accept USFL teams into the league is kind of a mystery to me. After all, from 1970 to 1985, the league grew in popularity and revenue, and in many people's minds and wallets surpassed baseball as the national pastime. Those were big questions that never got answered, but I think the NFL simply wanted to punish the USFL because the bidding wars and awarding of contracts in the USFL had forced NFL owners to open up their bankbooks and spend more than they wanted. They were out for revenge and they got it.

They also got a lot of really great football players from the USFL. The Dallas Cowboys must have been reading the writing on the wall, because in 1985, even before the USFL folded, they drafted me. That meant that later on, when the USFL ended its playing days, I wasn't eligible for what was called the dispersal draft. Guys like Reggie White and a few of my New Jersey General teammates were eligible, while other USFL players, whose rights were held by NFL teams, rejoined the NFL teams they previously played for.

I couldn't have been happier to join the Cowboys; it's the team I'd've picked if I had been able to choose where I was going to go. I've always said that God has had a way of taking care of me; whether it was via a coin flip or a shrewd move by a wonderful organization, I always wound up where I was meant to be.

One of the main reasons I felt so comfortable with the switch to Dallas was the presence of two men I respected greatly—Coach Tom Landry and Mr. Earnest "Tex" Schramm, the president and general manager of what became known as "America's Team." Mr. Schramm put together a team that in the 1970s appeared in the Super Bowl five times, winning it twice—the only NFC team to do so in that decade—and set a standard of excellence and innovation that few franchises in any sport could match. From using computer analysis in scouting, to advocating for instant replay, to creating the Dallas Cowboys Cheerleaders, Mr. Schramm was a powerful and well-respected leader in the game. He was smart enough to know that the USFL's days were numbered, and his drafting me in what was normally the selection of college players showed how shrewd he was. I also knew him as a fair and decent man who loved the game, loved the Cowboys, and treated me with respect.

If Mr. Schramm did one thing for which I will always be grateful—along with bringing me to the team—he hired Tom Landry as the head coach. To say I respected and admired Mr. Landry would be a serious understatement. In some ways, he lived a life that I aspired to. While at the University of Texas at Austin, he interrupted his education after one semester to join the military. He served in combat for the U.S. Army Air Force in England as a copilot of a B-17 Flying Fortress. Completing thirty missions and surviving a crash landing in Belgium when his plane ran out of fuel, he returned to UT after the war and played fullback and defensive back. He later enjoyed an all-pro career with the New York Giants as a defensive back and intercepted thirty-two passes in a brief eighty-game career. His last two seasons, he served as a player coach before turning to coach full-time in 1956.

Mr. Landry was a man I admired off the field as well as on. He was very active in the Fellowship of Christian Athletes and set high standards for his players. Mr. Landry's philosophy, which he stated directly to me on a number of occasions, was that he thought it was just as important, if not more important, to shape the men under his command into exceptional human beings as to turn them into exceptional football players. Some might consider the idea old-fashioned that shaping a person is a desirable trait in a coach, but I certainly didn't. I liked the kind of military-inspired discipline that he demanded as well as the respect that he demonstrated, and that respect was returned. He treated us like men and demanded that we behave like men. I guess that our shared beliefs about sacrifice and the military and our religious faith made me naturally inclined to agree with his practices, but I wasn't the only one who felt that way about him.

Even though I was only twenty-four years old when I joined the Cowboys and had never played in the NFL, I was more like a veteran than a rookie and I was treated that way. NFL players have all kinds of hazing rituals they put their first-year pros through—having to carry equipment to the practice field, singing their college fight song at the preseason training table—but just like at the University of Georgia, I didn't have to go through all that. A lot of ex-USFL players told me that they had to endure those rituals, but I didn't. I'd like to think that the reason for this was that the Cowboy players respected me and my work ethic. Guys like Randy White, Ed "Too Tall" Jones, Tony Dorsett, and Danny White were all veteran players who had a no-nonsense work-hard attitude that I shared.

Besides this, I'm sure that my Sentry alter was especially vigilant at this time. After all, I was in a new situation, and just like you might be if you went to work at a new job, I was pretty guarded at first, and more than likely, throughout my time with the Cowboys. That Sentry alter was the one who constantly told me that I had to be careful, to not trust anyone, to ask myself constantly why someone would want to be my friend, to look deeper at their motives to figure out what they might want from me. I'm not proud to say that this was my attitude, and I did let some people in behind the walls I'd built up, but they were few and far between. Maybe the other players sensed something about me that at the time I couldn't see about myself. They might have left me alone to do my own thing because I put off a keep-your-distance vibe. It's funny to think of it now, but one of the other reasons why Randy White and I got along so well is that we both had rottweiler dogs as pets. Some people believe that the pet you have says something about your own personality, and in many respects I probably came across as a rottweiler to my teammates. I looked fierce, was aggressive when challenged, was loyal to a select few people, and had a reputation for being someone not to mess with. So in a way, that Sentry alter is probably better described as a guard dog.

I don't remember any real run-ins with teammates or with opposing players on or off the field. Like them, I was always able to keep my dogs not exactly docile, but always under control. As I said before, one of the other alters I had was a kind of policemen or general who watched over the rest of the troops and kept them in line. He was not about to let anybody get to any one of us and stir things up. Believe me, lots of players tried to get me to lose my cool with trash talking, late hits, rabbit punches while in the pile, all kinds of nasty little tricks of the trade. I never let it affect me. Again, maybe that was one of the alters at work, taking me to a safe place where no one could get to me. I think my martial-arts training also played a big part in this self-control. On a practical level, I knew that one of the best things you could do in tae kwan do was to use your opponents' aggression and power against them. If I responded in kind to what was being said or done to me, I was going to lose power, and I was never going to do that. Also, as a Christian, I believed in turning the other cheek and the Golden Rule. Throughout my career, with few exceptions, I stuck with those guiding principles. Believe me, though: I wasn't all about goodness and light; I also knew my attitude gave me a competitive advantage.

In some ways, I wish that the Cowboys had been more competitive in my three years with them. In 1985, the year before I got there, the team had finished the season with a 10–6 record and lost in the conference semifinals to Los Angeles, 20–0. It wouldn't be until 1991 under new head coach Jimmy Johnson that the team would make the play-offs again. We stumbled to a 7–9 record my first year, which was a bit of an adjustment year for me. Tony Dorsett, the great running back and former Pitt Panther, and I were both in the same backfield. Tony and I were roommates in training camp, and he was a great guy and there was never any tension between us. The reality, however, is that there is only one ball to be given to one player on any given running play. With the two of us sharing those ball-carrying duties, my number of carries fell from 438 in 1985 with the Generals to 151 with the Cowboys, and my yards gained dropped from 2,411 to 737. I was okay with that, but only if we were winning, and we weren't. I didn't blame the coaches, the linemen, Tony, or anyone else. The fact was we had two backs who shared the ball-carrying duties roughly equally. Tony's production was down as well—he carried the ball 184 times for 748 yards. That was a drop from the previous season, when he gained 1,307 yards on 305 carries. Looking at those numbers, you can see we both had to sacrifice playing time and carries, and neither of us was happy with the team results. You play the game to win championships, and we weren't even making the play-offs. Much the same thing happened the following year—Tony and I split the ball-carrying duties, but the team still wound up with a losing record and missed the play-offs.

Tony moved on to the Denver Broncos for the 1988 season, and I was featured in the offense much more, with 361 carries and 1,514 yards gained. None of that mattered since we suffered through an incredibly disappointing season, finishing with a record of 3–13. That hurt. I hurt a lot. I would gladly have traded those carries and yards for wins. Playing on a losing team is no fun, but I think that my statistics show that I never gave up. Failing is not a part of my personality, and I dug deep and did as much as I could to help our team succeed. Sometimes, despite our best efforts, things don't go our way. That was what was happening with the Cowboys. For the most part, the effort was there, but we were getting our butts kicked.

So much of success in sports is mental, and I think the Cowboys collectively developed a bit of a losing attitude. It makes me sad to say that, but I can't come up with any other explanation. I hate to lose, and I am so extremely competitive that it's difficult for me to understand how some players can come to accept losing as a regular part of their reality. Maybe DID played a role in my personal success that year—I was able to block out all the distractions of losing and do my job to the utmost of my abilities. That was what I was getting paid to do, and maybe the alter who remembered what it was like to be down and out and picked on and insulted and punched and kicked rallied the rest of the troops to do what I'd done as a younger man. I was able to rise above those circumstances and do the best I could. And believe me, I wasn't alone in that. I don't think there was any "quit" in my teammates. I couldn't have gained those yards without their help. It's just too bad that my most successful year in the NFL came during the same year that my teammates and I experienced such horrendous results.

A lot of people believe that an athlete should be judged by the success of his team—the so-called making-everyone-around-you-better phenomenon. I don't buy that. I know that people talked about Michael Jordan's early career in this light. I believe that even if Michael Jordan had never won an NBA championship, he would still go down in history as the greatest basketball player ever. As supportive as I have always been of every one of my teammates, I also believe that sometimes players are saddled with playing alongside teammates who don't have the same talent, the same will to win, and the same mental determination as some of the "superstars." That's just how it is. I'm not comparing myself or my situation to Michael Jordan or the circumstances of his career; I'm simply saying that individual and team achievement aren't always linked. You can put a lot of pressure on an athlete to succeed and to make his or her team succeed, but it is never as simple as "individual accomplishment = team success."

Even though I had to insulate myself against the lack of success my team experienced in the first three years of my NFL career, I was still truly blessed by joining the Cowboys at that point in time. The experiences I had and the lessons I learned with that team helped me through the greatest challenge I faced in my pro career—my trade to the Minnesota Vikings. I'm grateful that I had Mr. Tom Landry as a coach, because his words proved true. At one point he said, "When you want to win a game, you have to teach. When you lose a game, you have to learn." We did a lot of learning in 1985, and I didn't know that I'd be, so to speak, enrolling in graduate school when the Cowboys and Vikings orchestrated one of the largest and most controversial trades in NFL, and maybe sports, history.

Say the words, "The Trade," to any Minnesota Vikings fan, and they will immediately know to what you are referring. It was the largest trade in NFL history, and many people believe it resulted in the Vikings team falling from a Super Bowl–caliber team to an also-ran and to the Dallas Cowboys rising phoenixlike from the ashes. To be honest, it's hard for me to be objective about any of this. In some ways, I was very sad to leave Dallas. I loved the community, Cindy and I made it our home, and I still live nearby today. What made my leaving easier was the fact that Mr. Landry was no longer the coach and Jerry Jones was the new owner. I have nothing against Mr. Jones. It's just that the Murchison family—the previous owners of the Cowboys—had a long-standing tradition in Dallas and their selling the team, coupled with Mr. Landry leaving the team, signaled the end of an era. What also made the trade easier for me to deal with was that the 1989 season was to go down in history as the worst the Cowboys ever endured—they won only one game.

So, when in October of 1989, the announcement was made that the Minnesota Vikings had acquired me in exchange for five players and six draft picks, I was a little bit relieved to be going from a team with no realistic chance of making the play-offs to a team that believed that adding me to their roster would propel them to the Super Bowl. To be honest, though, at first I thought that it was a joke—literally a joke, a publicity stunt of some kind. No team would give up that many players and draft picks for me. Maybe I should have been flattered, but I never really looked at it that way—that the Vikings were so confident in my abilities that they would, as pundits later said, mortgage their future on me.

I could write a whole book about my experiences in Minnesota. Let me give you the short version. I liked Minneapolis as a city and the fans were great to me. I liked the Vikings players and they treated me well. Chris Dohlman and Anthony Carter in particular were great teammates and became friends. I liked the Vikings upper management and ownership. But I don't think the Vikings coaching staff, and in particular head coach Jerry Burns, liked me or wanted me on the team. I base this view mostly on the fact that they didn't use me to the fullest extent possible. I don't know why you would trade for a player and then not use him, but that's what they did. If I was the missing piece of the puzzle, then the Vikings upper management and the coaching staff were working on two very different pictures.

I'll let the numbers paint a picture of my reality back then. In 1988, with the Cowboys, I carried the ball 361 times. In 1990 and 1991, my two full seasons with the Vikings, I carried the ball a total of 382 times. That's a difference of only 21 carries a game, but I played sixteen more games with the Vikings in those two seasons than I did in 1988. All I ever wanted to do was to contribute and to win. I would have returned kicks, played linebacker, carried water, whatever they asked, but they didn't ask me to do very much at all. I don't like to speak badly about people, but consider this. In the two full seasons that I was with the Vikings and Jerry Burns was the head coach, the team had a record of 6–10 and 8–8. The year after he left, and after I left as a free agent for Philadelphia, Dennis Green took over as coach and the team improved to an 11–5 regular-season record. With Coach Green in charge, the Vikings became one of the NFL's elite teams.

I'm man enough to take responsibility for my actions and my productivity. A coach's job is to put his players in a position where they can succeed and the team can win. As bluntly as I can say this, the Vikings coaching staff didn't utilize me the way they could have or should have. To further cement the point that it wasn't me who was washed up or underachieving, the year I left the Vikings and signed with Philadelphia, I gained 1,070 yards on 267 carries. The formula is simple: give me the ball more often and I will gain a lot more yards. We also went 9–5 and won our first play-off game before losing to my old team the Cowboys. Rich Kotite and his staff, along with the remarkable young quarterback Randall Cunningham and my dear, dear friend Reggie White, were instrumental in making that team a success.

I had a great run in Philadelphia and their passionate fans were great to me and my family. It was good to be back east and near Cindy's family. I'd continue to return full circle to my roots, later playing for the New York Giants and then returning to the Cowboys in 1996 and 1997. I believe that what you put out into the world comes back to you, and God saw fit for me to return to my adopted home in Dallas, and for that I am forever grateful.

When I look back on my career and the many shifts and turns it took, it reminds me of a classic Herschel Walker run—cutting back against the grain, juking and twisting, ultimately ending up in the end zone. At the same time, in looking back on things, I can only now begin to see that I was running from something I couldn't even begin to name.

Chapter Ten

Growing Pains

I started out this book by telling you that I wanted people to understand how DID functions and how it can be a force for good in a person's life. So far, I've concentrated on all of the positives it has done for me. Without DID and my alters—the Hero, the Consoler, the Judge, the Enforcer, the Sentry and his Watch Dog, the Daredevil, the Warrior, and the various combinations and offshoots of those facets of my personality, I could very easily have ended up in Wrightsville, another underachieving person crippled by some aspect of his past.

My alters functioned as a kind of community supporting me. As a result of the support I had from them and the lessons I learned about turning inward and marshaling my energy to focus on a goal, I was like a horse with blinders on. I couldn't see much beyond what was right in front of me. I was

189

rushing to get to the finish line, to multiple finish lines, and I seldom took the time to look around me—because I viewed it as a wasted effort or something that might slow me down and cause me to lose momentum and perhaps the race. I knew on an intellectual level that it was important to stop and smell the roses, but I was so focused and had so insulated myself from the outside world to such a degree that I didn't even know there were roses out there—save one, Cindy.

And even she had to take a backseat to my goals and ambitions. Even though Cindy was very much a part of my life and my thoughts, when we were dating, I still was primarily focused on school and sports. After I left UGA, my main focus was on my job, and that's really how I looked at football from that point forward, and a few other business opportunities and endorsement deals.

A lot of times, when somebody graduates from college and starts their career, it becomes "me" time—a place and space in your life when you devote yourself to getting a foothold in your future. Financially, you're just starting out and it makes sense to just take things easy and get established before you jump into things. Of course, there are other people who get married right out of college. It seems like you have that smaller group of people who have a wedding right away, then there's a lag time, then a whole bunch get married again five or so years later. I figured I was going to be a part of that latter group. Cindy felt like we should just go ahead and get married right away. As she pointed out, we weren't the typical couple in lots of ways. Why do things the traditional way?

We didn't have any financial worries. My contract with the Generals was only one of several benefits that came my way to make certain we were financially secure. If you remember, during my days running track and field, I was approached by a lot of apparel and shoe companies. I wised up a bit after a couple of seasons in Europe. I didn't take any money from

Adidas, but I did say that when I turned pro, I would sign an endorsement deal with them. I don't know if the Adidas representatives actually believed me or not, but a few days after I signed my football contract, I spoke with the management of Adidas and we made a deal. I like their shoes even to this day, so it made sense for me to go to them and not sell my services to the highest bidder. Besides, I told them I'd sign with them, and I always try to be a man of my word. I told them we didn't even need to sign a contract. We would just shake on it. I made a similar kind of deal with Franklin Sporting Goods. As far as I was concerned, it was a lifetime deal, and I needed no contract. The money from those deals made it even more difficult to use the I-need-to-get-established-first argument with Cindy. I wasn't really arguing with her, I was just a bit surprised by her suggestion. In retrospect, not waiting was the best thing I ever did. Having Cindy with me through every part of my pro career proved to be a real blessing.

By this time, Cindy's family was a part of her life again. They'd read a lot about me and decided I was a good guy. But they didn't like the idea that we were planning on moving to New Jersey together without being married. Her father used the old line about, "Why buy the cow when you're getting free milk?" Cindy didn't like that at all, and neither did I. That was just another variation on the old stereotype about men in general and athletes in particular—we were just interested in one thing and one thing only. Sex. To have your father making insinuations about the sexual nature of your relationship is not cool at all. If he was hoping he could drive a wedge between us, all he did was help us form a deeper bond.

I know I didn't want to admit it at the time, but I was a little scared about moving to New Jersey and being on my own. Even if we hadn't gotten married, Cindy would have come with me, but with those words of her father's ringing in both our ears, we decided it would be better to be married. We hadn't lived together when I was in Athens, and as a Christian, I didn't believe we should, and that figured in my decision as well. If she was going to come with me and live with me, then it had to be as my wife. Even before I went down to Florida for training camp, we went to the city hall in Verona, New Jersey, where we got married in front of a few friends who'd helped us make all the arrangements. Verona was both a romantic and practical choice of locations. I'd purchased a condominium in a building in Verona with the help of some people in the Generals front office. The fact that Shakespeare's tragic couple were from Verona wasn't lost on Cindy or me. I didn't see us as tragic, and our families certainly weren't feuding—the DeAngelis family never even made an attempt at that point to meet or speak with the Walkers.

No one from either family attended the wedding, and we had no reception or even a honeymoon. I had to get to training camp. I left Cindy behind, and she took care of furnishing and outfitting our new place. We had been staying in a hotel and only after I left did we finally close the deal, sign all the paperwork, and move in. I liked living in the Claridge House and in Verona. The building and area were predominantly Jewish, and I remember cracking up one morning when I came down in the elevator. A very sweet older woman got in on a floor beneath ours. She was fiddling with her pocketbook, and when she was finished fishing around in it, she looked up and saw me. Her eyes went wide with surprise.

"You must be new here," she said.

"Yes, ma'am, I am."

"What's your name."

"Herschel, ma'am. Herschel Walker."

"Herschel's a lovely name. My father was named Herschel. You must be Jewish, then, with a name like Herschel."

I shook my head, "No, ma'am, I'm not Jewish."

"Well"—she took a deep breath and sighed theatrically—

"we all can't be that fortunate, I suppose." She smiled, and when we got to the lobby, she patted my forearm and told me how lovely it was to meet me.

I guess her confusion over my heritage shows that I wasn't the only one struggling with my identity.

Verona was a beautiful place with a long history, and its tree-lined streets and well-kept lawns and brick and stone homes reminded me of the nicer parts of Wrightsville and Dublin. Cindy seemed pleased to be back in the Northeast, where she'd been brought up, and I was glad about that. I was too busy concentrating on my job to think that much about all the choices we'd made. Once again, it was full speed ahead. I'd cross the river into New York only to film television commercials or pose for print ads. I was working with Foster Grant—the eyewear people—Merrill Lynch, and I even did one spot with McDonald's. I could have done a lot more, but I wasn't in it for the money, and if I didn't really believe in the product, I didn't want my name associated with it.

I really did think of what I was doing as a job, just like anybody else's; it just so happened that I was the highest-paid athlete at the time. I didn't feel all that special, and Cindy and I lived a nice life, but we weren't extravagant at all. Our condo was a modest two-bedroom, and Cindy did a great job of decorating it, but it wasn't like we were living in a plush penthouse on Central Park West or something. Verona was nice and quiet and it was just a few miles from the Meadowlands Complex, where we played our home games. I wasn't used to all the crowds and congestion on the roads, and I was glad to have a short commute to work. To give you some idea of how unexceptional our lifestyle was, I was given a brand-new Buick Riviera as a treat for having made it in pro football. It was white, had a padded vinyl top and the classic oval opera-glass rear window. It had plush velour upholstery and a really nice cassette player. Only later, after I drove it to practice a few times and found myself parking alongside a few Mercedes, Porsches, and a couple of Corvettes, did I realize what my car looked like—a pimp-mobile. A couple of guys on the team teased me about it, but I already knew what they were saying was the truth. Funny how when you "arrive," what you think will be a symbol of having made it turns out to be a symbol of how far you have to go until you really arrive.

Eventually, I got rid of the Riviera and made arrangements with various automobile dealers to provide me with new cars every year. If I indulged myself in one area, it was with cars. I was still very much in love with them and the idea of going fast. Playing football and being able to afford them was cool, but they were my only real indulgence.

The game was the thing, and I loved the game. You could take all the rest of it—the contract negotiations, the endorsement deals, the media coverage, the betting on the games, the owners and profits, and all of that other junk—and just throw it out. I lived for Sundays. I lived for the moments when you strapped it on and went out there and competed and tested yourself against another man.

I've never taken a drug in my life, and competition was my high. If Xtasy, cocaine, heroine, or any other legal or illegal drug can produce a high like I experienced on the field, then I can understand why folks get hooked on them. I was a junkie. Whether it was the adrenaline or just the mental and emotional high that came from playing football, nothing in my life has come close to providing me with the kind of thrill that football did.

I say that, and I know how that sounds.

I took great pleasure in being married and now being a father. I took great pleasure in having friends and family and being able to help them out, and have them with me or near me. But those things didn't thrill me in the same way that playing football did. I got great visceral, heart-pounding, crestinga-hill-while-driving-fast, roller-coaster, dive-bombing, barrel-rolling, spleen-tingling FUN out of taking on another man in a contest of strength and will.

I talked earlier about how I felt about physical contact when I first transformed myself into a football player and what great pleasure I took in that. The intensity of those sensations was nothing in comparison to what I felt when I was out on the field as a professional facing guys who were, like me, at the pinnacle of their profession. I don't know if I can describe the soul-level satisfaction I got from those encounters. I hope that sometime in your life you've had what psychologists refer to as peak experiences—those moments when you feel so connected to life, when you know with every twitch of every cell in your body that you are doing the thing you were meant to do, love to do, and you are doing that thing with and against other people who feel the same way.

Because of DID and my tendency to be hypervigilant and not easily trusting of people—the activities of the Sentry and the Judge—I didn't develop really close, emotionally intimate relationships with many people. Men are typically like that, and a lot of the athletes I know are fairly extreme cases of these masculine traits.

Now that I'm removed from the game, and I have the clarity of mind that comes from knowing more about myself, I can say that I may not have had the respect or admiration of every one of my teammates or the guys I played against, but I felt something very close to love for every one of them. Maybe what I felt was even deeper and more powerful than love. I felt a kinship with them. It was as if we all shared a secret life because we'd experienced something similar. We formed a bond with one another based on our mutual experiences that we couldn't share with loved ones, spouses, or anybody else who hadn't played the game at the same level we did. In football, I found the kind of camaraderie that I'd always imagined I'd find in the military. I've spoken with a lot of soldiers, and they all tell me something about their experiences in combat that I experienced while playing.

In the middle of all that activity, they found a place of inner calm. They could be scared to death, but there was still this inner recess of placid control. The source of that calm, and the reason they could perform under pressure and in the face of their fear, was the knowledge that their fellow soldier, their teammate, needed them. When push came to shove in a game, you did what you had to do to win not just for yourself, but because there were other people depending upon you. Nothing else mattered but your teammates. The times you succeeded you experienced such a sense of satisfaction and sometimes relief. Nobody wanted to let the others down.

Here's where that tweenness, or I guess a better word is *duality,* enters again. The way to not let your teammates down and to really get the job done was to focus only on what you could control yourself. It was like you had this compartment of thoughts and feelings about the team, but you had to close and seal that up when you were actually in the middle of playing the game. You also had to have a somewhat selfish mentality—that you were the one everybody else was relying on because you were the one who could pull through when things got tough. You were the only one you could count on because it was your actions alone that you had direct control of. That's why I said earlier that I loved track because it was just me I was concerned with and relying on. Still, there was something about fitting that "I" into "team" that appealed to me so much in football. If this sounds contradictory and confusing, that's because it is. In order to succeed at a team sport, you have to be selfish as well. I mean, I wanted the ball all the time. I wanted to be the go-to guy, the one who had shoulders broad enough to carry not just my load, but the whole load. I don't think that anyone can be successful without having that kind of "me do" attitude I saw developing in my son, Christian, when he was first mastering his environment as a toddler. I have that same attitude, but it's developed to the nth degree. In a lot of ways, it has really helped me, especially professionally.

Much of what I've just talked about wouldn't matter so much if it weren't for the fact that a lot of these attitudes and beliefs and trends bled over from my professional life into my personal life. The alters who served me so well and allowed me to achieve so much on the field didn't do as much good in the rest of my life.

I mentioned before how that Indifferent alter, the one who didn't care so much about what other people thought of me and dealt with criticism so well, had another aspect to him that helped me succeed on the field but hurt me off the field.

I realize now how selfish I was in a lot of respects as a husband. When Cindy and I were first married and for a good bit of the time after, I was the planet at the center of the universe our lives revolved around. When we first moved to New Jersey, Cindy had a few friends nearby, but we spent most of our time together at home. I didn't socialize with the other players and Cindy and I seldom went out to eat, and I never went to bars. We loved to cook at home, and Cindy carried on many of the traditions of her Italian heritage and kept her and me well fed. Our daily routine was structured around me and my needs and the demands of my career. At first, Cindy seemed to love that. She traveled with me to away games, and sometimes she'd bring a friend or two along. We hadn't traveled much together, so each road trip was a new experience in a new town. Maybe Chicago, Los Angeles, Houston, Tampa Bay, and Jacksonville aren't the most exotic vacation locations, but for us and our friends they were new cities and sites to visit.

Even in the off-season, Cindy was subject to my schedule and my needs. If I had to go film a commercial, make an appearance somewhere, attend a meeting, she had to adjust her schedule to fit mine. She was basically running the household. I had financial advisers and things, but she ran the day-to-day operations exclusively. She wasn't working outside the home, and she was happy with that, but in retrospect, I now wonder how fulfilling all of those duties were for her. At the time, I was so busy focusing on what I had to do that I didn't really consider the effect my playing had on her. We were happy, and I did everything to make sure of that, but I don't know how fulfilled she really was. When the USFL folded and I wound up playing in Dallas for the Cowboys, we, of course, had to move. That's part of the life of a professional athlete, but it isn't easy on the athlete and has to be much harder on his or her family. I mean, Cindy had no control over these things. Neither did I, but it had to be different for her—I was still getting to do something I loved. We went from New Jersey to Dallas, then from Dallas to Minnesota, from Minnesota to Philadelphia, from Philadelphia to New York, then finally from New York back to Dallas. Even though we kept a permanent residence in Dallas, we had to have a place to live in season in all those other cities. That couldn't have been easy on her, being away from her family, from the friends she'd made in Dallas, but I didn't think much about it back then.

Because of all these trades and signings and things, Cindy had to do a lot to keep up with just maintaining a household while I was off at practice or at games. Don't get me wrong, Cindy and I had a great life, but given what happened between us later, I know that some elements of that lifestyle were taking a toll on her. Apart from close friends and family members, to the rest of the world, she was Herschel Walker's wife and not a real individual herself. That had to be hard. And, truth be told, I must have looked at her in that way, too, sometimes. She was my teammate, the one I supported and relied on. But here's where that tricky duality of selfishness and selflessness comes into play. Yes, Cindy was my teammate, and I wanted us to succeed as much as possible, and I didn't want to let her down, but that meant I had to focus so much of my time and energy on myself and what I was doing.

I was good at blocking out distractions, and I'm sure at times I made her feel like one of them. I was so used to not really caring about what other people thought of me that I must have blocked her and her opinions out as well.

We also lived life at the pace I was used to. I couldn't just sit around in the off-season. We took trips and things, but I think my experience with television's *Superstars* competition should illustrate this point.

The show was a spin-off of a British show that pitted athletes from various sports in a modified decathalon-style competition. In the American version, baseball players, football players, boxers, swimmers, track stars, etc., all square off against one another in events like cycling, golf, basketball, tennis, running, weight lifting, rowing, and a final obstacle course. IMG, my management company, produced the show, so I was invited to participate. For the first time since my transformation, I went into something with the wrong attitude. I figured I was a world-class track athlete, a professional football player, an incredibly fierce competitor, so I would do well in the event. I've never done anything where I think I don't have a chance to win. I may not win, but I always think I have a chance. Well, in 1986 in that *Superstars* competition, I got smoked. I didn't even make the finals.

The next year, I was playing for the Cowboys and had a Pro Bowl season. You'd think that I'd want to rest and recuperate from that. Not me. I was so determined to win the *Superstars* that year that I had been training for it all through the season and after. To give you some idea of how much I improved, I went from earning one point for finishing next to last in tennis in 1986 to winning the event for ten points in 1987. How'd I do that? I practiced like a maniac. Just about every chance I had, I went out and played tennis, took lessons. Cindy went along with it, and she started to play more seriously, too. To me, the *Superstars* wasn't about fun, it was about winning. Now it seems kind of funny that I spent so much time and effort on those games when I could have been taking it easy or traveling somewhere with Cindy. But that's how I was.

It was my restlessness and desire to compete and try new things that led me on another adventure that, in retrospect, was selfish and took me away from Cindy. My friend Willie Gault and I had shared a desire—to compete in the Olympics to represent our country. We both knew that making the Olympic track-and-field team was not likely to happen. We hadn't trained seriously for track in more than five years. Willie came up with another idea. He wanted us to try out for the Winter Olympics as pushers for the bobsled team. Willie had been trying since 1988, and other track athletes like the legendary hurdler Edwin Moses had also given it a shot. As track athletes, we had a real advantage: we were used to coming out of the blocks hard and fast. The one difference between a track start and a bobsled start is the surface. Ice was slippery. The other difference is that we would be pushing a sled. I figured I could make the adjustment. I didn't know a whole lot about a bobsled, other than that it went to a track on runners and that there were two kinds—two-man and four-man.

I had a great time and shared some wonderful experiences, despite some of the controversy that surrounded my participation in the Winter Olympics. Traveling to Germany, Austria, and then finally France for the '92 Albertville games was great, and Cindy was there every step of the way. In fact, the media picked up on her presence as my number one cheerleader. They reported on her being at the finals of the two-man competition wearing a T-shirt that referenced a famous and popular Nike ad featuring Bo Jackson. Her top said, BO DON'T KNOW DIDLEY, BUT HERSCHEL KNOWS SNOW.

Breaking Free

I know that being considered a man's cheerleader might seem demeaning to a lot of women today, and that certainly wasn't the role that Cindy played in my life, but it was so great to have her there and supporting me. She was my best friend, my confidante, and my rock of support. It's only when I look back on things now, knowing that our marriage ended, that I can see how some of these events could have contributed to that end. And I don't really mean the events themselves caused our divorce; I mean that it was the things I did that spoiled the years we had together.

I know it's obvious, but I have to say again: I loved to compete. The *Superstars* and the Olympics were as different as any two events could be, but both gave me the opportunity to test myself, experience new things, rise to different challenges. I said before that I was hooked on the high I got from competing. But I couldn't compete in sports all the time, and that's when my desire to test myself and my limits led me to explore some of the darker elements of life and competition.

I don't remember the exact date I bought the gun, but I know we were living in Dallas. This was during my time with the Vikings. Cindy and I still had a home there, even though I was spending most of my time in Minnesota. This was before I went to compete in Albertville, so it had to have been in 1991. To put it mildly, things hadn't gone as well as I or the Vikings had hoped after the blockbuster trade. I wasn't too happy, and I didn't realize the extent of how I was feeling until recently when I read a piece about me being elected to the University of Georgia Hall of Fame. The writer interviewed Cindy, and she talked about how down I was, and how upset I was. I don't really remember it that way, but I also came across an interview I did just before the Olympics. In response to a question about my competitive drive and why I was subjecting myself to a bread-and-water diet—I wanted to cut weight so that we could make the maximum allowable weight for the four-man crew plus the sled—I responded by saying, "I've had a lot of rage building up inside of me for the last two years. I came here ready to compete."

The writer assumed I was talking about my feelings regarding being traded from the Cowboys and how I was being treated by the Vikings. I've been interviewed so many times that its hard to remember exactly what I meant and what was going on in my mind at the time. Also, with DID, my memories of a lot of things are a bit fuzzy, and maybe my wanting to forget about what went on in Minnesota contributes to that, but I do remember sitting at my kitchen table in Dallas. Cindy had gone out for the evening with some friends. I was alone. The TV was on, but I wasn't paying any attention to it. Instead, I sat at the table with that .38-caliber Smith & Wesson revolver. It was an old police-issue double-fire center-action nickel-and-steel beauty that I'd bought as a collector's piece. I'd been looking for more of a military-issue-type gun, but when I saw this one at a gun shop in Dallas, I bought it on a whim. It had sat in a box in my closet for about six months before I took it out that night.

I sat at the table, with the gun in my hand turning it over and over, watching it catch and then throw back the light of the fixture above the table. I could smell the gun oil and the dusty cardboard odor of the box. I opened the chamber and slid a single round into it. I flipped it back shut and then spun it, like I'd see guys do hundreds of times on television. I sat there some more, just thinking. I could hear the voice in my head telling me to go ahead and try it. That voice kept telling me this would be the real challenge, the ultimate in competition. At first I resisted, but then I started wondering what it would feel like? I'd beaten most things in my life—my stuttering, my weight problems, people's low expectations of me. I'd won at football, track, the *Superstars*. I'd taken men on and beaten them. What would it be like to beat death? What would it be like to die?

I had a fascination with death for a while. Not that I was suicidal ever, and I don't think the first time I played Russian roulette I was despondent and wanted to end my life; I just looked at mortality as the ultimate challenge. Everybody is going to die. But did that mean that I had to? What would it be like to take on death on my own terms? If God has a plan for each and every one of us, and He knows the hour of our demise, could I take matters into my own hands? I know that as a Christian, the things I was thinking were blasphemous, and the presumption of thinking that I could alter God's plan is ludicrous to me now. Back then, it seems obvious to me now, my mind wasn't right. But sitting there with that gun and a single round chambered, I was thinking this wasn't much different from speeding around on a motorcycle, hurtling down a bobsled track, or taking any other kind of chance. I said all the usual things—you could easily die crossing the street, slipping in the shower, choking on a piece of food. Was that how I wanted to go out? Or would I want to go out this way, on my terms, by my own hand?

I truly didn't want to die, but I was like a junkie looking for that next and better high. Football, as it was unfolding in Minnesota, wasn't very satisfying at all. I was competing as best I could, but I felt like a horse with a halter placed on him and a jockey whose instructions were to not let him run free. If I was jittery or irritable or whatever Cindy detected in me, it was because I wasn't getting what I needed. I wasn't being allowed to go out there and do what I did best, what I loved most, and what fed some deep and unquenchable thirst in me.

I reached above me and flipped off the lights. I didn't want Cindy to come home and find me as the first thing she saw. I don't know how long I sat at the table in the hazy blue light of the television. At one point, I must have raised the gun to my temple, because I can remember feeling the coldness of the metal and the gentle pressure and my pulse pushing against the thing that could end my life. I didn't make any bargains, do any countdowns, and I don't recall having any thought that signaled to my hand and finger to pull the trigger. It was almost as if I'd done what I'd always done—flipped a coin. Before I could really register in my mind what my finger had done and my ears had heard, the click went off. It was lot louder than I expected—that's what I remember thinking first. Then I experienced a kind of thrill, an evil kind of thrill that I'd never experienced before. I didn't feel any relief, just a kind of warmth, a purely physiological sensation of heat, cascading down my body from my head to my feet. Before that sensation wore off, I spun the cylinder again, put the barrel to my mouth this time, tasted the oil and the steel on my lips, and pulled the trigger again. This time the sensations were even more intense.

Before I could make another attempt, I heard the garage door opener click and then whine and chatter. Cindy was pulling in. I packed the gun away and sprinted up the stairs to our bedroom and stowed the gun away. I know she never suspected a thing. Why should she? What I was doing was so out of character for me, both as a Christian and as a man who nearly everyone described as being upbeat and optimistic. I truly don't think I'm kidding myself by saying that I was not depressed, and was not suicidal; I was simply (if that word even applies here) thrill seeking.

I also believe that I engaged in that behavior because of my alters. If I didn't think I was infallible, I certainly came close to believing that I was nearly invincible. My alters and I had survived so much and attained such a high level of achievement, the only thing left for me to do was to take on death. Death was the ultimate enemy. I can't tell you how many other times I played Russian roulette in total. I don't have perfect recall, and since people with DID tend to have blank spots in their memories anyway, a count would be inaccurate at best. I do know that periodically, until I sought help and was diagnosed in 2001, I did engage in that behavior.

Obviously, playing Russian roulette—and the word *playing* now seems really weird to me—isn't the smartest, healthiest thing to do. I also know that as my playing career wound down, and it became clearer to me that at some point I was going to have to leave the game, the urge to test myself in that way increased. I know a lot of athletes who have struggled with lots of issues once they stopped playing their sport. I had a hard time leaving the University of Georgia, but at least I had something else to look forward to. What was so hard about leaving pro football was the feeling that I had, and still have today, that I could continue to compete. I felt I was in good enough shape and could continue to play indefinitely. Simultaneously, I saw the writing on the wall. The economics of the game dictated that a veteran player like me, one who was being well paid, was a liability. The thinking was that a younger (in other words, less expensive) player could contribute in roughly the same way that I was doing at a lower cost. It was kind of like a yards/tackles/receptions/sacks-per-dollar equation was being used all around the league. Everybody wanted to get the most for their dollar. As a man who runs businesses today, I can't really argue with that line of thinking. I also know that I brought a lot more to the game than the numbers can show, and it wasn't as if my numbers were bad.

The decline in my marriage coincided with the appearance on the horizon of the end of my career. I'd say that during the eighteen months before my last season of playing in the 1997 season, things between Cindy and me started to change. I don't blame her now, but at the time I did. I truly didn't understand what was going on. All I know is that toward the end of my playing career, Cindy and I weren't operating as smoothly as a team as we had before. I can't point to any major blowups between us, but I felt like things had eroded. Before things started to slide, Cindy had always been there for me, and we almost always did everything together. After I didn't show up for camp in 1998, I was going to be home full-time. Cindy was pleased to hear that. She kept saying to me that it was great that we were now going to have time to slow down and relax and really for the first time just enjoy the life we'd made together. I didn't say much at first, but to me, *slow down* and *relax* were as bad as any swearwords I'd ever heard on the football field. I realize now that not only did they shock me, they also scared me. I didn't know how to slow down and relax, I didn't know if I'd be any good at doing such a thing, and, most important, I didn't want to relax.

I also truly did not want to give up football. I didn't want to lose something that mattered so much to me. Moreover, I was always responding to another event in my life that served as a wake-up call. Ever since I'd made it in pro football, I'd been trying to help out my family in a number of ways. My brother Renneth was probably the best athlete among us Walkers. I told you that he earned a college scholarship but came back home after a while to be with his girlfriend. He also had a baby with a different girl, and he wanted to help support his child. He worked odd jobs and was never really able to get where he wanted to go or needed to go. He struggled for a bunch of years, and he and I were at odds over his lack of focus and direction. It was probably hard for him to hear such criticism coming from his little brother, but it hurt me to see him struggling. I was trying to be supportive and helpful, but he wouldn't listen.

My mother told me once that my problem was that I wanted for other people more than they wanted for themselves. She said that I had to accept the fact that some people didn't have to be on top like I always wanted to be. She is a truly smart lady, but it took me a long time to accept that truth. So Renneth and

I kept bumping heads and hurting feelings. One day in the fall of 1987, I was speaking with Renneth, and as things often did, the conversation descended into me telling him that he needed to get his act together. He'd married a woman by the name of Diane and she was a wonderful lady, and I didn't want to see him mess up. Renneth didn't appreciate my reminding him of his failures to really live up to what he could have been, and we hung up the phone, each one angry at the other. My mother was in Dallas visiting at the time, and when I got off the phone with Renneth, she told me to go easy on him, that he was trying, and that I couldn't change him. I had a game the day after the argument with Renneth. My mother flew home after the game, and Renneth and my older brother, Willis, Jr., picked her up at the airport. Later, my mother told me that Renneth had said to her that I was right, that he needed to get serious about his life and take advantage of the opportunities he had. He was going to get his stuff together.

Unfortunately, he didn't have any time left to make those changes. The very next day, Renneth was at work as a crew foreman for the railroad. They were doing some track repairs. As foreman, Renneth drove a pickup truck to the site instead of having to sit on the modified railroad engine and car they used to do the repairs and transport materials and tools and crew. One of the guys on his crew was celebrating his wedding anniversary, and as bighearted as Renneth was, he told the guy and the rest of the crew to take his truck back where they were parking their cars. Renneth would take the rig back to the yard. Because the tracks were never completely shut down, just had trains routed to different tracks, Renneth radioed in to the dispatcher to make sure that the track he was going back to the yard on was safe. He was told it was. It wasn't. The rig he was driving derailed and Renneth died.

My mother called me that Monday night and she was distraught. She could barely get the words out. I felt terrible when

I heard what had happened, but it was like somebody threw a switch. My alters immediately went into action mode, asking my parents what I could do and how I could help. They were both a wreck, and I knew I couldn't let on that I was hurting, too. I had a bunch of things to take care of, and between Cindy and me, we managed to make all the arrangements we could. We flew down to Atlanta on Thursday for services the next day. When I got there, my family was still in a highly emotional state. I had to be strong for all of them, and in the whole time since I'd learned of the accident, I hadn't shed a tear. I couldn't let myself. I don't know where I found the strength to carry on, but I did. Throughout that whole time, I kept repeating over and over again a few words from Psalm 71:

> Be my rock of refuge,
>> to which I can always go;
>> give the command to save me,
>> for you are my rock and my fortress.

God was my rock and my fortress, but in some ways He also tormented me. I admit that there were times when I let my defenses down and asked all the usual questions: Why would God let this happen? Why did this have to happen to my family? Why hadn't I been a better Christian and repaired my relationship with my brother before it was too late?

I asked Him how this could be fair and pleaded with Him for enlightenment. I felt as though I were walking in the wilderness, where the land was dry with no signs of refreshing water in sight. Yet deep inside me was that Living Water that never runs dry.

To say the least, losing my brother was a negtive occasion. I was comforted only when the thought occurred to me that I was being selfish. I knew God would take better care of him than I ever could.

I learned something positive when I came to that realization. God had helped me to see the good in an otherwise heartbreaking experience. The positive aspect was that my brother was in God's hands. What better place to be? I had to learn to let go and be firmer in my faith that what God had planned for him was more important than my loss and my desire to have him around me.

I began to try to dwell on the things in my life that brought me joy. I remembered carrying the football toward the goal line for a touchdown. I could not see the player just behind, running on my heels; but I could feel him, I knew he was there.

During this difficult period of adjusting to my brother's absence, I couldn't see him, but I knew he was there. I remembered then that it would be God, the God of whom I had been taught, the God I knew personally, who would get me through this sorrowful time.

It is the same God to whom I now give thanks. I thank Him for His faithfulness and for my everlasting assurance of eternal life. I thank Him that I am blessed and most of all, that I am free. I am free to tell my story of the joys of living, the tragedy of death, and the trials of contending with and surviving the effects of Dissociative Identity Disorder.

During that time I also put whatever pain and anger and frustration and sadness into a little box and put it up on a shelf. So, whenever I reached for that box with my gun in it, it was like I was taking all of those emotions out along with it. I can see now that my DID and my faith were battling one another, and in those dark moments I was facing a test I could not fail if I kept God on my side.

I couldn't stay long in Georgia. I had to fly out in order to make the final Saturday meetings and game day on Sunday. I acted when I got back to Dallas like nothing had happened—because of the coordinated efforts of my alters, in my mind it was almost as if Renneth hadn't been in that accident. I didn't dedicate the game to him. I wanted to keep to my same routine. I had to. I had a game to prepare for. A job to do. The alters who bore every bit of pain, sadness, anger, and frustration took over for me. I didn't feel a thing, just went about my business.

I do realize now that Renneth's death had an effect on me in lots of ways besides the obvious ones of missing a loved one. His accident reinforced in me the idea that in life we're promised nothing. We have no guarantee of the amount of time we'll be able to spend here. For that reason, you have to go hard all the time. You've got to get things done while you can. Wasting time will catch up to you at some point, and you don't ever want to be caught up short. I also realized that the military mentality I'd adopted would really help me get things done—especially at times of tragedy and sadness. If I showed no pain or fear, then I could accomplish what needed to be accomplished. My first mission in that situation was to show my family that things were going to be okay, that we were going to get through the ordeal. By maintaining control of my emotions and keeping my behavior within its habitual boundaries, I could create a sense of normalcy. I couldn't show my pain to anyone, never reveal any kind of weakness. When I flew into Cleveland for the game following my brother's death, I was certain that no one could tell that anything out of the ordinary had happened.

Of course, I realize now that I had other choices, that I could have responded in other ways, and that being strong has a lot more dimensions than simply being unemotional. I didn't know this then. Cindy tried to talk with me about Renneth, and how bad I felt about our last conversation. The fact that it was so negative just reinforced in my mind the idea that you have to get things done when you can and not wait. I don't think I really understood until later the subtler messages about expressing how you really feel, about letting go of your anger and frustration at how someone else is living their life, that offering encouragement and not criticism can work just as well if not better in assisting someone to make a change.

Any and all of those messages were lost in the clutter of finishing up that final season, of getting my job done. How my reaction to Renneth's death affected Cindy and my relationship, I can't really say. I just know that all those emotions that I had regarding his death went unexpressed at the time, but they were floating around me and may have had something to do with how far things slid before I reached out for help.

I never officially retired from football. I made no announcements, didn't hold a press conference, and like I'd done at Georgia, I kind of quietly slipped out the back door. I have no complaints to register about the Cowboys or how they treated me. I tell people this all the time. If I had to start my own football team or became the owner of one, I'd pick Jimmie Johnson as my coach. I liked how he handled players, I liked his approach to the game, and he always seemed to me to be a good man. I had almost as much respect and admiration for him as I had for Coach Tom Landry. It's really not fair to compare the two—they coached in different eras with different kinds of players. Mr. Landry was a fine Christian gentleman and some say his faith made it difficult to stay in touch with the younger generation of players. I know that we got along well, and he set a fine example for me.

What's puzzling to me is that for the most part, I was living a good, solid Christian life. Those outbursts of anger—like I described in the opening of this book—and flirting with death never seemed to be a part of who I was or how I conducted my life the rest of the time. All I know for sure is that when I stopped playing football, it was hard for me to shift gears. It seemed to me that Cindy wanted me to shift into neutral, to coast, and I didn't even have that gear. For somebody like me, going slow felt like going backward. So, instead of doing what Cindy wanted me to do, I kept charging ahead. This time, I went full speed ahead in getting my food-services business up and running. I had to do something, had to channel my energy somewhere, had to have some kind of challenge to keep me going. I don't think I could ever adequately explain to Cindy why that was necessary, but I also know I never told her about the dark secret hiding in our closet. I'm sure that if she knew that my running a business—what to her must have seemed just like more of me playing games—had been a way to keep me from playing another more serious and more deadly game, she wouldn't have objected to the kind of time I was spending at work. Of course, I never confided in her what I was doing with that gun. If she knew that I sometimes felt a literal gun against my head instead of just feeling like there was a figurative one urging me to always keep striving and doing, then things could have turned out differently between us.

The reason why I never told Cindy of those pressures is that I felt like she was betraying me. All she did was live her life, do the kinds of things a person would normally do, but I felt like she had turned her back on me. After I stopped playing and was working to get Herschel's Famous 34 Food Products off the ground, she wasn't sitting at home like she used to, and since I was spending more time at home I noticed that she wasn't there. We'd been a team, and now Cindy had other interests and other people she spent time with. Here's where that weird selfish and immature side comes in. I was like a little kid, expecting that my best friend would spend all of her time with me like she used to. I couldn't understand the change, and I didn't like it. I wanted things to be the way they were before, when the whole world revolved around me and what I wanted to do and what I needed to do. I was sad about not playing anymore, I had this big old hole in my life, and I felt like no matter what I stuffed into that hole to plug it up, things just kept leaking out. When I tried to plug up that leak in one area, another one sprang up someplace else.

And I mean it was the simplest and, I realize now, stupidest things that used to get to me. Cindy had kept up playing tennis after my *Superstars* training sessions. We'd played together a lot, but she had started to play with other people, too—when I was at practice or meetings. When I was home more, I expected her to play with me, but she kept up meeting with what I called her "tennis friends" and I didn't have anyone else to play against. I'd kept so isolated, I didn't have many friends in the area, so I wanted to monopolize her time. That wasn't fair, but that's how I felt. So I sulked a bit.

That's when that other part of my selfishness came in. I was faced with a challenge. The team I was on wasn't doing well, and I wanted more than anything for it to succeed. So I fell back on the old habits I had developed when I first transformed myself. I looked inside myself and remembered all the inner strength I had. I conveniently forgot how my brother Lorenza had helped and encouraged me, how Mr. Jordan had reached out to assist me, how Mr. Newsome had done so much for me and my family, how close I was with my sister Veronica and her husband, Bill. When Cindy and I began drifting apart, instead of saying what I wanted to say and should have said, I told myself, "It doesn't matter. You can go on by yourself. You've got to get a move on. You've got things you want to do. Don't waste time worrying over this. Get out there and do what you have to do."

And that's exactly what I did. If there was a wedge between us before that, I was the guy with the sledgehammer pounding on that wedge to divide us even further. I didn't really think of it that way at the time, and I don't think I was fully conscious of the consequences of my actions, but I did what I usually did when confronted with a situation. I worked harder. Instead of working harder at communicating with my wife, I spent more and more time focusing on my new business. I figured if Cindy wasn't going to be there for me to do all the things we used to do, I had to have something. I had to have some way of spending my time, some way to find satisfaction in building something instead of seeing something get torn down and destroyed. Whenever I had a moment of weakness and started to feel even the smallest amount of self-pity, there was that Consoler telling me, "You're going to be okay. You move on from this point. You've got to think about the future. You've got things to do. Get on 'em." And then the Judge would chime in, "If that woman doesn't want to be a part of this team anymore, then forget about her. If she can't be loyal to the cause, then she has to be cut out."

To my alters, Cindy had committed a terrible infraction of the black-and-white rules I'd live by—she'd been disloyal. If she didn't want to be a part of the team, if she wanted to go her own way and do her own thing, then we wanted nothing to do with her. One of the great things about my alters is how loyal they were to me. They looked out for my best interests all the time—or so I thought—and I exhibited that same kind of loyalty to the people in my life. I would never abandon a teammate. I would never speak badly of a teammate, a friend, a family member. In my heart, I knew that Cindy wasn't really disloyal, but in the context of how I lived my life, and how the alters interpreted and responded to her actions, she'd done a terrible, terrible thing. In retrospect, I realize how much the Judge and the Enforcer were influencing my thinking. The warrior code I lived by didn't allow for this. In addition, the isolation I felt, the perceived sense of abandonment, kicked into high gear all the machinations the Consoler, Hero, and Sentry had been refining and using all those years.

All of the skills I had learned to overcome my problems as a kid, as a teen, as an adult, all those lessons of fortitude and courage and defying the odds and gutting it out, and rubbing some dirt on it and getting back in there and giving your all, backfired on me. I was hurt and confused, and those were feelings I'd long ago stopped feeling, back when I was a kid. I'd put up such a wall of defense and kept so much negativity out of my life that when I was faced with it again, those alters did what they had done in the past—they built a wall around me, identified an enemy, kept it at bay, and ultimately figured out a way to eliminate her from my life.

In time, I did something so horrible that I can't believe to this day that I was the one who did it. I'm not trying to deny responsibility for my actions by saying that. I just want to convey that I knew right from wrong, and I did a very, very wrong thing that hurt my wife, another person, and in the end me. I went outside of my marriage and had an affair with another woman. She lived nearby in Irving, where Cindy and I had lived for quite a few years. We weren't close friends at first, but we socialized together and moved in the same circles, as the saying goes. I knew that we shared some of the same interests—running, working out, tennis. And that's how the whole thing got started. Cindy was with her crowd and I chose to be on my own, but I still wanted somebody to do the things with me that Cindy and I used to do together.

We enjoyed each other's company and being active in sports and things. At first, I didn't say much to her about what was going on with Cindy and me. I felt like doing so would be betraying Cindy, but I can see now that when I finally did open up to her, it was the first of what would be inevitable steps. Over time, as I shared the details of my life and what I was thinking and feeling, the two of us established some emotional intimacy. That was something I had with very, very few people. Even here, my kind of emotional intimacy wasn't what most people experienced. If it's possible, I maintained a kind of "distant intimacy" with a select few friends and family members. What I had with Cindy was a much deeper connection.

She was the only woman I'd ever dated, ever loved, and ever opened up to.

I guess I'm like a lot of men, and *immature* is a pretty good word to describe me when it comes to relationships, because I felt like once I was able to open up to this woman, there had to be a physical attraction there as well. I couldn't separate the two in my mind. The closer we got emotionally, the more natural it seemed to me that we would become lovers. I can analyze all of this now with a kind of detachment that I wasn't capable of then. I admit that I was swept up in a sea of emotions that had a depth and a tidal pull that I was completely unfamiliar with. That's no excuse, mind you, just a fact. But the alter who reads people knew the young woman I had fallen for was wonderful. I can say that now because with all the things I've been through she was the only one who stayed. Not the players I had been to war with, not the friends I traveled the world with. She became someone I also thought of as my soul mate.

Another fact, and one that troubles me so much, is that I knew that I wasn't just going around behind my wife's back with another woman, I was violating everything I believed in and that God said about marriage and fidelity. I could quote you chapter and verse on everything God and Jesus said about marriage. The only thing I can say is that I am weak and I sinned. I know that's not enough of an explanation, but it's certainly another fact. The other part of it, the element that makes sense to me even though it is completely illogical, is that in some ways, I felt like I was owed the chance to do something wrong, to commit adultery. I had lived a good and honest life to that point. I had always tried to be honest and to abide by God's word. I had been tempted by many people along the way—by opportunities to take money, to get involved in drugs and alcohol, to have relations with other women, to live a lifestyle completely contrary to the one that I was living. I never once caved in to those temptations. So wasn't I allowed this one mistake? I knew that God would forgive me. I knew that His only Son had died on the cross and shed His blood for me, but I wasn't going to use His sacrifice as an excuse. My having an affair wasn't the same thing as my tempting fate by playing Russian roulette. Or at least that's what I tried to tell myself. I sinned. I felt the excitement of sinning. But on the other side of those pieces of silver I took to betray my Savior, I was also racked with guilt and remorse. Good! I should have been and I was.

In looking back on this, I can see how my alters functioned in all of this illogic and excuse making. The Indifferent Daredevil, who didn't care about what other people would think or what was right and wrong, shut the Judge up or convinced him that there was something right about me doing something to punish Cindy since she had violated a cardinal rule by not being loyal to the team. I can see now that even all of my alters were jumbled up and acting out in ways contrary to the discipline they had enabled me to practice before.

In fact, I felt like my life was so out of control, that I was so angry at times, that I was risking my life with a gun at my head, that I was cheating on my wife, that I was behaving so out of character for me, that I had to go to someone. I turned to the Lord in the person of my minister. I knew I needed help and guidance. Instead of receiving those two things, what I got was a heap more trouble. My minister listened to my story, and I could tell that he was struggling to believe what he was hearing. He'd probably heard a lot worse, but hearing it from me had to be a shock, someone he knew to be so totally different from the adulterer who sat across from him, Unfortunately, my conversation with the minister may have forced a confrontation with Cindy I had not been expecting or hoping for. Cindy came home a day or two after my meeting with the minister and confronted me. She'd heard through a fellow church member that I was having an affair. I couldn't deny it, but I was completely knocked off balance by the thought that the only person I had told about this at the church was the minister himself. I couldn't believe that he would betray my confidence. I couldn't dwell on that for very long, I had one very seriously upset wife on my hands—and she had every right to be upset. Cindy was devastated, and naturally she withdrew from me a bit. I was still stuck in my alter rut and still thinking that much of what had happened between us was her fault. I was angry, I was the one who was wronged, I was the one who had been abandoned, so instead of expressing remorse, I was either angry or didn't say anything at all. More than anything else, my silence made her even angrier.

To Cindy's credit, she didn't abandon the marriage immediately. I know I would have done so if the situation had been reversed. I think in a lot of ways, my cheating on her made her realize that something was seriously wrong with our marriage and with me. She also knew that my behavior was so uncharacteristic of me that something else besides lust was at work. I still wasn't prepared to deal with any of this. I knew in my heart that I was wrong, but I still wanted to understand better why I'd done these things. Cindy and I managed to declare a kind of truce for a while. Things between us weren't even close to normal, but they were at least civil. I can't tell you the number of times Cindy accused me of being a rock. I can remember sitting across from her and listening to her plead with me to just talk to her, let her know what I was thinking and feeling. All I could manage to do was shrug my shoulders and say, "I don't really know" or something equally unproductive and evasive.

To make matters worse, I lost a very good friend when it was revealed that I'd had an affair and that our marriage was troubled. Jim Jeffcoat, a teammate from my Cowboys days, and I were very good friends. We worked out together a lot and hung out, and so did our wives. The four of us had a lot of fun together. I felt like he turned his back on me and sided with Cindy. He stopped taking my phone calls, stopped working out with me, and essentially ended our friendship. That added to my sense of being the party who was wronged, the one who was the victim of other people's abandonment, their inability to dig in the trenches and get dirty and fight alongside me. But how did I respond? With the usual words and actions of my alters: "That's okay. You don't need him. You're going to be okay. Just keep moving forward. If a friend doesn't have your back when you need him, how much of a friend can he really have been?"

I see now that my thinking was all twisted, but I still clung to the idea that I got through the worst of it. I survived. This was about more than survival, however. I really did want to be happy.

Eventually, I did turn to someone else for help. I first met Dr. Jerry Mungadze back in the early 1980s when I was still running track. Dr. Jerry was originally from Zimbabwe and was competing internationally while attending college in the United States on a track-and-field scholarship. We spoke to each other a few times, and I was intrigued by his story of coming to the States. Our lives took very different paths after that, but they would eventually intersect. Dr. Jerry, obviously, went on to graduate school. He obtained a Ph.D. from the University of North Texas, as well as certification as a licensed professional counselor. He had focused his undergraduate and graduate studies on cults, theology, counseling, and psychology. I learned this and more about him when we met at a dinner party in Dallas. He had stayed in Texas after his graduation and established the Mungadze Association, a nationally known and respected outpatient counseling center specializing in the treatment of individuals suffering from dissociative disorders, childhood trauma and abuse, post-traumatic stress disorder, and ritual abuse. He is both its founder and president, and remains so today. In 1989, Dr. Jerry established the Dissociative and Trauma Related Disorders Unit at Cedars Hospital in DeSoto, Texas. It is one of only a few intensive programs in the country for the treatment of dissociative disorders.

When, shortly after meeting him again at that dinner party, I found myself sitting across a desk from him, it wasn't as a friend but as a client. I went to Dr. Jerry not because I knew anything about his work with dissociative disorders, but because I didn't know where else to turn for help. We both agreed to some ethical and legal ground rules before he could begin to treat me. Over the next weeks, Dr. Jerry observed my behavior and ran tests; and we had long sessions of intense counseling. Finally, he disclosed his diagnosis: dissociative identity disorder.

For the first time in my life, I had a name for my condition and realized I was not alone. Now I was eager to know the truth about the voices in my head that had become a part of me.

Dr. Jerry described his procedures and proposed treatment for the part of me I had never truly understood. He said his treatment would focus on the whole person rather than the separate parts or personalities I had created.

He assured me it was possible to achieve emotional stability based upon the approach and methods he had developed. First, I had to be held accountable for my behavior. I needed to admit that my behavior was not in anyone's best interest, that I was out of control emotionally, and that I was in a personal crisis. He characterized my psychological condition as poor.

Dr. Jerry's goal for all of his patients is to improve how they function day by day while waiting for what is known as "integration" to occur. This must be accomplished before the patient can entirely concentrate on the concerns of everyday life.

He explained how dissociative identity disorder can be compared to a broken leg, in the sense that the cast cannot be removed until the leg begins to heal. With DID, you may have created alters who have been with you for all of your life. You cannot let the alters go until you have completed a healing process that may sometimes be lengthy.

When the life of a person with DID is unstable and out of control, his alters must be available to him. If not, he would react like an individual with a broken leg and no cast. The leg would fail and be useless to the body. The whole person would be crippled and unable to function at his full potential.

It's not true that a person who uses alters cannot be helped. These alters have been cultivated over a lifetime of severe pain, loneliness, fear, and trauma. That process did not occur overnight and cannot be eliminated overnight. Just like a person with a broken leg, an individual with DID must have the proper care. Healing and wholeness come with time and hard work.

These are some of the things I learned during our early sessions. Since that time, Dr. Jerry has played an important role in my healing process. I consider him one of my best friends, and probably the most essential. He also arranged for me to go to the Del Amo Hospital in Torrance, California, for outpatient treatment. There, the doctors confirmed his diagnosis. I also met and worked in group therapy sessions with others diagnosed with DID. I was glad to see, on the one hand, that I had a relatively mild form of the disease. On the other hand, it was sad to see people who were not able to function at a high level like I was. I remember meeting one woman while there who seemed really nice and well adjusted. A few days later, I bumped into another woman in the hallway. As I usually do, I said hello to her. She turned to me and let out a stream of curses. I was with a doctor and I said that I was sorry for upsetting that woman. He turned back and said, "You mean Ann?"

I couldn't believe it—that angry, bile-spewing woman was the same one who had been in my group. Her transformation was astounding—physically and emotionally. I counted my blessings that I was going to be able to go home after a short stay. For Ann, it seemed, the rest of her life was going to be a series of plagues.

My treatment was also supplemented by my faith in God. During the most trying times, when I was struggling with the diagnosis and the stigma of having a mental illness, I called upon my lifelong faith and the lessons my mother taught me. I remembered Mama sitting in an old rocking chair, slowly rocking back and forth with that big black book, the Bible, in her lap.

My siblings and I listened intently as she read aloud about God and his angels. She taught us that each individual is assigned his very own guardian angel to protect him from harm as well as to dissuade him from harming others.

She said there are two kingdoms in the world: the kingdom of light and the kingdom of darkness. The kingdom of light is the realm of God and His angelic beings; the kingdom of darkness is ruled by Satan and his demons. In my case, the alters I developed as a result of DID were a lot like the angels and the fallen angels and Satan doing battle in my mind. They were capable of doing great good and great harm, of being a positive or a negative force in my life. Being able to put things in a spiritual context greatly helped me to come to terms with what I was learning about myself. And I worked very hard to understand better intellectually and spiritually what was going on in my life, for as Proverbs 8:11 tells us, "for wisdom is more precious than rubies, and nothing you desire can compare with her." My faith and the knowledge I gained formed a potent team. Unfortunately for me, my diagnosis, treatment, and understanding occurred too late to help me save my marriage. Although Cindy tried and tried to work with me, there were parts of me that were still so broken that I couldn't do what was really needed to help her heal the wounds I'd inflicted on her. Our divorce was finalized in 2003. I've been miserable about the end of my marriage ever since. I function well in most parts of my life, but knowing how much pain I caused her is difficult to live with. We share a son, Christian, who was born in 1999, when Cindy and I were still working to reconcile. He has been more than a blessing to us both, and I've remained in the Dallas area to continue to feel the love and grace of God through him.

It's not possible for me to undo the past. I'm more than sorry for what I did to Cindy and to our marriage. I still struggle with isolating myself too much. I probably work too hard and too much. I still haven't really slowed down completely. I realize that the mistakes I made were painful, but I'm making progress. I wanted to charge ahead and conquer DID as quickly as I could. There were times when I denied that I had it. I'm working hard to understand and apply the new things I'm learning about myself every day. I have to resist the urge to use the lessons I learned in transforming myself as a young boy and later refined on the football field of the Southeast Conference, the USFL, and the NFL. As my mother always said, "There's a time and a place for everything." I definitely know now that there is no time and no place for me to put a gun to my head. I'm in the process of becoming a different me, a better me, but I still think I could go out there today and gain a hundred yards a game. Some other things, like God's love for each and every one of us, never change, and I don't think they should.

Epilogue

Running in a New Direction

Since my initial diagnosis, nearly ten years ago, I've been on a roller coaster. I have to admit that at times I felt a great deal of shame and uncertainty about my diagnosis. As I did with so many other things, I read widely and passionately about this new element in my life. I had to know the ins and outs of the condition, and I learned a great deal from Dr. Jerry and in my consultations with other mental-health researchers and practitioners. It has taken me a long time to come to terms with what I did and what I've experienced. I would hate to waste it by not sharing this story. I also realize that I could have gotten help much sooner if I had opened up to those closest to me as I have in this book. Sharing this story with all of you has been a part of my journey toward healing. I've always been a very private person, but I feel the need to share my story and what

I know of DID with the world. I've accomplished many things in this life. I wanted to make a difference in the world through serving in the military. I thought that taking lives would be the way that I accomplished that mission of service. I know now that I can be of better service by helping others to heal.

The ultimate goal for a DID patient is integration. Dr. Jerry says that integration is not about ridding oneself of alters, but of the mind coming together as a unified whole. It is a healing rather than an elimination process. The patient must be reassured that the disappearance of an alter during therapy is not something to regret or be wistful about, because it is a step toward healing. The patient may mourn the loss of the alter, but the therapist will regard it as meaningful progress.

One way to think of dissociative identity disorder is in terms of the effect it has on the "self"; that is, all that we are, the entire wholeness or completeness of an individual. Self involves the body, the emotions, the thoughts, and the sensations that make up the identity of a person. Simply put, DID is a condition in which intrusions into a person's sense of self occur.

It is common for the DID sufferer to be aware of the presence of other personalities, but that is only one part of the entire dissociative experience; although it is clearly the most sensationalized and misunderstood.

In discussing the initial diagnosis with a patient, experts recommend describing normal dissociation and then the link between trauma and dissociative disorders. It is important to explain the symptoms and where dissociation comes from, to state that it is treatable, and to assure the patient that it is not a form of insanity. The therapist must be careful to keep emotions out of the process.

The patient should be told that "dissociative identity disorder" is simply a label applied to the experience of having separate parts inside who feel like different people, even though they are not. It should be emphasized that they are all parts of one person, and the goal of therapy is to integrate the personalities. Educating the patient about dissociation is an ongoing process, a continuing conversation between the patient and therapist.

The therapist should impress upon the patient that they are not equal in the context of therapy. The treatment occurs in a cooperative environment, but not in a democracy. The patient needs to be a participant in the treatment, but there may be times when he must yield to the greater expertise of the therapist.

It is important to form a treatment coalition with as many alters as possible. The "host" and rational adult alters can be worked with on an adult level, whereas it may be necessary to play games, read books, or go for walks with child alters. The therapist must ensure that this is only a means to an end and that such game playing ultimately lead to integration.

The therapist often includes the persecutor alters in the patient's therapy, reminding them that they all have the same goal, which is to end the suffering.

Persecutors often resent the therapist as an intrusion into their territory. They may think he believes they have failed to take care of the host. The therapist might address this by stating that he recognizes that they know the host much better than he. Then he will seek their permission to ask them questions to help him know the host better. He might mention that everyone needs a helping hand sometimes.

Hostile alters act tough, but most of them really want to be loved. One of the best ways for the therapist to form an alliance with personalities is to try to discern their sadness and pain, and make a comment about it. In most cases, hostile alters are suffering children and adolescents who are only pretending to be antagonistic. Another tactic to gain their trust is to ask them to act as enforcers, to prevent the stronger alters from harming the less powerful ones.

As stated before, in most cases, those who develop dissociative disorders have histories of overwhelming and repetitive trauma during their formative years, typically prior to the age of ten. Dissociation is usually the result of extreme physical, emotional, and/or sexual abuse.

However, it may also be caused by other types of trauma, such as natural disasters, war, kidnapping, and torture. Dissociation may be a child's only lifeline to survival by allowing him to "go away," or escape internally. In effect, he creates another personality to deal with the pain, enabling himself to continue functioning.

Dissociative identity disorder is an extraordinarily creative "device" that enables the child to maintain some degree of healthy functioning while enduring a situation from which there is seemingly no escape. Children who regularly practice this type of dissociation over a long period of abuse may become so conditioned to the process that they automatically use it in all uncomfortable or anxiety-producing situations.

Although the experiences that originally triggered DID may no longer occur when one reaches adulthood, the pattern of dissociation continues. In extreme cases, this causes problems in work and social environments, and may even interfere with the ability to perform everyday tasks. Thankfully, this has not happened to me. Some aspects of DID, as I have argued, actually aided me for much of my life.

Another ramification of using dissociation repeatedly is that, over time, the alters initially created for survival take on individual identities and often have names. It may seem to the person with DID that each personality has his own way of thinking and behaving.

Those who frequently engage in dissociation may find their sense of identity and their personal history affected. They may be unable to recall certain segments of their lives. In my case, there are still parts of my childhood I cannot remember.

In dissociation, information normally associated with other information fails to make the proper connection in the brain. For example, the memory of the time and place of a traumatic experience and the circumstances of the event may be disconnected, resulting in a memory gap surrounding the incident. Mental-health professionals refer to this as amnesia for the abuse.

Alter personalities serve many functions for the person who has suffered traumatic experiences. They may insulate the host from feelings of pain or fear. They may serve as children or adolescents who "act out" in a way the host would not, enabling the host to remain "good" while the alters' behavior is "bad." This was the nature of my reckless teenage alter.

In some instances, hostile alters will act aggressively toward the adult host to punish him for perceived bad behavior. This could be the consequence of long-harbored, subconscious guilt that was instilled by an abuser and internalized by the child.

Some people with a dissociative disorder may have a tendency toward self-sabotage and self-persecution, both emotionally and physically. Others may experience depression, mood swings, suicidal tendencies, panic attacks and phobias, alcohol and drug abuse, visual and auditory hallucinations, or sleep and eating disorders.

Many dissociatives endure years of misdiagnoses. Research indicates that people with dissociative disorders spend an average of seven years in the mental-health system before finally receiving an accurate diagnosis. This is unfortunate but understandable, because the symptoms of dissociation are similar to those of other psychological conditions.

There are general symptoms that most people with DID exhibit to some degree. Various types of amnesia are common. "Losing time" occurs when they have no recollection of traveling, say, the last ten miles of a trip. Most "normal" people have probably done this at some point in their lives.

A more extreme version is known as a "fugue," finding one-self in a location with no memory of the journey. This happened to me often when I drove back and forth between Wrightsville and the university in Athens.

Other examples include meeting someone but not remembering them when you meet again, and being told of an action you performed and having no memory of doing it.

Some people with DID forget how to execute tasks they have done hundreds of times before, such as starting a car or writing a check. They might discover personal items are missing, or come across objects they do not recall purchasing. It is very common for portions of one's childhood to be hidden away by amnesia, as in my case.

Another common characteristic of dissociative identity disorder is what professionals call "somatoform conversions." Simply stated, these are changes in a person's body for which there is no medical explanation. These usually involve an impairment of movement such as paralysis or difficulty with swallowing or walking. It can also manifest as unexplained pain or the inability to feel pain, such as my experience with a dislocated shoulder during the Sugar Bowl game. There can be tunnel vision, deafness, blindness, and the inability to feel any physical sensations whatsoever.

Another phenomenon associated with DID is hearing voices. Although some patients claim they do not hear voices, most mental-health professionals suspect they rationalize the voices as if they were hearing their own thoughts.

The DID patient who admits to hearing voices typically describes them as being inside his head, as opposed to the schizophrenic, who hears inanimate objects speaking.

Dissociative identity disorder has been misdiagnosed by many doctors as schizophrenia, but, in fact, DID does not entail the degree of detachment from reality that characterizes schizophrenia.

Some patients with extremely severe DID do experience psychotic-like symptoms such as auditory hallucinations (hearing things that are not being said) and visual hallucinations (seeing things that are not there). They, too, may be mistakenly diagnosed as schizophrenics.

Typically, people with schizophrenia will hear their own thoughts being spoken aloud by others, or they will think they are being controlled by others, much like a robot. They may insist that feelings they have are not their own, but have been injected by others. Schizophrenics may also believe everyone knows their private thoughts, or that others have put their own thoughts into their minds. They may believe their thoughts can be stolen by an outside entity. Some report being able to hear two or more people arguing about them, or a voice commenting about their behavior.

Some people with DID suffer out-of-body experiences, trances, and/or flashbacks. These are particularly common in those with post-traumatic stress disorder.

Severe flashbacks can cause an individual to lose contact with his current circumstances and relive the trauma of the past. Some medical experts believe flashbacks are probably at the root of a person's compulsion to self-medicate or injure himself in an attempt to escape the pain and anguish being revisited upon him.

The "big three" of dissociative identity disorder are amnesia, depersonalization, and derealization.

In depersonalization, the individual feels disconnected from his body and actions. His body has somehow changed and is not his own; it is strange and unreal. It operates on its own and has stopped being controlled by the self.

Derealization is the feeling that the world is distant or disappearing; has become foreign, unreal, and strange; and that time has slowed down or even stopped.

Any of these symptoms experienced alone or in conjunction

with others can be troubling. They are unsettling invasions of a person's mind, and can wreak havoc with one's sense of self. The good news is, one can have a fulfilling and satisfying life, WITH THE PROPER TREATMENT.

During treatment sessions with a qualified and compassionate therapist, individuals can learn to use dissociative identity disorder to their advantage and derive many benefits from it. It does not have to be a source of desperation and hopelessness leading to self-destructive behavior and thinking. I'm convinced that I never would have accomplished the many things I did in my life if it weren't for DID. I'm also convinced that, to one degree or another, many other people use the same techniques to cope with painful pasts, to motivate themselves, to find a focus and center for their powers of concentration, to set and achieve goals, and, in many ways, to move mountains. They may or may not have DID, but if along with those positives they are experiencing some of the negative effects of the disorder, I hope that my story will help them make the decision to seek professional help.

I also hope that you will understand that while I've been diagnosed with DID, it is not my identity nor is it my destiny. I've always battled against the idea of being labeled, and I continue to resist this one. I am much more than a complex of behaviors and symptoms. I never sought treatment as a way to find an excuse for mistakes I've made—I simply wanted an explanation. I walked into Dr. Jerry's office hoping he could answer a very simple question for me: "Doctor, am I crazy?" I think I've gotten the answer, and I hope that any of you who have struggled with that same doubt will be able to find the answers that you've been looking for.

I'd like to conclude with a section of a speech that I use fairly often when I'm asked to appear at various gatherings. (Yes, H-H-H-Her-sh-sh-sh-el the g-g-girl-sh-sh-sh-sh-el now gets paid to travel around the country to deliver inspirational speeches.) I think it sums up nicely a lot of what I've been trying to say and reflects who I am in my many dimensions.

If you have shopped on Rodeo Drive in Beverly Hills, walked along the cobblestone streets of England, or ridden in a rickshaw through the narrow streets of Hong Kong, you have undoubtedly passed sophisticated boutiques featuring the porcelain sculptures of the Lladró Brothers of Spain.

When Juan, José, and Vicente Lladró began a sculpting business in their tiny village near Valencia, they could not have foreseen the passionate following their work would inspire from around the world.

The first time I saw a Lladró figure, I was drawn to it like a magnet. It touched my soul in its expression of the human experience. One can actually perceive the love of one person for another in the sculpted faces of valuable Lladró creations.

These pieces depict the joy of giving, and of living life to the fullest. The delight of proud parents holding their newborn child; the elation of a young lady in an elegant ball gown waiting to dance with her Prince Charming; the bliss of an elderly couple gracefully growing old together. You can sense the love they share as they live their lives as one.

Sometimes I sit in silence and study the one-of-a-kind figurines in my Lladró collection. They never fail to remind me of how God so graciously made each of us a unique individual and a beautiful part of His masterful creation and plan. I recall His Word saying we are "wonderfully made."

Perhaps this analogy is what captured my interest in the porcelain sculptures. God made man, man made the figurines, and both were planned in the minds of their makers before they were created.

The difference between the sculptures and man is simple. Once a figurine is broken, it cannot be restored to its original beauty and elegance. However, when a man is broken by life's traumas, the great Master Potter can repair and restore him as if completely unscarred by life's suffering. When God picks up the pieces of our lives, he reshapes, refines, and reconstructs us. Then we become the vessel God intended us to be.

By contrast, a Lladró piece, although beautiful, does not feel pain or sorrow. It has known neither disappointment nor loneliness, nor ever shed a tear. If it is never touched by life, it will retain its beauty forever. However, once it leaves the Lladrós' hands, it becomes very vulnerable. If it is broken, its creator cannot restore it to perfection.

When God repairs our lives, we become the person He created us to be, with the ability to help transform other lives we touch. Unless we allow God to repair us, we will never know the uniqueness of ourselves and the abilities we have to offer mankind.

For those who struggle with dissociative identity disorder, life can seem at times like looking into a broken mirror. The face reflected appears to have been broken into hundreds of tiny pieces, and you see more than one reflection of yourself. You may see different faces and different personalities looking back at you. Looking into that mirror of life, a person may become afraid of what they see.

At such times, the question may arise, "Am I crazy?"

Perhaps this is because you have not come to a clear understanding that those many faces compose the beautiful and unique person you really are. I believe that knowledge is the key to helping an individual with DID live the successful and fulfilling life of a productive person in our society.

When you hear another language spoken and comprehend its meaning, it is literally more beautiful than just hearing the words. When you look at a painting on a wall and truly understand what you are seeing, you distinguish the concept beyond the painting.

I think of life as a locked treasure chest filled with precious stones. Everyone has some type of treasure inside that is simply waiting to be unveiled. Each person holds a different set of keys. If you do not use the keys to unlock the chest, the jewels will remain hidden; and no one will ever see their brilliance and beauty. The most important key I hold unlocks the truth about DID.

When I am asked to describe dissociative identity disorder, I explain that I sometimes see it as a "diamond in the rough"; not the kind that has been birthed from a mine, but from the depths of the abyss in the ocean.

There it lies dormant as debris gathers around it, completely obscuring the diamond and its beauty. It has been buried by tumultuous currents, the victim of harsh surroundings. It remains there until someone reaches deep down within that darkness and brings it to the surface to display the brilliance of its many prismlike facets.

Life, like the sea, is a place of constant change, capable of being calm one minute and swamped with turmoil the next. The deeper the water, the darker the environment. It is almost as if there is another world beneath.

The depths of the ocean contain creatures we have come to respect, as well as those we have learned to fear. There are species of marine life men have yet to discover.

Under the surface of the water, there is a tremendous amount of activity. Schools of shimmering fish of all shapes and colors constantly struggle to evade predators, even as they seek out their own prey.

A stingray glides across the ocean floor searching for food. Amazingly, seaweed flourishes and sways to the ever-changing motion of the sea. Coral reefs have formed to provide a safe haven for various ocean dwellers.

Dolphins swim playfully, while the killer whale is always nearby, threatening those around him. He seems to be the one most respected by other fish; the one who rules his surroundings.

Considering all of this activity, one may ask what lies beneath the ocean floor. Could something be hidden deep under the sand?

Some may wonder the same thing about a person with dissociative identity disorder. What is hidden deep inside the world of a DID sufferer, and how can it be uncovered to reveal the true person?

I envision something extraordinary amid the chaos of the sea and the countless creatures that inhabit it. I see a diamond of the rarest quality that was not formed in a mine or mountainside.

This diamond is hidden deep beneath the sand at the bottom of the ocean floor. No one knows how long this precious stone has been there, or how long it will remain hidden; but when it is uncovered, its transparent light will be seen.

One may ask what this metaphoric diamond, this gem, this rare jewel is. This one-of-a-kind creation is YOU! And me. All people with DID are "diamonds in the rough."

If you have been diagnosed with DID, you may feel hidden and insignificant. However, we must consider that there is a forming and shaping taking place in our lives, and it is not all bad. *Your* life has value and, unlike a diamond, bears no price tag.

Just as the undersea world is constantly changing with shifting winds and tides, chapters in our lives open and close without warning, shifting from one event to another like sand on the ocean floor.

With each shift and shuffle, the diamond in the rough stays in place; although with work and patience, the debris trapping the diamond can be removed.

Once a person comes to terms with DID and allows this debris to be removed, nothing can prevent him from becoming whole and complete.

The diamond is the purest stone known to man. When properly cut, a diamond gathers light within itself; a light that reflects back in a shower of fire and brilliance.

There may be times when our lives seem as cold and dark as the deepest ocean. We may feel as if killer whales and sharks live within us and surround us. However, beneath the turmoil are real people. I am such a person; and if you have DID, so are you.

A true diamond is formed deep underground under tremendous heat and pressure. The movement of magma, or volcanic rock, beneath the earth's surface causes deposits surrounding the diamond to erode and lift off, thus pushing the diamond up toward the surface.

As a person with DID, I have been in places of unbelievable pressure, and have suffered extreme disappointment and humiliation. When a person with DID allows God and medical science to be the magma, he is carried to the surface at the appropriate time.

With help, you and I, just like the diamond, can be polished to become a reflection of hope to others who live with alters day after day.

One of the first steps to recovery is to recognize and

admit the presence of DID, and be willing to be exposed to the ramifications of that acknowledgment. That will be the beginning of great changes in your life.

If you have been fighting a battle with dissociative identity disorder, you may have been broken by something traumatic in your life. I would like to help you become that beautiful vessel God intended you to be.

I hope I have given you something to hold on to, and helped you come to terms with your diagnosis. Most important, I hope you have come to realize that you are *not* crazy.

Dr. Jerry Mungadze taught me not to be afraid to look into my mirror of life and face the issues that have haunted me. I had to confront my alters and say to them, "I'm not going to run from you any longer. I will work this out with you, because Herschel is the one in control. I will not think weird things, because I'm not crazy. I will not be afraid of the challenges that lie ahead."

I am certain that one day I will be able to go through life without the assistance of alters.

If you feel that DID has shattered your life and your vessel is broken, there is hope. With the help of the medical profession, knowledge, understanding, and especially the Master Potter, you can live life to the fullest.

There is an account in the Bible of Jeremiah going to a potter's house to observe him remaking a broken vessel. The craftsman turned the clay on the wheel and formed it with his hands until it was without blemish. As Jeremiah watched the transformation of the clay, the Lord said to him, "Just as the clay is in the potter's hand, so are you in My hand."

Now when I look in the mirror with the knowledge that I am in the Master Potter's hands, I realize that Herschel is just a piece of clay spinning on the Potter's wheel. I am being remade, reshaped, and worked into a new vessel. When I see cracks and chips, I simply remind myself that I am a work in progress.

I sincerely believe that God is creating a special vessel who will be able to transcend geographic and cultural borders.

This has been a lengthy process and no one knows the amount of time it will take to complete the task. When it is accomplished, I will feel that I have endured a grueling twist on the Potter's wheel and can say along with the psalmist David, "I am fearfully and wonderfully made, a beautiful work of art to be displayed in the gallery of life."

I will continue to educate people regarding dissociative identity disorder and the everyday battles faced by those with DID. I will offer myself as a tool to help others become whole and take over their own lives without relying on the "others."

Some of the Lladró figurines bear the original signature of their creator, whereas you and I have been tattooed into the palm of God's hand with His own unique signature on our lives.

Each year, certain Lladró pieces are retired; but we can rest in the assurance that we will never be retired by our Master Potter.

May God's love be with you, always.